Bahá'í Heritage Series

# Against Incredible Odds

## Life of a 20th Century Iranian Bahá'í Family

with love to Joan on
her birthday
20 October 2007
Lori

# Against Incredible Odds

## Life of a 20th Century Iranian Bahá'í Family

by

Baharieh Rouhani Ma'ani

GR

George Ronald
Oxford

George Ronald, *Publisher*
Oxford
www.grbooks.com



*A catalogue record for this book is available from the British Library*

ISBN-10 0-85398-504-9
ISBN-13 978-0-85398-504-4

Printed by Cromwell Press, Trowbridge, Wiltshire

# Contents

For Sovaida, Kenneth and Giselle Ruḥíyyih Ewing

# Introduction

The 1979 Islamic Revolution in Iran brought to the fore one of the long-standing issues the country had faced since mid-19th century: the ever-growing presence of the Bahá'ís in a country tightly in the grip of dictatorial rulers and Islamic ecclesiastics. The despotic rulers and the radical Muslim clergy of Iran shared a complete disregard for the rights of the Bahá'í religious minority. They often joined hands to suppress the followers of a religion that believe in and work for the establishment of the unity of humankind, universal peace, elimination of prejudice of every kind, universal and compulsory education, gender equality, harmony between science and religion, abolition of priesthood, elimination of extreme wealth and poverty, the establishment of a universal auxiliary language and so on.

The Bahá'í Faith, founded in the middle of the 19th century, has not been recognized in the land of its birth and although its members form the largest religious minority, it does not enjoy the protection accorded in the constitution to the followers of other religions. Consequently, the perpetrators of hate crimes against the followers of Bahá'u'lláh have generally enjoyed impunity. And when the government and people of malice have worked together to repress the Bahá'ís, the outcome for the believers has been dire in terms of their loss of life and material belongings. This has been true since the inception of the Bábí–Bahá'í Faith more than 160 years ago. The introduction of the constitution in 1906 made very little, if any, difference in the situation of the Bahá'ís who were used as scapegoats whenever a pretext was needed to divert the public's attention from issues threatening the authority and power of either the clergy or the government. The generality of the inhabitants of Iran have followed the example of the rulers, temporal and spiritual alike, and benefited from the injustices perpetrated in the name of Islam.

Forced by the cruel treatment they received at the hands of the people and government of Iran, the persecuted Bahá'ís scattered first to different parts of the country then to the neighbouring lands and beyond. They took with them, wherever they went, the light of Bahá'u'lláh's Revelation. By the time World War I broke out, the Cause of Bahá'u'lláh was established in the Middle Eastern countries, Central Asia, Russia, India, Burma, a number of European countries and North America. 'Abdu'l-Bahá's divine plan mobilized the Bahá'ís of North America to arise and take the light of Bahá'u'lláh to lands beyond their shores. With the onset of the Formative Age, Shoghi Effendi formulated plans with specific objectives for the execution of the plans revealed by 'Abdu'l-Bahá. The Universal House of Justice has continued the process and made it possible for the Cause of Bahá'u'lláh to reach every corner of the globe.

The executors of various plans, as explained time and again by Shoghi Effendi and the Universal House of Justice, have been Bahá'ís of all ranks and backgrounds who have responded to the call and helped to lay the foundation of a new world order brought by Bahá'u'lláh. The account of the life of the Bahá'í family attempted here covers the whole of the 20th century and portrays the challenges they met, the sacrifices they made, the sufferings they endured and the blessings they enjoyed.

The account starts with the eventful life of two people coming from very different backgrounds. They are Touba (Ṭúbá) Khánum and Mírzá Muḥammad-Shafí', who later adopted Rouhani (Rúḥání) as a surname. They are my parents and both come from Nayríz, a small town in the province of Fárs, where the fort of Khájih episode[1] took place in 1850 and Jang-i Jibal (the Battle of the Mountain)[2] in 1852. After those two wars the believers in Nayríz were systematically persecuted and repeatedly attacked, their property plundered, their means of livelihood threatened and some were savagely put to death.

My purpose in writing an account of the life of my parents and discussing in brief who their forebears were and what happened to their offspring is this: The story portrays what our parents and ancestors went through to pass down to their children the precious legacy we possess today. It is a story of lifelong struggle against incredible odds, of renouncing worldly pleasures to achieve higher aims, of accepting material deprivations to gain spiritual strength and of foregoing the desire of wanting to be physically close to one's children – the cherished desire of every parent – to enable them to scatter far and wide and work towards the achievement of Bahá'u'lláh's pivotal goal of unifying humankind.

The span of father and mother's lives covered all of the 20th century, designated by 'Abdu'l-Bahá as the century of light. Their lives until their marriage are discussed separately; after their marriage their lives are discussed together, along with their children, as one family.

Some parts of this book that deal with events in the first few decades of the 20th century in which father was a participant are based on information provided in his memoirs.[3] Passages and sentences directly translated from his memoirs are indicated and page references given. The parts about mother are based on information provided by my older siblings and from my own observations during childhood and later years. Other parts come from my own memoirs.

# Nayríz – Land of Soul-stirring Events

The Báb declared His mission in S͟híráz on the eve of 23 May 1844. Nayríz was effectively touched by the message of the Báb only in 1850. As the town is situated in close proximity to S͟híráz, one may wonder why it took so long. One reason may be the slow means of communication between different parts of Iran at that time. Postal services and newspapers as we know them today did not exist. When necessary, messages were sent back and forth by couriers and news travelled by word of mouth. Yet five years is too long for news of the magnitude of the coming of the promised Qá'im to reach the inhabitants of a town less than 250 kilometres away from where His advent was proclaimed.

The claim of the Báb and the events associated with the declaration of His mission had plunged the country into turmoil. The adherents of the new faith were persecuted and brutally killed in provinces as far away as K͟hurásán, Ád͟harbáyján and Mázandarán. It seems rather strange that Nayríz and its inhabitants had been generally oblivious of what was happening to the Báb and Bábís in other parts of the country. One plausible explanation is that news of the Báb's claim had reached Nayríz and many other places in Iran through rumours designed to create consternation in the hearts, thus keeping people away from investigating the truth and preventing them from embracing the new faith. This is how humanity has always dealt with new Manifestations of God whenever and wherever they appeared. The persecution of the founders of new religions and their followers has ever been based on the false hope that brutality, massacre, deprivation and intimidation will help extinguish the new light. The same treacherous theory was put into practice when the Báb appeared and was later applied to Bahá'u'lláh and His followers.

The person who proclaimed the Bábí Faith in Nayríz in 1850 was Áqá Siyyid Yaḥyá Dárábí, entitled Vaḥíd (unique). He was the special envoy of Muḥammad Sháh sent to Shíráz to investigate the truth of the Báb's mission. After embracing the nascent faith, he arose to spread the glad-tidings to other parts of Iran, including Yazd where he had a home and where his family lived. His teaching activities in that town aroused the animosity of the religious leaders. Their persecution of him was so severe he was forced to leave Yazd for Nayríz where his second wife, Ṣughrá Khánum, and her family lived. On his way to Nayríz, Jináb-i Vaḥíd stopped in places where he found people who were receptive and taught those souls who were eager to hear about the new faith. Nayríz was the last place on this earthly plain that he visited.[1]

The events that took place in Nayríz involving the followers of the Báb and their opponents changed the destiny of that small obscure place and transformed the lives of its inhabitants. As a result Nayríz gained prominence on the map of episodes associated with the history of the Bábí–Bahá'í Faith. As Nayríz is where my parents were born and where they lived a good part of their lives and is the town where some of the major episodes covered in this book took place, some basic information about it seems necessary.

Nayríz is a small town about 228 kilometres to the east of Shíráz in the province of Fárs in Iran. It is built on a plateau and is the centre of a division (*bakhsh*) of the same name that includes 47 villages and townships. The division of Nayríz is one of the four divisions that form the district (*shahristán*) of Fasá. There are eight districts and 32 divisions in the province of Fárs. Nayríz is strategically placed between Bavánát and Zarqán on the north, Sírján on the east, Iṣṭahbánát on the west and Dáráb and Iṣṭahbánát on the south. In the early 1970s the population of Nayríz proper was 15,391 and the division was 27,000. However, harsh economic conditions and the movement of the population towards urban areas have caused the population to dwindle.

Nayríz was an important and famous town in ancient times. It enjoyed a good climate and its soil was fertile. It was renowned for its flourishing agriculture. It produced tasty and juicy fruits that were exported to other parts of Fárs. The inhabitants of Nayríz were resourceful and industrious. The town was also famous for manufacturing steel. It made swords, as well as iron and wooden tools. One section of the town was called *suhádkhánih* (the abode of steel makers and ironmongers).

In the 19th century the town of Nayríz was divided into four distinct sections or quarters, called *maḥallih*. The four quarters were separated one from the other by orchards. Each quarter had its own distinguishing characteristics and was identified by a name:

1) Maḥallih Ábádzartusht, less developed and poorer than the other quarters.

2) Maḥallih Chinársúkhtih, also called Chinársháhí. The name was later changed to Maḥallih Pahlaví. The inhabitants of this *maḥallih* were mostly Bahá'ís.

3) Maḥallih Bázár, the largest and most affluent of the four. This *maḥallih* has always served as the seat of the local government.

4) Maḥallih Sádát, also known as Kúchih Bálá. The inhabitants of this *maḥallih* were predominantly fanatic Muslims notorious for their animosity towards the Bahá'í Faith and its followers.

Before the introduction of Islam the inhabitants of Nayríz were Zoroastrians. Their temple, the *atashkadih* (the place where fire is kept alive), was in the Chinársúkhtih section of the town. It was converted into a mosque after the Muslim conquest. The building was renovated in 362 AH (circa 985) and renamed Masjid-i Jámi'-i Kabír (the Great Jámi' mosque). In 560 AH (circa 1184) it underwent more repairs. This is a significant site, for the Cause of the Báb was for the first time proclaimed in Nayríz from the pulpit of this mosque by Jináb-i Siyyid Yaḥyá Vaḥíd in 1850.[2]

A celebrated artist by the name of Aḥmad-i Khushnivís and a religious figure who achieved national renown for his commentary on the Qur'án and author of *Majma 'u'l-Baḥrayn*, Shaykh Arshadu'd-Dín Muḥammad bin 'Alí, who died in Shíráz in 604 AH (circa 1228), came from Nayríz.[3]

The author of *Lama'átu'l-Anvár* writes that Siyyid Yaḥyá Vaḥíd was attracted to Nayríz because it was a place where knowledge, art and technology flourished. Jináb-i Vaḥíd's second wife, Ṣughrá Khánum, was from Nayríz and he had established a second home in the town. The prominence that Nayríz enjoys among the Bahá'ís is owed to a considerable degree to Jináb-i-Vaḥíd, for he taught its inhabitants the Bábí Faith. Jináb-i Vaḥíd's valiant acts and the heroism evinced by his supporters in promoting the Bábí Faith and defending it against the onslaught of the enemy makes Nayríz well known in the annals of Bábí–Bahá'í history.

Under the influence of Bahá'u'lláh's teachings the Bábí warriors of Nayríz, after they accepted Him as the one whose advent the Báb had presaged, were completely transformed. They changed their way of life and preferred to be killed for their faith than to kill, as many of the episodes covered in this book will reveal.

## Father's Family and Early Life

According to his birth certificate, obtained many years after his birth, father was born in Nayríz in 1894.[4] The accuracy of this date is uncertain. According to his account of a historical event, which will be discussed later, he was about eleven or twelve years old in 1909. Thus he may have actually been born in 1896 or 1897.

Father was named after his grandfather (his mother's father) and called Mírzá Muḥammad-Shafí'. His grandfather, Mullá Muḥammad-Shafí', was a prominent believer in Nayríz. He was about nine years old when the fort of Khájih episode took place in 1850 and eleven when the Battle of the Mountain (Jang-i Jibal), also known as the second Nayríz episode, occurred in 1853.[5] Mullá Muḥammad-Shafí' later embraced the Cause of Bahá'u'lláh, whose advent the Báb had heralded. He rendered outstanding services to the Bahá'í Faith in Nayríz and parts of Kirmán, attained Bahá'u'lláh's presence and was honoured with many Tablets from Him and from 'Abdu'l-Bahá. The following is the provisional English translation of one of Bahá'u'lláh's Tablets revealed in his honour:

N. Y. (Nayríz)
He is the Most Holy, the Most Great!
O Muḥammad-Shafí'! The Intercessor hath turned His Countenance to thee from His luminous habitation, the Spot wherefrom the Lord of Destiny pronounceth the mysteries of all that hath been and will be. We have sent thee a Tablet to which no created thing can compare, and this is yet another one proceeding from My Preserved Tablet. Is it in thy power to thank God befittingly? Nay, by My all-encompassing knowledge, which remaineth concealed. We render praise to God in this glorious station on behalf of My chosen ones.

O Shafí'! This is the Day in which God's most excellent favours have been vouchsafed and the showers of His grace are constantly pouring down from the clouds of His bestowal. Well is it with those who have recognized Him. O thou who hast turned thy face to God! The Herald made the people aware of the Truth but now they are seen to have strayed. Today steadfastness in the Cause is regarded as the greatest of all deeds. Blessed is the one who hath attained unto it. Counsel all the friends regarding this lofty and exalted station that they may not be hindered by the feeble attempts of the debased from attaining the Lord of the end, just as a single letter hath held back such a one from the Mother Book and the croaking of the raven deprived him of the cooing of the Celestial Dove. We enjoin all to abide by everything that hath been revealed in the Book of God. Whosoever doeth this today, that one is of the people of Bahá. Say, ye are bidden to what is praiseworthy. Ye are bidden to do what is right. Through it the Cause of God, the Supreme Protector, the Self-Subsisting, is made manifest.

Glory be upon thee and upon the servants of God and His handmaidens in that land. Rejoice for this bounty and say: Praise be to thee O Thou Counselling Prisoner.[6]

Father's life spanned almost all of 'Abdu'l-Bahá's ministry, all of

Shoghi Effendi's guardianship and 21 years of the Universal House of Justice's rule. He was the first child born to Mírzá 'Abdu'l-Ḥusayn and Núríján Khánum, both members of outstanding Bahá'í families in Nayríz who traced their lineage to the early adherents of the Bábí–Bahá'í Faith in that town. Father had one sister and four brothers. The name of the sister who died in childhood is unknown. One of the four brothers, Mírzá Ismá'íl, died young. The other three brothers, in order of age, are Mírzá Khalíl, Mírzá Jalál and Mírzá 'Alí-Akbar.

When father was growing up, schools providing systematic education did not exist in that part of Iran. Therefore, as was the practice in those days, tutors were engaged to teach him the basics. Being the first born, father had to help at a young age with the daily chores and could not spend full time on his studies. His keen interest in furthering his education suffered a setback with the untimely passing of his father which left him at the age of 20 in charge of the affairs of the family and raising, together with his mother, two brothers who were minors. As we will see later, father managed to continue his education at a later date and became proficient in Arabic and those branches of knowledge current in Iran in the early years of the 20th century. Father was a resourceful person. He was good in the fields of agriculture, business and accountancy. He had wonderful public relations skills. He was a great Bahá'í teacher and also a historian, writer and poet.

When father was a young boy of about eleven, Mírzá Ṭarázu-'lláh Samandarí, later designated by the Guardian of the Bahá'í Faith as a Hand of the Cause of God, and Mírzá 'Alí-Akbar Rafsanjání, a prominent Bahá'í teacher, visited Nayríz. During their visit many public meetings were held attended by Bahá'ís and non-Bahá'ís alike. At times the crowd was so large that many would occupy rooftops to listen to what the Bahá'í teachers had to say. Father said those meetings served as a catalyst awakening in him at that young age spiritual feelings and making him realize the responsibility the Bahá'ís bore for establishing love and unity among members of the human race. It was then that he and many of his peers dedicated themselves to the growth and consolidation of the Bahá'í Faith in and beyond Nayríz. He later realized the timeliness of the visit of those devoted teachers, for soon after their departure from Nayríz the chalice of calamity was passed around and the wine of sacrifice touched the lips of all the believers in that town. Some quaffed it to its last dregs and offered up their souls for their belief. Others had a lesser share of the cup of sacrifice. The event which claimed the lives of 18 Bahá'ís in Nayríz coincided with the interment on Naw-Rúz 1909 of the remains of the Báb and His companion, Mírzá Muḥammad-'Alí Zunúzí entitled Anís, in the Shrine that 'Abdu'l-Bahá had built on Mount Carmel for the purpose. According to 'Abdu'l-Bahá, the interment of the remains of the Báb on Mount Carmel needed sacrifice. The believers in Nayríz, who twice previously had proved themselves in the arena of sacrifice, won the honour one more time.

On that fateful Naw-Rúz three believers from Nayríz were on pilgrimage and attained 'Abdu'l-Bahá's presence. Upon returning to Nayríz they related how 'Abdu'l-Bahá was aware of what was happening in the town on that day. Two of the three pilgrims were the writer's grandfathers. Their recollections will come later.

## The Gruesome Events of Naw-Rúz 1909

During the latter part of the reign of Muẓaffiri'd-Dín S͟háh (1896–1907), the movement for democracy in Iran gathered momentum. Many Iranians, tired of the despotic rule of the Qájár kings and the inordinate influence of the clergy, supported the movement and demanded modernization. Finally, Muẓaffiri'd-Dín S͟háh and his crown prince, Muḥammad-'Alí Mírzá, signed the decree for democracy and the establishment of parliament in December 1906. Muẓaffiri'd-Dín S͟háh died five days after the signing ceremony and Muḥammad-'Alí Mírzá became the king. The reign of Muḥammad-'Alí S͟háh (1907–9) was short and chaotic. Those who were unhappy with the prospects of democracy, among them the royalists and some prominent clergy, began to agitate and put up strong resistance. To reestablish dictatorship, Muḥammad-'Alí S͟háh closed the parliament in 1908 and ordered a number of prominent supporters of democracy killed. But the period of his absolute rule was short-lived. In 1909 he was dethroned and sent into exile. After Muḥammad-'Alí Sháh, his underaged son Aḥmad Sháh became the king. Aḥmad Sháh ruled over Iran from 1909 to 1925.

The period 1906 to 1925, marking the end of the Qájár dynasty, is the most turbulent in the contemporary history of Iran. During this time in some provinces certain elements took advantage of the weakness of the central government and raised the banner of rebellion. Among them were clerics who worked with tribal heads looking for opportunity to spread their influence and enrich themselves by extorting money and plundering property. Emboldened by a deterioration of the security situation and inspired and encouraged by clergy who opposed the advent of democracy and modernization in Iran, some tribes in Fárs revolted against the central authority and wreaked havoc on the regions they brought under their control. Nayríz was one of the worst affected areas and suffered devastation. The rebellion there soon turned into an organized attack against the Bahá'ís.

The governor of Nayríz at that time was Mas'údu'd-Dawlih, son of Áṣifu'd-Dawlih. The Shí'ís of the area paid allegiance to Ḥájí Siyyid 'Abdu'l-Ḥusayn-i Lárí, who was inspired by Shaykh Faḍlu'lláh Núrí, a Muslim ecclesiastic and opponent of modernization and the movement for democracy. Ḥájí Siyyid 'Abdu'l-Ḥusayn lived in Lár, a town in the district of Láristán. His area of influence included the mountainous region of Nayríz. He took advantage of the chaotic situation caused by the central government's weakness and ordered Shaykh Dhakaríyyá Kúhistání to raise the banner of rebellion. Shaykh Dhakaríyyá was happy to comply and did as ordered. He and his gunmen moved towards Nayríz where Shaykh Dhakaríyyá intended to expel the governor and establish a kind of national government. Nayríz was besieged and fighting began between the forces of the governor supported by the inhabitants of Nayríz on the one hand and the rebels supported by tribesmen living in the surrounding area on the other. The Shaykh's army was reinforced constantly, while the governor's force dwindled steadily. Communication between S͟híráz, the capital of the province of Fárs, and Nayríz was cut off, making it impossible for the governor to seek and receive support.

While father's father, Mírzá 'Abdu'l-Ḥusayn, was on pilgrimage, father and his siblings lived under the care and supervision of their mother, Núríján K͟hánum, and maternal uncle, S͟hayk͟h Muḥammad-Ḥusayn. After three days of fighting, the rebels took the northern highlands and strongholds. S͟hayk͟h D͟hakaríyyá invited the inhabitants of the town to the fort of Sayfábád, which he had conquered. The people of Nayríz responded to the invitation and attended the meeting. In his speech the S͟hayk͟h introduced Ḥájí Siyyid 'Abdu'l-Ḥusayn-i Lárí as the defender of Islam and the supporter of the national government and himself as the standard-bearer of Islam. In the same speech he roused the Muslim population of the town against the Bahá'ís. By so doing he planted the seed of hatred and dissension in their hearts and diminished support for the local government, whose forces were already steadily losing ground. Then, in a surprise attack by night, he took a section of the town known as Maḥallih Kúc͟hih Bálá. A few days later another section of the town fell into the rebels' hands and they moved closer to Maḥallih Bázár, the seat of the government. The governor of Nayríz, Mas'údu'd-Dawlih, and his brother-in-law, Muḥammad Ḥasan K͟hán-i Sartíp, grandson of Ḥájí Zaynu'l-'Ábidín K͟hán,[7] fled Maḥallih Bázár and moved to Maḥallih Pahlaví where the Bahá'ís lived. They chose the Jámi' mosque, which was a mighty stronghold, for their defence. Intimidated by the approaching forces of the S͟hayk͟h, the governor and his brother-in-law fled Nayríz by night and left the Bahá'ís at the mercy of the advancing forces of the S͟hayk͟h. Thus Maḥallih Pahlaví became the battlefield. Fighting began around the Jámi' mosque between the inhabitants of that *maḥallih* and the rebels. One of the Bahá'ís, Muḥammad-Ḥasan, son of Raḥím, was killed. After the *maḥallih* fell to the rebels, the S͟hayk͟h issued a decree making it a religious duty to kill the Bahá'ís, plunder their property and set fire to their homes. The Muslim inhabitants of the *maḥallih* joined hands with the S͟hayk͟h's forces in carrying out the decree. The Bahá'ís, in obedience to Bahá'u'lláh's teachings prohibiting His followers from taking up arms against their assailants and engaging in a holy war, left Nayríz and moved to the mountains to the south of the town, where the early Bábís had defended themselves against their enemy. However, a few of them stayed in the town and went into hiding.

Father, his mother, grandmother, four aunts and two uncles took off for the mountains and took with them a servant who carried some provisions for them. They started off early in the morning of Naw-Rúz 1909. Father's mother, a devoted and valiant soul, knowing the gravity of the situation, related stories about the heroic deeds of the early believers, awakening in them the spirit of heroism and sacrifice. Before noon they reached a valley known as Tang-i Láy-i Ḥiná and took refuge in a small cave. When night fell, everywhere was pitch black and no sound could be heard except the water and the wind. Frightened and bewildered, they counted the hours and minutes. About midnight, a Muslim relative – the husband of one of father's aunts – visited them and said that the area was unsafe. He also confirmed the Shaykh's decree and added that the Shaykh had announced that whoever presented a severed head of a Bahá'í would receive the reward of a hundred túmáns; if a Bahá'í were captured and taken to him alive, the captor would receive 300 túmáns.[8] However, he said, the women and small children were not to be harmed. The Muslim relative suggested that while it was still dark the men should take an unfrequented mountain route to Sarvistán and the women return with him to Nayríz. Everyone agreed. There was some doubt as to whether father, who was about twelve years old and could not keep pace with the men who were going to Sarvistán, would be treated as an adult or a child. So it was decided that he would wear a *chádur* and accompany the women.

As the men were about to depart, Shaykh Muhammad-Ḥusayn, father's uncle, addressing his Muslim brother-in-law, saying:

> Now that we are saying goodbye and moving towards an unknown destiny, God has willed that you take charge of these defenceless and shelterless women and children. I adjure you to hide them in

> an obscure and deserted place in Nayríz. If you see that the enemy is likely to find and dishonour them and you are unable to provide protection, throw them into a well and cover it with debris that no blight may touch this family.[9]

Had the women been consulted, they would have agreed with the suggested course of action. They would have preferred death to being dishonoured. A woman's life at that time revolved round her 'honour', as defined by tradition. Without honour a woman's life was worthless. Indeed, death was preferred to life without honour. It was different for men. They were considered honourable if they could protect their womenfolk from other men. To fulfil their honourable duty, at times they felt obliged to take drastic decisions, as can be seen from this account.

That night in the Tang-i Láy-i Ḥiná was spent in fear and uncertainty. No one had the appetite to eat anything. However, spiritually all were ready for any eventuality. The next morning father wore a *chádur* and, accompanied by his mother, other women and two younger brothers, started walking towards Nayríz. With them was Mas͟hhadí Ḥasan, the husband of father's aunt, as well as a servant, whose name was Muḥammad-Taqí. On the way they heard gunshots and saw fire raging in the part of the town where the Bahá'ís lived. They realized that their houses had been set on fire. Then the mule, which carried their provisions, carpet and bedding, was wrested out of the servant's hand and the servant himself stripped of his clothes. Fortunately, the women were not disturbed in that attack. About noon the group, exhausted, hungry and without necessary provisions, reached the ruins of a house where they decided to stay for a while. They spent the night in that spot without food or water. Fear of being discovered kept everyone awake. Every time they heard a footstep they all rushed to a dry well within the ruins of the house and stood ready to throw themselves in, to honour the parting words of S͟hayk͟h Muḥammad-Ḥusayn.

The plunderers and opportunists were hard at work that night searching every corner of the town to find the Bahá'ís, turn them in and receive their reward. The next morning another Muslim relative by the name of Mírzá Muḥammad-i Shu'á', who had heard that his aunts were staying in that forsaken place, rushed to their rescue and took them to his home.

As they were passing through the town, father saw from under his *chádur* deplorable and tragic scenes, especially around the Jámi' mosque. Opposite the mosque he saw a body hanging upside down from a mulberry tree. The corpse was bright red, like freshly barbequed meat. There was also a heap of stone gathered underneath the body. Father was curious and wanted to know who it was. In response to his inquiry he was told that it was the corpse of Mullá Muḥammad-'Alí who, together with his son-in-law Mullá Ḥasan, had been killed in Maḥallih Bázár the previous day. The corpse of Mullá Ḥasan, he was told, had been similarly hung in Maḥallih Bázár but Mullá Muḥammad-'Alí's corpse had been dragged to Maḥallih Pahlaví near the mosque, where it had been set on fire, hanged and stoned. The scene and the explanation he received in response to his question so affected father that after he reached the home of his Muslim cousin, he fell ill and developed a temperature.

At the cousin's house the women were accommodated in a room and father in a storeroom. An opening large enough for him to crawl into was made under saddlebags that were filled with dried fruit, nuts and grain. He spent 13 days and nights in that hole until Shaykh Dhakaríyyá left Nayríz. The only time he could leave his hiding place for a brief time was late at night. The Muslim relatives kept the refugees abreast of the news. More Bahá'ís were killed every day. Even ten-year-old Bahá'í boys were not immune, father was told. If one were found alive, he would be burned rather than killed. Father saw clearly that this could happen to him but instead of being fearful he was so filled with the spirit of faith and sacrifice that he found himself ready to offer up his life for his belief. He attributed his state of readiness for sacrifice to the visit of the two prominent Bahá'í teachers, Mírzá Ṭarazu'lláh Samandarí and Mírzá 'Alí Akbar-i Rafsanjání, who had visited Nayríz before the incident. Their visit had prepared the Bahá'ís of the town for such a day, he believed.

Father's father, Mírzá 'Abdu'l-Ḥusayn, mother's father, Mírzá Aḥmad, and another pilgrim from Nayríz[10] had the honour of being in 'Abdu'l-Bahá's presence on Naw-Rúz 1909 when He interred the Báb's remains in the mausoleum He had built on Mount Carmel for the purpose. They related, upon their return to Nayríz, that on that portentous day 'Abdu'l-Bahá had singled out the three pilgrims from Nayríz for extra consideration and loving care. The special treatment they received astonished all others. For instance, after the ceremony, in spite of the fact that there were many prominent Bahá'ís and well-known teachers of the Cause present at the event, 'Abdu'l-Bahá had chosen by drawing lots the three pilgrims from Nayríz to sit in His carriage and accompany Him on the journey home from the Shrine. The Nayrízí pilgrims were at that time unaware of the real reason they received so much love and consideration.

The day after the interment of the remains of the Báb, 'Abdu'l-Bahá called the Nayrízí pilgrims to His presence and, while walking along the seashore, looked at the sea and said, 'There is a storm, a severe storm.' He repeated, 'The storm is extremely severe.' The pilgrims looked at the sea, saw no storm and thought 'Abdu'l-Bahá was referring to a storm in the making, completely unaware that He was referring to the ongoing storm in Nayríz. That storm had claimed the lives of a number of Bahá'ís, put to flight many others, destroyed sources of their livelihood, devastated Bahá'í homes and left women and children without shelter and at the mercy of the sworn enemies of the Bahá'í Faith. After His brief address 'Abdu'l-Bahá told the pilgrims that they were dismissed. He instructed them to leave immediately and said that on the way back they were to tarry nowhere. Father said it was here that the following verse found true expression:

> He has killed His lovers and seated Himself over their blood
> He has then said prayers on their corpses, one by one.[11]

During the 13 days that Shaykh Dhakaríyyá was in Nayríz, i.e. from 21 March to 3 April 1909, 18 believers were brutally killed for no reason other than their adherence to the Bahá'í Faith. They were Mullá Ḥasan, son of Mullá Áqá Bábá; Mullá Muḥammad-'Alí, uncle and father-in-law of Mullá Ḥasan; Áqá Muḥammad-Ḥasan-i Kuláhmál, son of Muḥammad-Raḥím; Mullá 'Abdu'l-Majíd; Mullá 'Abbás, son of Muḥammad-Sharíf; Áqá Ibráhím, son of Ḥáj Muḥammad; Áqá Ismá'íl, son of Ḥáj Muḥammad; Áqá Asadu'lláh, son of Áqá Ibráhím; Mullá Ḥusayn, son of Zaynu'l-'Ábidín; Áqá Mihdí, son of Mullá Ḥusayn, who had been martyred earlier; Áqá 'Alí-Akbar, son of Mashhadí Naw-Rúz; Ustád 'Atá'u'lláh; Jináb-i Muḥammad-'Alí Darvísh; Áqá Muḥammad-Ibráhím Darvísh; Ustád 'Alí Ṣabbágh; Jináb-i Amru'lláh, son of Salmán; Mírzá Akbar, son of Mírzá Ismá'íl; and Áqá 'Alí, son of Muḥammad-Ismá'íl, who had been martyred earlier.[12]

Before Shaykh Dhakaríyyá left Nayríz he installed a man there as his deputy. The rule of the Shaykh and his deputy lasted for a month. During that time pressure was maintained on the Bahá'ís. Those who were in hiding could not come out. The properties, which had been confiscated, stayed in the rebels' hands and the women and children, through necessity, lived on the barest minimum. Father and the members of his group lived for a month on a daily ration of figs and a little coarse bread. After a month news was received that a new governor had been installed in Fárs, that Qavámu'l-Mulk-i Shírází had been put in charge of keeping law and order in the province and that his force was moving towards Nayríz and the areas under the control of tribal chiefs. As this news spread, the situation changed, enabling father and two other Bahá'í boys of his age to venture out. Father was then able to run errands for his mother outside the home. But whenever he risked going out, he faced the abusive language of the children who roamed the streets and inflicted on him and other Bahá'ís as much harm as they possibly could. One day he met another Bahá'í, Ḥájí Mír 'Alí, who had just come out of his hiding place. He whispered into father's ear, 'Some relief supplies have arrived from Shíráz. Tell your mother to send someone to my home to receive a saddlebag of wheat (about 75–80 kilos).' Father was overjoyed, ran home and gave his mother the glad-tidings. His mother said in response, 'My husband is in the Holy Land, I cannot degrade him by accepting handouts.'[13] The young hungry boy, who was longing for a piece of good bread, was naturally disappointed.

Gradually the inhabitants of the town discovered where father and his family were hiding and exerted pressure on their hosts, who were their close relatives, for having sheltered them. One day their landlady suggested to grandmother Núríján that in order to put an end to the talk circulating in the town, she should consider going with the womenfolk to the mosque. She stressed that her mere presence in the mosque would suffice to ease the pressure. Grandmother refused to comply, saying, 'I will leave your home and stay in the wilderness but will not visit the mosque. I will not bring upon myself the blight of people thinking that I have abandoned my faith.'[14]

Several weeks after the Shaykh's conquest of Nayríz, which turned the town into a living hell for the Bahá'ís, Qavámu'l-Mulk and his force proceeded to Sarvistán, where about 80 Bahá'í refugees from Nayríz had gathered. He encouraged them to return to Nayríz and resume their activities. He assured them of the restoration of normality and issued severe orders empowering the newly appointed deputy governor of Nayríz, Riḍá Qulí Khán, entitled the Mushír-i Díván, to chase the Shaykh and his supporters out of the town.

It was close to mid-May 1909 when grandmother Núríján took the hands of her three young children and returned to the ruins of her home. The first night was spent on the debris with no bedding but to them it looked like paradise, for they had been freed from confinement and could breathe a sigh of relief. Another month elapsed before grandfather 'Abdu'l-Ḥusayn returned from the Holy Land and found his partner, Mullá Ḥasan, martyred, all accounting books, records and documents destroyed, harvests demolished, agricultural produce devastated and his family without shelter. The Nayrízí pilgrims, upon re-entering Iran, had heard of the disturbances in Nayríz but did not know the details until they arrived in Shíráz. Even then they did not know the extent of the devastation that had taken place.

In a Tablet revealed during those frightful days, 'Abdu'l-Bahá wrote:

> O ye Friends of God! In these days Nayríz hath become the place for blood-shedding. Sanctified souls among the loved ones of the Lord have sacrificed their lives and hastened to the field of martyrdom in the path of the conspicuous Light. For this the eyes are tearful and hearts burn with sorrow. Sobbing and sighs have soared to the highest heaven and extreme sadness hath caused lamentation to appear anew. 'Abdu'l-Bahá's highest wish is to quaff a drop of the chalice of faithfulness and to be intoxicated with the wine of sacrifice, that the end of His life may be the beginning of infinite grace . . .
>
> O ye friends of 'Abdu'l-Bahá! In these days, through a felicitous event and confirmations from the Lord of the highest Heaven, as well as assistance from the unseen Kingdom, the sanctified body of His Highness, the Báb, was interred in its Shrine on Mount Carmel. Therefore, sacrifice was necessary and martyrdom required. The loved ones in Nayríz, inebriated by this brimming chalice and with the rod of high resolve, have won the trophy of excellence. Happy are they and blessed is this chalice, which is overflowing with the wine of the love of God. Upon them be the Glory of God . . .[15]

## The Worldwide Bahá'í Response

When the news of the devastation suffered by the Bahá'ís of Nayríz reached the Bahá'ís in the East and West, donations started pouring in to help the survivors of the martyrs and those who had lost their homes and means of livelihood. The phenomenal solidarity shown by the Bahá'ís of the world helped the teaching work in Nayríz, for non-Bahá'ís saw that what the Bahá'ís preached was put to the test and proved by deeds. The success of the teaching activities spearheaded by prominent teachers such as Mírzá Faḍlu'lláh, son of Ḥáj Muḥammad Raḥím, and Shaykh Muḥammad-Ḥusayn, son of Mullá Muḥammad-Shafí', increased understanding between the inhabitants of the town and created a loving atmosphere which continued for some time.

During the period of calm that followed, the first Local Spiritual Assembly of Nayríz was formed and took charge of the affairs of the community. The Assembly, comprising devoted believers, started a campaign of educating the friends and familiarizing them with their spiritual, personal and social duties. In a short time the affairs of the community flourished such that it became the envy of the inhabitants of the town, who showed special respect for the Bahá'í Assembly. In one instance two non-Bahá'í parties to a dispute, who were unsuccessful in settling their case in the civil court, asked the Assembly to adjudicate. The Assembly acted as a just arbiter. Its decision was accepted and respected by both parties, thus relieving them of exorbitant legal expense and raising the Assembly's prestige in the eyes of the public.[16]

The rectitude of conduct of the Bahá'ís, especially their honesty in dealing with one another as well as with members of the public, and the trustworthiness they evinced in their business transactions attracted the attention of local and foreign traders and businessmen, who showed special interest in dealing with them. Such was the degree of trust that transactions with Bahá'ís were often carried out without a formal contract and major traders willingly sent them goods on credit, to be paid for in easy instalments.

## Renewed Onslaughts

When Shaykh Dhakaríyyá Kúhistání heard that the people of Nayríz associated freely with one another and that Bahá'ís enjoyed the respect and trust of the inhabitants of the town, he was outraged. To reverse the tide and check the influence of the Bahá'ís, he sent to Nayríz a force headed by his brother, Shaykh Abu'l-Ḥasan-i Kúhistání. His purpose was to conquer the town and renew the atrocities committed earlier. The deputy governor of Nayríz, Mushir-i Díván, who had been installed by Qavámu'l-Mulk, secured the support of all the inhabitants to defend the town and stand firm against the onslaught of the enemy. A battle took place between the forces of the government and Shaykh Abu'l-Ḥasan in Gudar-i Ḥasanábád. In that battle the Shaykh was defeated and his forces retreated. He was astonished to see the inhabitants of the town firmly behind the governor. The Shaykh, however, did not give up his ambition of reconquering Nayríz. He waited for the central government's authority and control to decline. After one year he felt the time suitable for an attack. On this occasion he sent Shaykh Kamál together with a group of armed men. They pretended that the Shaykh's aim was the supervision of the spiritual affairs of the inhabitants and that they were sent at the invitation of a group of people from Nayríz.

Upon arrival, Shaykh Kamál declared that he had come to exterminate the Bahá'ís and assured the Muslims that they had nothing to fear. He then conveyed Shaykh Dhakaríyyá's message that the Bahá'ís were either to pay *jizyih*, a special religious tax exceeding 20,000 tumans, or, failing that, 20 of them were to be beheaded and their heads sent to the Shaykh. The headman of Maḥallih Pahlaví conveyed the message to the Baha'is. The decree was met with repugnance by the inhabitants of the *maḥallih*, Bahá'í and non-Bahá'í alike. The headman and a few influential people convened a meeting at the home of grandfather Ḥájí Mírzá 'Abdu'l-Ḥusayn to discuss the matter. Not only did the participants express their repugnance regarding the decree but declared their willingness to help raise the money. After the decision was made and the sum raised, Shaykh Kamál was invited to lunch in the home of Mírzá 'Abdu'ṣ-Ṣamad, known as the Vakílu'r-Ru'áyá (the peoples' deputy). The raised sum was delivered to him at that meeting and he returned to his abode in the Kúhistán.

As the chaotic situation continued, it became clear that the local government was unable to provide security for the inhabitants. Instability was widespread throughout the province. Qavámu'l-Mulk's attention was turned to Shíráz and the surrounding areas. The Arab tribes of Fárs decided to conquer Nayríz. Amír Qulí Khán-i 'Arab made a pact of cooperation with the chiefs of a few other tribes and together they attacked the town. The armed forces of Nayríz unitedly thwarted this assault as well and prevented a certain massacre. However, the repeated assaults of the enemy over such a short time depleted resources and diverted the believers' time and energy away from pursuing business and agricultural interests and into defending their lives.

## The Governorship of Manṣúru's-Salṭanih

The situation improved when a new governor was instated in Shíráz. Qavámu'l-Mulk was again charged with establishing order in areas occupied by various tribes in Fárs and Manṣúru's-Salṭanih Arab-i Shaybání was appointed the governor of Nayríz. Manṣúru's-Salṭanih was very familiar with the Bahá'í Faith. Some believe he was a Bahá'í.[17]

The Local Spiritual Assembly of Nayríz and Manṣúru's-Salṭanih enjoyed friendly relations. Consequently, the relationship between Bahá'ís and non-Bahá'ís improved markedly. The inhabitants of the town enjoyed security and freedom. Bahá'ís and non-Bahá'ís met in fellowship and amity; many were attracted to the Bahá'í Faith. No one was impeded in his efforts to earn a livelihood through trade and crafts.

Father said that one of the most important contributions made by Manṣúru's-Salṭanih to the people of Nayríz was building the system of education and establishing the Manṣúrí School. Before the establishment of the school, the children in Nayríz were taught how to read and write by tutors who held classes in private homes. Religious students studied in mosques and seminaries. The subjects taught were Persian and Arabic, the Qur'án and the poetry of Ḥáfiẓ and Sa'dí. Those who wanted to continue their studies further had to go to Shíráz. The Manṣúrí School was established through the generosity of Manṣúru's-Salṭanih and some prominent people of the town. Once the school was ready, two people from Shíráz were invited to become the principal and the Arabic teacher; Mírzá 'Abdu'l-Ḥusayn, son of Mírzá Áqá Buzurg-i Bázyár, and Shaykh Áqá, known as Fáḍil-i Qaṣru'd-Dashtí, respectively. They were both Bahá'ís. The operational budget of the school was provided by charging monthly fees, as well as by donations received from wealthy citizens. Other teachers were chosen from among the inhabitants of the town. Soon the school became famous and was recognized as one of the best in the province of Fárs. Up to this time a school with six grades had existed only in Shíráz. Other towns had either no school or one with only two grades.

The number of Bahá'í students registered in the school reached 25. Although the fee was high, they paid it happily and continued their education with excellent results. Father and another Bahá'í youth who had previously studied Persian and Arabic registered in the highest class. The school operated for two years as a private enterprise and attracted much favourable publicity. Then the government stepped in and took over. Afterwards it continued operating under the aegis of the Department of Education in the province of Fárs. Father's insatiable quest for learning was somewhat satisfied during those happy years of his life. As his Arabic improved he was able to immerse himself further in the ocean of the Bahá'í writings and enjoy the sweet savour of unravelling their meaning and purpose.

At the Manṣúrí School, Bahá'í and non-Bahá'í students associated freely with one another. They were invited to and visited each other's homes. When the Bahá'í youth visited Maḥallih Kúchih Bálá, quite a distance from Maḥallih Pahlaví, they stayed overnight. The depth of trust between them was such that although Maḥallih Kúchih Bálá was notorious for previously having shown animosity towards the Bahá'ís, now the youth gathered there and freely discussed subjects of interest, including the Bahá'í Faith. During this time two residents of that *maḥallih* became Bahá'ís. One was Siyyid Maḥmúd, son of Siyyid 'Ísá. He died during an influenza epidemic. The other was his cousin, Siyyid Muḥammad. He later taught at the school. As he lived among Muslim fanatics, he did not make his newly-found faith publicly known. Others from among the students and teachers at the school learned a great deal about the Bahá'í Faith. Father said that those years were the best period of his life, for he was consumed with Bahá'u'lláh's love to the degree that he wanted nothing but His good pleasure, and teaching His Cause was his highest wish and aspiration.

During the governorship of Manṣúru's-Salṭanih, law and order reigned in Nayríz and calm prevailed. Under those conditions people enjoyed freedom to conduct business without fear of harassment. Consequently, the Bahá'ís did very well, which caused resentment in the hearts of the people of malice.

As Manṣúru's-Salṭanih's rule lengthened, the traditional agitators began sowing the seeds of dissension. Among them were members of the family of Fatḥ-'Ali Khán, the grandchildren of Zaynu'l-'Ábidín Khán. They considered the governorship of Nayríz their birthright.[18] When differences between the two opposing camps over leadership deepened, those highly resentful of the freedom enjoyed by the Bahá'ís joined the opponents of Manṣúru's-Salṭanih and voiced objection to the Bahá'ís holding meetings and having activities without any impediment.

Encouraged by the support he enjoyed, the deputy governor raised the banner of rebellion but was chased out of the town by Manṣúru's-Salṭanih's forces. The deputy governor fled to Dáráb and sought refuge with two Bahárlú chiefs, 'Abdu'l-Ḥusayn Khán and Amír Áqá Khán, whose clans and Manṣúru's-Salṭanih's clan had been at odds for a long time. Gradually others from Nayríz and Dáráb joined them and created a formidable force, which moved towards Nayríz and laid siege to the town.

A fierce battle took place between the assailants and Manṣúru's-Salṭanih's army, which was supported by many Nayrízís. The battle raged for several days. Manṣúru's-Salṭanih sought and received military assistance from the Lashanís, traditional allies of his clan. He also called to his aid his nephew, Lieutenant Muḥammad-Taqí Khán, who was stationed in Shíráz. As reinforcements arrived and the number of combatants increased, the battle intensified until one night the enemy, in a surprise attack, took one of the quarters of Nayríz, which bordered Maḥallih Pahlaví. The next morning the combined forces of Manṣúru's-Salṭanih, led by his nephew, together with the Lashaní gunmen and the local forces supporting the governor, moved towards the vanquished *maḥallih* and surrounded it. A fierce fight began, claiming many lives on both sides.

Then suddenly there was silence. Both sides simultaneously laid down their arms and left the battleground. As the governor's forces were retreating to their base, they advised the inhabitants of Maḥallih Pahlaví to leave, for they said the enemy was about to take over the *maḥallih* and massacre the Bahá'ís. Upon hearing the news, father's father rushed home and conveyed the message to his family. But it was too late for them to escape. All they could do was to resign themselves to their fate and offer supplications to Bahá'u'lláh to save them from the claws of the ferocious wolves intent on tearing them and other innocent Bahá'ís apart.

At that fateful moment a person came running from the *maḥallih* where the battle had raged earlier and announced that the assailants were in retreat. Father and his family rushed to the rooftop and saw the enemy retreating to their base. The government forces were informed of this favourable development. They moved back to the *maḥallih* which the enemy had vacated and took control. Thus a calamitous event was averted.

The battle continued for a few more days. Finally, with the mediation of the benevolent Ḥájí Mírzá Muḥammad-Qulí Qurá'í, the two sides ceased fire and signed a peace treaty. According to the terms of the agreement, Amír Ḥusayn Khán, grandson of Fatḥ-'Alí Khán, who was the main cause of the trouble, and his supporters were to return to Nayríz and enjoy immunity from prosecution. In exchange, they were to desist from taking up arms against the government. Both sides honoured the terms of the agreement. Thus a long-standing dispute came to an end, at least temporarily, and the hand of providence saved the Bahá'ís from a terrible fate.

## Deterioration of Security

The governor of Fárs, Niẓámus-Salṭanih, and the man in charge of keeping law and order, Qavámu'l-Mulk, were rivals and exploited events each to his own advantage. The general situation in the province deteriorated as differences between them deepened. Finally, hidden hostilities boiled over and resulted in open warfare between them and their supporters. One of the repercussions of that war was the deterioration of the security situation in different parts of Fárs. Qavámu'l-Mulk was defeated and fled the country.

Manṣúru's-Salṭanih, the governor of Nayríz, replaced Qavámu'l-Mulk, and his brother, Amír Salím Khán Arab-i Shaybání, was appointed the governor of Nayríz. The rule of Amír Salím Khán was of a short duration. Those appointed after him were self-serving, greedy and cruel. The Bahá'ís of the town were again at the mercy of tyrants who used various pretexts to exert pressure on them and make their lives intolerable. They often used extortion and made the Bahá'ís pay exorbitant fines.

One of the Bahá'ís who was repeatedly required to pay fines was grandfather 'Abdu'l-Ḥusayn. When the inhabitants of Maḥallih Pahlaví, Bahá'í and non-Bahá'í alike, saw that there was no end to the governor's unjust demands, they refused to pay any more fines. The governor issued orders for cannonballs to be fired at their *maḥallih* and for the place be plundered. The inhabitants resisted and succeeded in protecting their homes and property. In the ensuing battle one soldier was killed. The governor made the inhabitants of Maḥallih Pahlaví pay compensation. One Bahá'í, Mullá Ḥusayn, son of Ḥájí Qásim, was also killed. Finally, all the inhabitants of Nayríz united against the tyrannical governor and forced him to flee.

The man responsible for firing cannonballs at the homes of Bahá'ís also fled. To protect him from harm when he returned, grandfather 'Abdu'l-Ḥusayn hid him in his home for one month. During that time the fugitive studied many Bahá'í books and wrote a brief account of his life at the back of a copy of *Iqtidárát*.[19] After one month he went to Shíráz and was not heard of again. According to father, grandfather was not a dynamic teacher of the Cause of God but taught many with the force of example and true love. One of the people he taught was Mullá Ḥusayn-i Ustádí, a fanatic and staunch follower of the Imám Jum'ih. He had a farm next to grandfather's orchard. Every day, on the way to his farm, he was greeted lovingly by grandfather and shown some act of kindness, which caused him to look seriously into the tenets of the religion that had made grandfather such a good person. His investigation led him to the Faith of Bahá'u'lláh.

When father was in his late teen years, a perilous event occurred on the first day of Muḥarram, which coincides with the anniversary of the birth of the Báb according to the lunar calendar.[20] On that day, after the celebration of the holy day, the Bahá'í men went to one of the orchards near the fort of Khájih to have a picnic. The non-Bahá'ís who were looking for pretexts to agitate the people found the occasion suitable for carrying out their evil design. The trouble started when the daughter of Mashhadí Hádí and the wife of the Ḥishmatu'l-Islám, the mujtahid of Maḥallih Pahlaví, had an encounter with grandmother Núríján (father's mother) in the public bath. The exact nature of the encounter has not been recorded but from the stories I heard many years later it seems that the incident had to do with the fact that the attendant served grandmother first because she had arrived earlier. The wife of the Ḥishmatu'l-Islám perceived this as an insult. She became insolent and used abusive language. Grandmother, realizing the gravity of the situation, briskly dressed and left the bath. This incident and the fact that Bahá'ís celebrated the anniversary of the birth of the Báb on the first of Muḥarram served as pretexts for the enemies to attack the Bahá'ís. The agitators immediately organized a group, took up position in the Masjid-i Jámi' and fired shots at the home of father's parents.

On that day grandfather was recovering from an illness and had not gone out to celebrate. Father, too, had stayed at home to look after his father. As soon as their home was fired on, grandfather sent father to seek help from his nephew Mírzá 'Alí-Muḥammad and two other friends who owned guns. Luckily, they too were at home. As soon as they heard the news, they came with their guns and responded to the fire. Their defensive action gave time for the Bahá'í youth to return from their outing, for grandfather had sent an envoy to apprise them of developments. In less than 30 minutes 80 men arrived and reinforced the ranks of the small number of Bahá'ís defending themselves. As they advanced towards the enemy's position, the attackers realized that they were unable to resist the counterattack. They sent a message to the inhabitants of Maḥallih Bázár and sought their assistance for the assault they had initiated under the guise of *jihád* (holy war). The wise men of the Bázár refused to get involved. But when they saw the situation getting out of control, they mediated a truce. One of the mediators from Maḥallih Bázár was Siyyid As͟hraf, the Shayk͟hu'l-Islám, who was a believer at heart. He and two others among the 'ulamá, accompanied by a representative of the governor and several other notables, went to the home of father's parents and summoned Mas͟hhadí Hádí, his sons and several other agitators and warmongers. During that meeting, reconciliation was achieved.

The popularity enjoyed by grandfather 'Abdu'l-Ḥusayn made him a target for persecution by those who wished him ill. Some malevolent governors singled him out for maltreatment. One of them, Ḥis͟hmatu's-Sulṭán, threw him into prison and had him tortured. He then fined him the sum of 80 tumans, an exorbitant amount of money in those days. The fine outraged the inhabitants of Maḥallih Pahlaví. To show sympathy and solidarity with the Bahá'ís, the non-Bahá'ís initiated a response. They spread a tablecloth in front of grandfather's shop and invited the inhabitants of Maḥallih Pahlaví, Bahá'í and non-Bahá'í alike, to place on it whatever sum of money they could afford. Many participated in this benevolent act. The amount of money collected was more than that demanded by the governor. The money was placed in a bag and taken to the seat of the government. It was presented to the governor with a message: 'Since Mírzá 'Abdu'l-Ḥusayn is innocent, we have considered his fine a collective one.' The governor took note of the solidarity that existed between Bahá'ís and non-Bahá'ís and thereafter exercised restraint in his treatment of the Bahá'ís.

## The Famine and the Passing of Grandfather 'Abdu'l-Ḥusayn

Grandfather suffered many hardships at the hands of the enemies of the Bahá'í Faith. His family endured with him the consequences of the malevolent deeds perpetrated against him. Then came the famine with its devastating effects on the poor and needy. Although grandfather had suffered the severe and successive restrictions imposed upon him by the local government and had been deprived of many trade and agricultural benefits, when the famine made everyone's life miserable, he opened up his warehouse of dried figs and distributed the prized commodity among those whose survival was at stake, both Bahá'ís and non-Bahá'ís. His concern for the plight of the poor and needy was phenomenal. He let nothing stand in his way to extend assistance to them, not even the tremendous love he had for his children. The following story tells the extent of his concern.

One day during the month of the fast father returned home from a hard and long day of work. It was close to sunset and the time for breaking the fast was drawing near. After the long Tablet of the Fast was chanted, father told his parents that on his way home from the orchard he had seen two hungry men eating weeds to satisfy their hunger. They had had little clothing to keep them warm in the cold weather. His father reprimanded him for not bringing them home and instructed him to go immediately and fetch them. His mother objected. She wanted him to go after breaking his fast. His father wanted him to go right away. In the end his father prevailed. Father went and brought the two men home. Then he broke his fast. The two men stayed with the family for several days. They were fed and clothed. Unfortunately, one of them who had suffered beyond his endurance died; he was given a decent burial.

The continuation of the famine caused by lack of rainfall and accentuated by a swarm of locusts which stripped all trees of their foliage and fruit, coupled with the cruelty of tyrannical governors, increased grandfather's woeful ordeals and affected his health. He developed severe, persistent stomach ache. The primitive medical care available in Nayríz in those days could not save his life. After several days of pain, he passed away in 1334 AH (circa 1916).

Grandfather 'Abdu'l-Ḥusayn received several Tablets from 'Abdu'l-Bahá, including this one:

In care of Jináb-i Mullá Shafí'[21]
Nayríz, Jináb-i Mírzá 'Abdu'l-Ḥusayn, nephew of Jináb-i Áqá Siyyid Muḥammad, upon him be Bahá'u'lláhu'l-Abhá
Alláh-u-Abhá! O thou servant of God! Render praise to the Lord

of wisdom that thou wert led to the sheltering shade of the divine Lote Tree and enabled to take refuge under the protective shadow of the Tree of Life. He caused thee to drink from the eternal Kawthar and watered thee from the crystal clear spring. Now thou shouldst spread across the world, with absolute ecstasy and attraction, the soul-stirring fragrances of the Covenant, and protect thyself and others from the whisperings of those who have turned away therefrom. The glory of God be upon thee.
*'Ayn 'Ayn.*[22]

Father attributes his father's success in mirroring forth in his deeds the teachings of Bahá'u'lláh to the training he received as a child from his mother, a devoted, virtuous, decent and meek woman.

The name of grandfather 'Abdu'l-Ḥusayn's mother was Fáṭimih Bagum. Her father was Siyyid Ja'far-i Yazdí, who embraced the Cause of the Báb through Áqá Siyyid Yaḥyá Vaḥíd. He was one of Vaḥíd's companions in the fort of Khájih. After Vaḥíd was martyred, Siyyid Ja'far was imprisoned and his properties confiscated. After two years' imprisonment, Siyyid Ja'far was exiled from Nayríz. Fáṭimih Bagum and her family later returned to the town. On the way there, her husband, Mírzá Ismá'íl, was killed in Qaṭrúyih at the instigation of the governor of Nayríz. After her husband's death, Fáṭimih Bagum, a single parent, raised her three children – one son and two daughters – with great difficulty. Her son, grandfather 'Abdu'l-Ḥusayn, was then one year old. Since Fáṭimih Bagum was the daughter of Siyyid Ja'far, the believers in Nayríz received her honourably and showed her special regard. She rendered many valuable services in Nayríz and was the recipient of several Tablets from the Blessed Beauty. The following is one of them:

Amatu'lláh Fáṭimih Bagum
In the name of the Peerless Friend
The world is engulfed in the flames of tyranny and injustice. The heedless have chosen worldly vanities to everlasting bliss. The people of equity are wronged by and captured in the hands of

the followers of tyranny. What happened in the land of Ṣád is a testimony to the truth of what hath been said.[23] Blessed is he who hath not been held back from the Exalted One by the agitation of the misguided.

O Amatu'lláh! Thou art residing in thy abode and the Wronged One of the world hath turned His attention to thee from the Most Great Prison and made mention of thee. If thou renderest thanks with the tongues of all the inhabitants of the world, thou shalt find it as naught compared with this most great bounty. Do thou appreciate the value of this favour and cling thou to the cord of His bestowal.

Convey this Wronged One's greetings to all the handmaids of that land, i.e. those who believe in God, and hail them with the glad-tidings of His mention that all may happily and joyfully engage in chanting praise during the days of His manifestation. At this time the Pen of the Most High mentioneth thy daughter.[24] Happy is the one who in this day of God hath quaffed the wine of His love and turned unto His horizon. Glory be upon thee and upon her, and upon the one who hath been named Mírzá,[25] and upon the servants of God and His handmaids, those who have turned to the Highest Horizon when the Lord of the universe appeared with conspicuous sovereignty.[26]

## Mother's Family and Early Life

The exact date of mother's birth is unknown. The reason for it is that, as stated earlier, the registration of births was not a requirement in Iran until the late 1920s, therefore no government agency or office had been assigned the task. Although people of stature and rank had titles, nobody had a surname, nor was it necessary to have one. When mother was born, Iran was in the grip of Muslim orthodoxy, which had no respect for women's rights and hence their identity did not generally matter. Children were usually identified as the sons or daughters of their fathers. In my mother's case, she would have been known as Ṭúbá, daughter of Ḥájí Mírzá Aḥmad-i Nayrízí. Women were generally treated as adjuncts to the male members of their families. For example, a girl would first be referred to as the daughter of her father, then as the wife of her husband, later as the mother of her firstborn son. If the first category of male relatives was absent, she would be referred to as the sister of her brother, especially if he were well-known. If none of the male categories were present, then she would be called the mother of her firstborn daughter. But this was indeed a rare occurrence.

Some families, especially those who were literate, kept track of their children's birth date as they were born. They wrote the name, date of birth and other pertinent information in a book the family held dear. The illiterate – and the majority fell into this category – made a mental note of it. With the passage of time people's memories faded and became blurry and confused, especially if several children were involved. And in those days people had lots of children. Moreover, adequate protection against natural disasters did not exist. How often it happened that floods and earthquakes destroyed everything, including precious records. In the lifespan of my parents Nayríz witnessed devastating floods, which divested many inhabitants of the town of almost everything they had.

When it became compulsory for Iranian parents to acquire birth certificates for their children, some chose arbitrary dates for those born several years earlier. Those who wanted their sons to enjoy exemption from military service inflated their ages and adjusted the ages of their siblings accordingly. My mother is a case in point. When birth certificates were acquired for her and her siblings, including her younger brothers, they were reported to be several years older than their real age. Her Persian birth certificate, issued in Nayríz in 1308 AH (1929), shows her birth date as 1276 AH (1897)! A more accurate date would be 1905–6.

According to mother's own recollection, when her father returned from the Holy Land after attaining 'Abdu'l-Bahá's presence, she was young enough to sit on his lap and hear him talk about that momentous visit. Her father was on pilgrimage in March 1909 when, as described above, on 21 March (Naw-Rúz) 'Abdu'l-Bahá placed the remains of the Báb in the Shrine He had built on

Mount Carmel. Although mother remembered her father's return from that highly significant trip, she did not remember anything about the disturbances that had engulfed the Bahá'í community of Nayríz during the uprising of Shaykh Dhakaríyyá, which culminated in the martyrdom of 18 believers. The reason may be either that she was too young to recall the event or because her mother's relatives, who were staunch Muslims, during her father's absence from Nayríz provided protection to the family. Owing to this, mother's family, their home and property were untouched in the uprising. Mother said that she could not have been more than four when her father returned from pilgrimage. Thus 1905–6 seems a more realistic birth date for her.

Mother was named Ṭúbá, meaning blessedness, at birth. She passed away in Shíráz on 16 March 2001. Her life covers all but five years of the 20th century, described by 'Abdu'l-Bahá as the 'century of light' and the 'blessed century'. Her long life was full of challenges and adventures. Although semi-literate as a young woman, she broke away from the traditions and conventions holding the female population of Nayríz in its tight grip. When she married the forward-looking and erudite man that my father was, she made mighty efforts to be a befitting partner and companion for him. Together they travelled extensively in Iran and abroad. Wherever they went, she gained valuable experiences and adjusted herself to the conditions of the area. At the beginning of the Islamic revolution in Iran, she and father left their beloved homeland and settled in India. After father passed away in India in 1984, she moved to the United States, and except for a brief stay in Saskatoon, Canada, spent some ten years in that country. Three years before her passing, she returned to Shíráz, where she had lived for many, many years. She is buried in the Bahá'í cemetery there. What happened during the 96 years between her birth and death is the main reason for writing this account.

Mother's father was Mírzá Aḥmad and her mother Farrukh Khánum. They were both from Nayríz. Her father embraced the Faith of Bahá'u'lláh in his youth and dedicated the rest of his life to its service. As explained above, he visited 'Abdu'l-Bahá in 1909 and was among the three pilgrims from Nayríz who witnessed the interment by 'Abdu'l-Bahá of the Báb's remains. He also visited Shoghi Effendi twice. During one of these visits he requested and was granted permission to donate carpets for the Báb's Shrine.[27] Mírzá Aḥmad married Farrukh Khánum before he embraced the Bahá'í Faith. She came from a staunch Muslim family. Although a supporter of the Bahá'ís, Farrukh Khánum never registered as one. She bore five children, three girls and two boys. They were Ṭúbá Khánum, Mírzá 'Abdu'l-Ḥusayn, Tábandih (Munavvar) Khánum, Mírzá Jalál and Bushrá Khánum. The children were raised as Bahá'ís and all but one established Bahá'í families who are now scattered in different parts of the world. Mírzá Aḥmad had three children from another marriage, one girl and two boys: Rúḥá Khánum, Mírzá 'Abbás and Manṣúr, who died young some 60 years ago. Mírzá Aḥmad's second wife, Laqá Khánum, came from a Bahá'í family. When Shoghi Effendi enforced the law of monogamy, she and Mírzá Aḥmad divorced.[28]

Mother's early years were spent in Nayríz. She received elementary education at home. In the early years of the 20th century formal education in Iran was a novelty enjoyed only by the elite. It was generally unavailable to the female population, especially to those living in smaller towns and villages. Girls rarely received instruction in the arts of reading and writing. Those who were fortunate enough to receive elementary education were mostly taught how to read, not to write. It was considered morally wrong for girls to learn how to write, for the ability to write, it was argued, would enable them to engage in clandestine communication with their lovers and undesirable elements, making complete monitoring and controlling of the women's lives impossible.

Mother, although able to read the Qur'án and the poetry of Ḥáfiẓ and Sa'dí, could not write for a good part of her life. The inability to write became a major problem when her children grew up, got married and moved away. Whenever she wanted to write to her older children who had left the country, she would dictate her message to one of her younger offspring. She would then read the letter, ensuring that it contained everything that she wanted to say and asking that deletions or additions be made before mailing it. This situation became untenable when all but one of her children left home. She knew that the day was not far off when her youngest daughter, Firishtih, would follow in the footsteps of her siblings and leave the country. So, at the age of 65 she attended adult education classes and learned how to write. Her letters, although profound in content, were written in a handwriting resembling that of an elementary school child.

Mother was a quick learner and had an excellent mind which remained sharp to the end of her life. She combined high intellectual ability with practicality. She had a way with words. She expressed herself in short sentences and easily made others feel what she was going through. Had she received proper education, she would have achieved wonders. She was well aware of the limitations that tradition imposed on her generation and was content with all that life had offered her. She did not dwell on the unpleasant things in life and focused on the tasks at hand. Although obedient to authority and respectful of the rights of others, she was not intimidated by those whose academic and scholastic achievements made them arrogant and intolerant. She was dignified and well respected for who she was.

## The Marriage of Mírzá Muḥammad-Shafí‘ and Ṭúbá Khánum

Since young women and men of marrying age could not traditionally meet, get acquainted and choose their life partners, it was left to parents to look out for and find suitable spouses for their children. The marriage proposal usually came from the man's family. The woman's family had the luxury to agree or reject it. Marriage between members of one family, such as cousins, was common. The children of families with business ties and those who enjoyed similar social stature stood a better chance of marrying one another. Mother was fortunate to have a Bahá'í father and a mother who did not go against the wishes of her husband. She was also fortunate in that her father had friends among the Bahá'ís with whom he had business ties. One such family was that of Mírzá 'Abdu'l-Ḥusayn and Núríján Khánum. Mírzá Aḥmad was a close associate of Mírzá Abdu'l-Ḥusayn and together they had travelled to the Holy Land to visit 'Abdu'l-Bahá in 1909. The two fathers had high hopes that their eldest children, Ṭúbá Khánum and Mírzá Muḥammad-Shafí', would marry and this was not hidden from the rest of the family, including the bride and groom to be.

Since birth certificates when they were first introduced in Iran did not always reflect accurately the birth date of their holders, it was not easy to establish the exact age of the parties to a marriage. The age of maturity in the Bahá'í Faith for boys and girls is 15 but in those days the Bahá'ís had to do the best they could to establish accurate ages of the bride and groom. In some cases they may have had to go by an approximation of their ages. Mother may have been barely 15 when she got married in 1298, corresponding to 1919.

Mírzá 'Abdu'l-Ḥusayn, the father of the groom, Mírzá Muḥammad-Shafí', had passed away when Mírzá Muḥammad-Shafí' was about 20 years old. Being the eldest son, he had to become the breadwinner of the family and help his mother, Núríján Khánum, to raise his four siblings, the youngest being five years old.

The marriage of Mírzá Muḥammad-Shafí' (my father) and Ṭúbá Khánum (my mother) took place after the end of World War I. At that time father was still in charge of the affairs of his own family and mother therefore moved from her parents' home to that of her husband, sharing it with her in-laws, including two minors. Mother's parents were well off, lived a comfortable life and enjoyed the respect of the populace. Father's parents were well known for their allegiance to the Bahá'í Faith and were often targeted by those who persecuted the Bahá'ís for their beliefs and inflicted upon them financial and material loss. As stated earlier, father's father was singled out for persecution. Therefore, although renowned for the staunchness of his faith and the uprightness of his character, he was not financially as well off as mother's family. And when his father passed away, father voluntarily forewent his firstborn privileges and waited until the two minor siblings came of age before dividing his father's estate equally among the surviving offspring.

## Mother's Initial Challenges

Mother's struggles began when she was barely 15 with the adjustments she had to make to her new situation. She suddenly had to leave behind the sheltered life of a young girl in her parents' comfortable home and be the wife of a well-known and erudite Bahá'í who was also the mainstay of his mother and brothers. In her father's home, mother had a nanny who also served as her adviser and confidant. When she had puzzling questions to which she sought answers, she turned to her nanny who unfailingly resolved her perplexities. In her new home she did not have the benefit of her nanny's 'magical' and comforting words, which worked like a soothing medicine for anything that she found unsettling. However, she soon discovered that she had the benefit of a loving and understanding mother-in-law who helped her meet the new challenges with considerable ease. Grandmother Núríján, who had lost her only daughter in infancy, treated her daughter-in-law like her own and, together with father, helped to nurture her spiritual growth and development, something that her non-Bahá'í mother and nanny had been unable to provide. Another person in father's family who had a benevolent effect on mother's life was father's youngest maternal aunt, Fáṭimih Khánum, who later married father's best friend, Mírzá Aḥmad 'Irfán. Mother and aunt Fáṭimih remained good and close friends till the end.

Mother's first challenge as a married woman was to deepen her understanding of the tenets of the Bahá'í Faith. Her ability to read well and her keen interest to learn were her greatest assets in this regard. When prominent Bahá'í teachers visited Nayríz, she participated, with the support and encouragement of father, in the deepening classes they offered. For example, she spoke about attending the deepening classes offered by Jináb-i Fáḍil-i Yazdí when he visited Nayríz. And since her first child was not born until about three years after her marriage, she had ample time to devote to the pursuit of knowledge.

## Father's Pilgrimage

Several years before his marriage father had sought and received permission from 'Abdu'l-Bahá for him and his mother to go on pilgrimage. Thus towards the end of World War I they travelled to Shíráz on their way to the Holy Land. The means of travel in those days was by mule and the trip from Nayríz to Shíráz took a week. The journey was particularly hard and arduous for grandmother. When they reached Shíráz they were informed that, owing to the war, pilgrimage to the Holy Land had been suspended and that they were to postpone their trip. Exhausted and disappointed, they returned to Nayríz. Father and grandmother were both heart-broken that they were not able to fulfil their heart's desire. Father in particular felt that his inadequacy had prevented him from attaining the bounty of pilgrimage. He sent a missive to 'Abdu'l-Bahá expressing his feelings and received the following response:

> Nayríz
> Jináb-i Mírzá Muḥammad-Shafí'
> He is God!
> O thou who art steadfast in the Covenant! Thy letter was well written, its contents filled with spiritual meaning and expressive of thine inner feelings.
>
> Look not at thy inadequacy, rather fix thy gaze on the bounties of the Almighty. The confirmations of the Ancient Beauty, like unto the refreshing breeze, bestow new life on the trees of existence and confer upon leafless and barren trees blossoms, foliage and choice fruit. He turneth the black earth into the highest heaven by adorning it with flowers and vegetation.
>
> Some of you have sought permission to put on the garb of pilgrimage and visit the Sacred Threshold. At present travelling is fraught with endless hardship. Be patient. Ye are permitted to come next year. And upon thee be glory. 'Abdu'l-Bahá 'Abbás.[29]

After a year the means for travelling abroad were in place but taking a trip inside Iran was most difficult for the authority of the central government had weakened considerably and the security situation had worsened drastically. Since travel conditions were most unfavourable for women, grandmother could not join father and six others, all men, who were to make preparations for the trip. It was in the winter of 1920–1 when the seven pilgrims from Nayríz started their long and arduous journey. Father had to leave behind his young bride, whom he had married the previous year. Since it was not deemed appropriate for mother, a young and newly-married woman, to be left behind in a house inhabited by young men – her four brothers-in-law lived in the same house – grandmother decided to forego pilgrimage at that time and remain with her daughter-in-law, making it possible for father to fulfil his heart's desire. Her decision not to accompany her son on pilgrimage was also influenced by the experience of her first trip to Shíráz on mule back, which she found laborious. So, she willingly stayed behind in the hope that when better means of transportation were available, she would make her pilgrimage to the Holy Threshold. Unfortunately that pilgrimage never materialized, for 'Abdu'l-Bahá passed away on 28 November 1921, six months after father's pilgrimage. And although father sought and received permission during the ministry of Shoghi Effendi to go on pilgrimage again, he was never able to undertake the trip owing to family obligations and financial and other difficulties.

The trip from Nayríz to Haifa took several months. Father and his fellow pilgrims travelled by mule from Nayríz to Shíráz and from there to the port of Búshihr. From Búshihr they travelled by steamship to Bombay, then to Alexandria and finally to Haifa in the Holy Land. Their return trip likewise was long and arduous. Their stay in the Holy Land was extended from 19 to 39 days. Father wrote memoirs of his pilgrimage and excerpts have been translated into English by the present writer and appear in this book as appendix 2.[30]

## The Ascension of 'Abdu'l-Bahá

Father was away from Nayríz from December 1920 to June 1921. A few months after his return 'Abdu'l-Bahá ascended to the Abhá Kingdom. This tragic event devastated father, who six months earlier had been in His presence, and made him acutely aware of the vital importance of the Covenant and obedience to the provisions of His Will and Testament. Thus mother learned at an early age and from an ardent lover of 'Abdu'l-Bahá the crucial significance of the Covenant which became the brilliant light guiding the course of their life to the end.

The news of 'Abdu'l-Bahá's ascension was conveyed to Manṣúru's-Salṭanih, the governor of Nayríz, by a special courier sent from Shíráz. The governor apprised Shaykh Áqá Fáḍil-i Qaṣru'd-Dashtí, a Bahá'í who taught Arabic in the Manṣurí School, and asked him to inform the Local Spiritual Assembly of the sad news. As most Bahá'ís, including members of the Local Assembly, were celebrating an elaborate Bahá'í wedding in the house of the bridegroom, Shaykh Áqá summoned the members of the Assembly to a quiet corner on the rooftop and shared with them the news. Upon hearing it the Assembly asked the bridegroom's family to immediately suspend the festivities. This was done and the music band was dismissed. That evening the bridegroom and his father went to the house of the bride's family and quietly accompanied her to her new home.

To avoid disturbances by the non-Bahá'ís, who were ever waiting to find a pretext for disturbing the peace of the town, the ascension of 'Abdu'l-Bahá was not publicly announced. However, after one week, when the Local Spiritual Assembly of Shíráz confirmed the news and forwarded the Greatest Holy Leaf's telegram to this effect, the real reason for the suspension of the wedding festivities became known and befitting memorial gatherings were held. When non-Bahá'ís learned the news they began making plans in secret against the Bahá'ís. Since the governor was a Bahá'í, there was not much they could do. Also, the Local Spiritual Assembly of Nayríz was vigilant. While mourning day and night the grievous loss the Bahá'í community had suffered, it awaited further news about the person who was to lead the worldwide Bahá'í community and carefully watched every development locally. When the Greatest Holy Leaf informed the Bahá'í world that 'Abdu'l-Bahá had left a Will and Testament which would be read on the fortieth day after His ascension and that the name of His successor would be made known then, she also advised that the friends study the Tablet of the Holy Mariner. As the Bahá'ís of Nayríz studied the Tablet with Jináb-i Fáḍil-i Qaṣru'd-Da<u>sh</u>tí, they felt that the Greatest Holy Leaf herself might be the successor. One night Jináb-i Fáḍil shared with the friends his understanding that she would be 'Abdu'l-Bahá's successor. Upon hearing this, an old man named Ma<u>sh</u>hadí Zaynu'l-'Ábidín, illiterate but divinely inspired, who had visited 'Abdu'l-Bahá twice, stood up and said:

> I am illiterate but 'Abdu'l-Bahá's successor cannot be anyone but the child I saw in the cradle. He captivated my heart then. That child is Shoghi Effendi, and it cannot be anyone but him. In his childhood he so enraptured my heart that I called one of my sons Shoghi. When I wrote to 'Abdu'l-Bahá about it, he did not allow it and bestowed upon him another name.

His statement was not favourably received. The audience felt uncomfortable that he persisted in what he understood to be the case. To put an end to speculation, it was decided that thenceforth no one would express an opinion until such time as the Will and Testament had been received.

After 40 days the Will and Testament was read to a select number of the believers in the Holy Land. Several days later the news of the appointment of Shoghi Effendi as the authorized interpreter of the writings and Guardian of the Bahá'í Faith reached the Bahá'ís of Nayríz. The joyous news made everyone without exception exceedingly happy. The Bahá'ís of Nayríz bowed their heads in obedience to him and congratulated one another that they were not left without a shepherd. They also realized and praised the insightfulness of that old man who had recognized the authority of Shoghi Effendi while an infant. And when a copy of the Will and Testament arrived, the Bahá'ís got together and studied its contents with great joy, gratitude and delight.

## The Early Years of Shoghi Effendi's Guardianship

The enthusiastic reaction of the Bahá'ís of Nayríz to the appointment by 'Abdu'l-Bahá of Shoghi Effendi as the Guardian of the Bahá'í Faith, as well as their unflinching allegiance to him, disappointed those who thought the situation was favourable for sowing seeds of doubt in the hearts and benefiting from dissension and disunity among the Bahá'ís. Contrary to their expectation, the community remained united and strong. Consequently, in the early years of the guardianship the Bahá'ís of Nayríz continued to enjoy comparative freedom, which helped them to achieve unprecedented success. With the help of prominent visiting Bahá'í teachers, such as Mírzá Munír-i Nabílzádih, the Bahá'ís of Nayríz made financial pledges for the establishment of two schools, one for boys and one for girls. Each school started with four or five classes and about 40 students. Further classes were added later. Father was appointed as the honorary principal of both schools. He held these positions in addition to membership of the Local Spiritual Assembly of Nayríz and several committees. Moreover, he had responsible and demanding occupations, such as farming and trade.

The two schools advanced rapidly and received repeated praise from the director of education in Nayríz, Mr Ṭughrá'í. When Qavámu'l-Mulk visited Nayríz, schoolchildren together with their teachers and principals went out to welcome him. Students from different schools read welcoming speeches. The director of education admitted that the two Bahá'í schools were superior to others. Upon hearing this Qavámu'l-Mulk instructed his secretary to present the Bahá'í schools with a monetary donation. In discharging his duties as the principal of the two schools, father enjoyed the invaluable assistance and full cooperation of two outstanding Bahá'ís, Mr Amír Khán Ḥisámí and Mrs Nuṣrat Mí<u>th</u>áqí.

The busier father became, the harder and more challenging were the duties of mother, who had to perform additional functions and shoulder extra responsibilities. When visitors stayed in their house, mother was the hostess and responsible for their comfort. When receptions were held in honour of authorities and prominent individuals, she had to supervise the work and make sure that everything was done according to protocol. She also had to attend to the needs of the children and supervise the family's domestic affairs. When evildoers and agitators envious and resentful of the success of the Bahá'ís gained the upper hand and targeted her husband, she stood firmly by his side and together they suffered the consequences.

## The Failed Plot

The first attack organized against the Bahá'ís after the marriage of father and mother was aborted during the second visit to Nayríz of Jináb-i Nabílzádih. Abu'l-Ḥasan-i Kúhistání, a sworn enemy of the Bahá'ís, was invited to Nayríz by the hostile elements of the town to organize an attack against the believers. He was only too happy to comply. He arrived in Nayríz and started agitating the populace against the Bahá'ís. His plan was to gather together in Maḥallih Bázár subversive groups from various quarters of the town and on 10 Muḥarram, the day of the martyrdom of Imám Ḥusayn, attack Maḥallih Pahlaví where the Bahá'ís lived, pillage their belongings and shed their blood. The reason Muḥarram was chosen for the attack was the ease with which people's religious fervour could be exploited during this holy month of mourning for Shí'ís. When the fire of fanaticism and prejudice is fanned into flames at moments of people's vulnerability, they are likely to do things they ordinarily do not commit. Some religious leaders know this and exploit it fully.

Mother was concerned about her husband. He was a prominent Bahá'í in Nayríz and had many enemies who wanted him dead or exiled from his home town. She was also concerned about her family, a target for those who were determined to inflict harm not only on father but also on his next of kin. Fortunately, the governor of Nayríz, Manṣúru's-Salṭanih, who was either a Bahá'í or very sympathetic towards Bahá'ís, watched the situation carefully. Mr Nabílzádih also followed the developments with keen interest and, in consultation with the Local Spiritual Assembly, took a number of steps. In a public meeting attended by many Bahá'ís and non-Bahá'ís, Mr Nabílzádih delivered a speech, saying that the enemies of the Bahá'í Faith had wrongly imagined that since 'Abdu'l-Bahá had passed away the Bahá'í community was left without a leader. What they did not know, he said, was that 'Abdu'l-Bahá had left His young and mighty grandson in charge, who was under the protection and guidance of the Báb and Bahá'u'lláh and received his inspiration and authority from 'Abdu'l-Bahá.

He also said that the adversary had heard that Bahá'ís prefer to be killed rather than kill and that they would not defend themselves against attacks. What the adversaries did not know, he said, was that the Bahá'ís who followed this law had a refuge to which they turned. That refuge was the Universal House of Justice, which was not yet established. In its absence, he continued, Local Spiritual Assemblies performed the duty of looking after local communities. The Local Assembly of Nayríz, he said, would defend the Bahá'ís of the town against any attack. It would first appeal to the authorities and seek protection. If those in charge of keeping law and order failed in carrying out their duties, the Local Assembly would have no choice but to defend the Bahá'ís.

Mr Nabílzádih's speech served two purposes. It prepared the Bahá'ís for defending their lives and renewed in them the spirit of heroism. At the same time, it sent a message to the non-Bahá'ís that it was not as easy a task to attack the Bahá'ís as the enemies of the Faith had made it appear.

Another important element in pacifying the populace was the wise course of action adopted by the governor of Nayríz. Whenever Manṣúru's-Salṭanih met with the prominent people of the town he talked about the heroism the Bahá'ís of Nayríz had shown during the three bloody episodes that had taken place there. He reminded everyone that Bahá'ís had stood firm against their adversary previously and that they would do so again if they had to. He then encouraged the influential people to find an amicable solution to the problem he saw brewing.

In the meantime, the fire which external subversive elements had started was spread rapidly by people of malice and was smouldering in Nayríz. The month of Muḥarram was approaching and the agitation continued unabated. The Bahá'ís were under pressure, for they could not go to work, conduct business or engage in trade. But Bahá'í activities continued better than before.

On the first day of Muḥarram, Mr Nabílzádih asked that the Bahá'ís refrain from going out unless they had essential and urgent things to do. He also asked the Local Assembly that 50 young and heroic souls be placed at his disposal and that four houses with strong defences, each in one of the four corners of Maḥallih Pahlaví, be selected as gathering places for the believers. He further asked that sufficient foodstuffs be stored in those houses and that a number of armed men guard them day and night. When all was done, he and the 50 chosen young men took position in the first stronghold facing the usual route the attackers took.

On the ninth day of Muḥarram, called *tású'á*, a large number of agitators gathered in Maḥallih Bázár and made plans to attack the Bahá'ís the next day (*'áshúrá*). The plan, which was conveyed by informers to Mr Nabílzádih and the Local Spiritual Assembly of Nayríz, was this: Several groups of mourners were to start the procession from different quarters of the town, converge in Maḥallih Bázár and from there move to Maḥallih Pahlaví, where they were to attack and massacre the Bahá'ís. Upon hearing the plan, Mr Nabílzádih put in motion the scheme he had devised. He instructed the 50 valiant souls who were with him to go at midnight to Maḥallih Bázár, the centre of conspiracy. He told them to use unfrequented routes to get there, surround the place before dawn and make it impossible for the groups to converge there in the morning. They did as instructed. The next day the groups found themselves unable to carry out their plan. Disappointed, they returned to their quarters.

When the threat was averted, Mr Nabílzádih praised the youth who had participated in the successful completion of the task, then asked for seven self-sacrificing volunteers to accompany him to Maḥallih Bázár. The seven came forward and together visited the *maḥallih*. They marched unhindered through lines of armed men who were standing guard, entered the house of the director of the post, visited with him for a while, and walked back to their base in Maḥallih Pahlaví. With a series of well-planned and well-executed actions, Mr Nabílzádih demonstrated the heroism of the Bahá'í youth and struck fear in the hearts of those who meant to do the Bahá'ís harm. Consequently, for a considerable time, the agitators dared not plan another attack.

Mr Nabílzádih left Nayríz a few days after that episode. By then calm had replaced agitation and law and order prevailed, enabling the Bahá'ís to go about their work, hold meetings and successfully pursue the projects in hand. The two Bahá'í schools continued to flourish. They enjoyed such a favourable reputation that non-Bahá'í parents pulled their children out of government educational institutions and registered them in Bahá'í schools.

The period of calm and tranquillity that ensued provided a wonderful opportunity for fostering love and unity among Bahá'í families of diverse backgrounds and between them and the institution of the Local Spiritual Assembly. This was an important element in attracting the attention of non-Bahá'ís to the Faith. Another achievement was the establishment of friendly relationships with the inhabitants of the town. In both these achievements the families played an important role. Bahá'ís and non-Bahá'ís enjoyed fellowship and associated with one another freely.

## The Role of the Women

The Bahá'í women played a critical role in fostering the spirit of love and unity. In addition to bearing and raising children and managing the home, they provided loving hospitality, an important ingredient in bringing people together in harmony and fellowship. Although their contribution was completely overshadowed by the men's work, which was performed openly, they were a significant factor in ensuring the success of the ongoing programmes. They often worked quietly behind the scenes, rendering valuable assistance to the male members of their families and expecting no acknowledgement, praise or reward. This characteristic was phenomenal, especially among older Iranian Bahá'í families. My own mother is a good example. By virtue of her husband's prominent position in society, she had a giant share in providing loving services so crucial to ensuring father's success in his work. Her energy for carrying out services behind the scenes seemed inexhaustible. She was tireless in face of the daunting tasks she performed. One of the reasons for women remaining generally absent from early Bahá'í history is their self-abnegation. They worked hard, at times beyond what ordinary human beings could endure, to keep the light of the Faith shining brilliantly in the hearts of their offspring but they never thought what they did was important. That is how they were raised to think and that is what they believed. When the early history of the Bahá'í Faith is rewritten to present the true value of the contribution made by the women believers, future generations will know the significant role their female forebears played.

Having said that, I must add in defence of my father, who has written the history of the Faith in Nayríz, that he did not follow the general trend and, within his limitations and powers, tried to do justice to the cause of womankind. In his memoirs he paid glowing tribute to mother and in his history book he wrote about the women in Nayríz who played such an important role. When possible, he included their photographs.

During the period when the Faith enjoyed freedom, progress in all aspects of community life was evident. Under the guidance of Shoghi Effendi who encouraged Assemblies to set up committees to carry out various functions, the Local Assembly of Nayríz appointed several. One was the committee for the advancement of women. The appointment of similar committees by Assemblies throughout Iran was a necessary step towards preparing women to be elected to Bahá'í institutions at the local and national levels, which finally materialized in 1954. Before this date, women could vote but could not be elected. Some Bahá'ís assume that this late development was due to the women's spiritual immaturity and unpreparedness, which may be true to a certain degree, but men's traditional mind set and presumed superiority, which needed to be gradually tempered, had a lot to do with it. The fact that a man, no matter how backward, ignorant and unlettered, was eligible for membership of the Local Assembly but a woman, no matter how accomplished, learned and able, was ineligible says a lot about the true reasons for women's lack of participation in the decision-making process of the community until the mid-20th century.

Nayríz was blessed with the visit of another well-known Bahá'í teacher, Fáḍil-i Yazdí. He stayed in Nayríz for a while and held classes to deepen the understanding of the believers in the tenets of the Bahá'í Faith. Mother attended the classes held by this renowned teacher. The classes increased the knowledge and understanding of Bahá'u'lláh's Revelation by the young believers, men and women alike, who participated in them. This was in itself a revolutionary stage in the development of the Bahá'í community of Nayríz. It provided opportunity for the men and the women to go beyond what tradition dictated. It afforded the women the opportunity to experience the exhilarating and liberating advantages of receiving an education; and it taught the men to look upon women as members of the community having the right to be educated. The women welcomed the opportunity and the men not only allowed but encouraged their spouses and daughters to attend the classes offered. The result was the enjoyment of the salutary effects of the programme by both sexes.

## The Flood

For older people who were mostly illiterate and could not remember the date of the events that had occurred in the distant past, natural disasters served as landmarks and provided a point of reference for relating an event to a date. In the first decades of the 20th century the people of Nayríz used floods to give a past event a time frame. They often referred to three ruinous floods and, to give an indication during the course of a conversation regarding the approximate date of an important event, they would say it was before or after the third flood, something they all seemed to remember without difficulty. The first of the three floods had happened in 1310 AH (1893), the second in 1315 AH (1898), the third and fiercest in the winter of 1924–5. During the latest flood, torrential rain had fallen for seven consecutive days and deeply concerned those who had experienced previous devastating floods. Soon the inhabitants' worst fears were realized. A fierce flood forced its way through the town, washing away everything in its path. Three of the four main quarters of Nayríz were destroyed. The devastation was so extensive that newspapers reported it both at home and abroad. The houses of my parents and many other Bahá'ís were completely destroyed by the flood. Referring to the flood, father wrote:

> The destruction caused by the flood was so bad that the boundaries of the flattened houses could not be determined. At the time of reconstruction, trees were the only marks they could use to ascertain the original boundaries. Property, movable and immovable, including food warehouses, were either washed away to the sea or buried under the debris. Excavation would have recovered unusable goods and the cost would have been prohibitive. I sustained more loss than all. My family and I had no house to live in. We stayed for some time in the house of my father-in-law, Mírzá Aḥmad. In addition to the house and its furniture, I sustained tremendous loss as several of my food and produce warehouses were buried under the debris.[31] The situation was so bad that many friends felt sorry for me . . .

Newspapers in Iran and abroad carried the news and it soon became the news of the day. The government in those days did not have the financial ability to extend effective help to the victims.

The Local Spiritual Assembly of Shíráz informed the Spiritual Assembly of Ṭihrán, which conveyed the news to the beloved Guardian.[32] He issued emphatic instructions to Ṭihrán, cabled the National Spiritual Assembly of the United States and by letter invited Bahá'í communities in the East and West to make

> contributions to relieve the sufferings of the flood victims. He designated the Local Spiritual Assembly of Shíráz as the central agency for receiving and disbursing funds.
>
> The Bahá'ís of the East and West immediately arose to assist. The collected contributions were sent to the Local Spiritual Assembly of Shíráz. That Assembly sent one of its members, Mr Muḥammad Riḍá Vakhshúrí, with a considerable amount of cash to Nayríz. Under his supervision and with the approval of the Local Spiritual Assembly of Nayríz, the money was spent on reconstructing to a higher standard than before the houses that had been destroyed in the flood. The Local Assembly of Nayríz prepared a list of the houses that had been destroyed but many of the well-to-do Bahá'ís refrained from accepting financial assistance. They merely accepted a token sum as a blessing.[33]

Father says in a footnote that he accepted a token sum as a blessing but donated a piece of land to make possible the construction of an access road to the land acquired as the site of the future Mashriqu'l-Adhkár.[34] He adds that other Bahá'ís who were well off also manifested financial independence and showed self-sacrifice.

Mother, too, lost all her worldly belongings, including everything she had brought with her as a dowry when she got married. One day she had everything that a woman of her stature could desire, the next she had nothing. All of a sudden, she, her husband and two children had become homeless. How could they start to rebuild? Where could they begin? She was well aware of the magnitude of the burden on father, who felt that he alone had to shoulder the responsibility of building everything anew. She knew that they had to start from scratch and rebuild brick by brick what they had once possessed.

She was lucky, though, that her parents lived nearby and happy that she and her family could take shelter there until they again had a place of their own. Fortunately, her parents were among the wealthy in the town, so taking their daughter and her family in for some time imposed no hardship on them. But father was a proud and independent man when it came to caring personally for his wife and children. Mother was well aware of this and fully appreciated it. She tried to make the burden easy by showing love and understanding. She cooperated fully and with her wise attitude made the transition to normality as smooth as possible.[35]

When their house was rebuilt, father, mother and their children returned to it and resumed their busy schedule of daily activities. The positive aftermath of the flood continued for some time and the inhabitants enjoyed a period of peace and tranquillity.

## The Renewal of Hostilities

The subversive elements among the population who resented the existing good relations between the adherents of all religious backgrounds and creeds were intent on halting the progress, so they began to agitate. Under the guise of protecting Islam, they aroused religious fervour and rekindled in the hearts animosity towards the Bahá'ís. As the holy month of Muḥarram approached, Siyyid 'Azíz-i Yazdí visited Nayríz and started preaching. In his sermons he attacked the Bahá'ís. The Local Spiritual Assembly of Nayríz complained in vain to the local authorities. It then complained to the authorities in Shíráz, the provincial capital. Father was then secretary of the Local Spiritual Assembly of Nayríz. He was chosen to hand carry the written complaint to Shíráz. He complied with the decision of the Assembly. Mother and the children remained in Nayríz, knowing the dangers latent in the mission that father was undertaking. Fortunately, his trip to Shíráz and the complaint he lodged with the authorities produced the desired result. Instructions were issued to the governor of Nayríz by the provincial authorities to take severe action. As a result, Siyyid 'Azíz was sent whence he had come from, and his efforts to provoke hostility against the Bahá'ís were frustrated.

The following year another cleric from Yazd was invited to Nayríz to preach. His name was Shaykh Muḥammad-i Yazdí. He began to incite the inhabitants against the Bahá'ís. Different groups met in secret and plotted to exterminate the friends. Father's movements were under surveillance. Those who remembered vividly the frustration of their plans the previous year were determined to succeed this time. The Local Spiritual Assembly of Nayríz lodged fresh complaints with the local authorities. The actions taken averted a massacre of the Bahá'ís but did not completely wipe out the threat. Father was a businessman. To purchase goods for his trade he had to frequent the Maḥallih Bázár, which was a centre of anti-Bahá'í activities.

One day he went there to buy sugar cubes. He bought ten sacks and had porters carry them out of the Sarví caravanserai, whence they were to be taken to Maḥallih Pahlaví, where he worked and lived. In the vestibule of the caravanserai a crowd had gathered with the aim of causing him harm. They first attacked the porters and threw the sugar cubes on the ground. The merchant who had sold father the sugar cubes heard the commotion and offered to hide him among his merchandise. Father remembered how in Yazd the fanatics had pulled out the innocent Bahá'ís from their hiding places and mercilessly put them to death. He thanked the merchant but declined his offer. In those days a person would wear an *'abá* (cloak). Father pulled up his *'abá* and with brisk steps advanced towards the crowd. Thinking that he was carrying a gun under his *'abá*, they let him pass unharmed. Incited by Hidáyatu'lláh, son of Siyyid Muḥammad, the prayer leader, the crowd pursued him with insatiable anger. Father increased his speed and took refuge in a local government office nearby. The police intervened and scattered the enraged crowd.

Father returned to Maḥallih Pahlaví and reported the incident to the Local Spiritual Assembly, which concluded that the problem was deeply rooted. After deliberations, it decided to remain alert and ready to defend the believers, if necessary. It also chose several houses as gathering places for the Bahá'ís and stockpiled food.

The next day there was a religious sermon in the house of Mírzá 'Abdu'ṣ-Ṣamad, entitled the Vakílu'r-Ru'áyá. He was a good-hearted person and favourable towards the Bahá'ís. <u>Sh</u>ay<u>kh</u> Muḥammad ascended the pulpit and, unaware of the fact that two Bahá'í members of Vaklu'r-Ru'áyá's family were present, started his verbal attack on the Bahá'í Faith. One of the Bahá'ís present at the sermon objected to his abusive language. His objection caused the sermon to be interrupted and the crowd dispersed. Angered by what had happened, some of the dispersed crowd turned their attention to the Bahá'í objector, wanting to teach him a lesson. As he was related to the owner of the house, his relatives hid and protected him from the rage directed at him. Those intent on taking revenge went to Maḥallih Bázár and waited there to meet and harm any Bahá'í who passed by. Another group took to the streets and thoroughfares in search of Bahá'ís they could kill. That day, according to instructions from the Local Assembly, the friends were not to be seen on the streets or in the marketplace, lest a tragedy occurred. Since there was no Bahá'í anywhere to be seen, the crowd stopped at every Bahá'í house they came across, shouted abuse at the people inside, threw stones at the entrance and moved on to the next house. As my parents' house was on their route, several Bahá'í youth had been appointed to guard it. They were instructed not to respond to the mob's abuses and stoning. However, if the agitators tried to break down the door and force their way in, the Bahá'í youth were to prevent it. The members of the Assembly on that day and several subsequent days were living and meeting in that house and were on hand to consult and make decisions on the spot.

The mob stopped at my parents' house for a considerable time and with every passing minute increased the verbal attack. Since there was legitimate fear that they would break down the entrance, uncle Khalíl, one of the youth in charge of guarding the house, went to the edge of the roof to look down and assess the situation. Father pulled him back but the crowd saw that Bahá'í youth were standing guard, ready to defend the house, so they dispersed, went to Maḥallih Bázár, got organized and devised a new scheme. The next day the mob gathered in an Imámzádih (a Shí'í Muslim shrine) in Maḥallih Bázár with the intention of moving towards Maḥallih Pahlaví. Realizing the gravity of the situation, the governor himself went there and addressing the mob, said, 'If your aim is to get hold of the person who yesterday insulted the Shaykh, I will bring him here and punish him with several lashes in your presence. However, if your intention is to create unrest, I will prevent you with the weapons at my disposal.' The governor's statement caused the crowd to disperse but that afternoon the Shaykh ascended the pulpit again and aroused the mob against the Bahá'í community, as well as the local government. Emboldened by the Shaykh's incitement, some of the crowd positioned themselves at strategic points and prevented vehicles from leaving Nayríz for Shíráz. They also cut off telephone lines and prepared for a big attack.

That evening the governor of Nayríz sent the headman of Maḥallih Pahlaví with several armed guards to the house of my parents, where the meetings of the Local Assembly were held. The headman carried a message to the Assembly from the governor. It said that there was unrest in the town and asked that three members of the Assembly go to the seat of the local government at midnight for a meeting, using unfrequented routes, lest they be spotted by the mob and harmed. The Assembly chose three young members, one of whom was father. When mother and the wives of the other two members of the delegation were apprised of the selection, they remarked, 'Older members of the Assembly are sitting tight and sending younger ones to welcome the enemy's shaft!'[36] The women, who had no part in the decision-making process, were well aware of the potential hazards that their husbands faced and were extremely worried. Nonetheless, they obeyed the decision of the Assembly and did not stand in the way of their husbands carrying out the task. Their complaint, however, produced a salutary effect, for as soon as the delegation left, the Assembly dispatched several young Bahá'í guards to ensure that the members of the delegation were not harmed en route to the government house.

Father and the other two members of the delegation were fully aware of the dangers facing them and had little hope of returning home safely. They could be cut into pieces if spotted by the enemy, yet with full reliance on Bahá'u'lláh's bounties, they said goodbye to their wives, children and colleagues on the Assembly, then proceeded to the seat of the government. To avoid being spotted, they did not take the normal route. They passed through orchards by climbing over walls. It was summertime and the governor was staying in the centre of the garden of his official residence.

When the three Bahá'ís reached the governor's house, the guards who were awaiting their arrival ushered them into the presence of the governor who, after greetings, explained how he was going to calm the situation. He said he had promised the mob that he would punish in front of them the Bahá'í who had insulted the Shaykh by interrupting him and asked that Mr Muḥammad Quddúsí, the believer in question, be delivered to a guard he was going to send the next day for the purpose. He promised that he would have the lashes administered in such a way that none would touch his flesh. He added that this would buy him time to request and receive assistance from Shíráz. He then added, 'Since you have contacts in Shíráz, such as Jináb-i Suhráb, who serves as aide de camp in the army for the southern division, and other influential Bahá'ís, immediately send a messenger to Shíráz and ask that a number of armed soldiers be sent to Nayríz, to get here before *arba'ín*.[37] If armed assistance is not received in time, we will not be able to prevent a planned onslaught.'[38] The Bahá'í delegation thanked the governor and promised to consult with the Assembly and let him know its decision.

It was a considerable time after midnight when the three members of the Assembly left the governor's house. As they started walking back towards Maḥallih Pahlaví, they saw several brave Bahá'í youth who, unbeknown to them, had followed them to the governor's house and waited until they finished their meeting. So together they returned to Maḥallih Pahlaví. The Assembly met that very night and made the following decisions:

1) To silence those who were stirring up trouble, Mr Quddúsí was to be delivered to the headman of Maḥallih Pahlaví, who was to take him, accompanied by armed guards, to the seat of the government where he was to be lashed by police in public, according to the plan agreed upon with the governor.

2) To save lives as well as the Faith's integrity, and to forestall an

incident in which the lives and property of all would be endangered, all Bahá'ís were to sacrifice their material possessions. The Assembly members would pledge to spend what they had to the last penny and other Bahá'ís would give as much as they could afford to enable the Assembly to request the dispatch of additional armed forces from Shíráz.

3) The Bahá'ís of Nayríz were to be advised to remain indoors and to have adequate provisions for several days in their homes. If hostilities erupted, they were to take refuge in the four houses that the Assembly had appointed.

4) Since the telephone lines had been cut and means of transportation to Shíráz stopped, a competent messenger was to carry the Assembly's report on foot to Iṣṭahbánát, using a mountain route, and from there travel by automobile to Shíráz. For this task they had to find someone who was clever and had connections in Iṣṭahbánát. Mírzá Ḥusayn Bahín'á'ín volunteered and was chosen for the job.

5) Since the expense of any army detachment was to be pledged in advance, the Local Spiritual Assembly of Shíráz was to be informed that the Local Assembly of Nayríz was ready to pay the expenses of the dispatched army up to 100,000 túmáns.

The letter was prepared and given to the messenger, who left. In the meantime, Mr Quddúsí was sent to the government house and received the prescribed lashes, which pleased the governor. The other measures decided upon by the Assembly were carried out. Members of the Assembly were to stay alert and be ready for emergency meetings. So the Assembly members continued to live in my parents' house where the meetings were held. Father was busy with the Assembly work and mother worked around the clock providing loving care and hospitality to the guests.

As *arba'ín* drew closer, all the Bahá'ís gathered in the four appointed houses guarded by fearless Bahá'í youth. The crucial day was almost to hand. The members of the Assembly and the governor were waiting impatiently for the army detachment to arrive. Hours and minutes were spent in fear and hope, the fear of being attacked by a relentless enemy and the hope that military assistance from Shíráz would avoid an onslaught. The ferocity of the hostile elements of the town increased as the appointed time drew nigh. Danger was imminent. Everyone knew that if the enemy had its way, a massacre would ensue and not a single Bahá'í life would be spared.

The eve of *arba'ín* arrived. The Assembly was in session and anxiously awaited the outcome of the actions the Assembly of Shíráz had been requested to take. Suddenly there was a knock on the door. Father asked the visitor to introduce himself.

A familiar voice said, 'Open up. This is Ḥusayn, the special messenger.' When father opened the door Mr Bahín'á'ín stepped in and said, 'You need not close the door anymore. Praised be God, more than what was expected has been achieved. Two truckloads of soldiers commanded by Captain Ḥusayn Áqá 'Azímí have, according to orders from Mr 'Aṭápúr, arrived to deal with the transgressors and evildoers. I was with them. I am hungry. Give me lunch, then I will talk.'[39]

Mr. Bahín'á'ín was served lunch. He then explained that after leaving Nayríz he had taken a mountain route and traversed the distance between Nayríz and Iṣṭahbánát on foot. When he arrived in Iṣṭahbánát the next morning, a car was about to leave for Shíráz. He managed to get on it. By the evening of that day he was in the city. He immediately contacted two members of the Local Spiritual Assembly of Shíráz and apprised them of the situation in Nayríz. An emergency meeting of the Assembly was held that night and it was decided to take immediate action. As the commander of the army for the southern division, Jináb-i Maḥmúd Ayrum, was in Kirmán and Brigadier-General Muḥammad Ḥusayn Mírzá was acting in his place, the Shíráz Assembly immediately presented the matter to him and requested the urgent dispatch of an army detachment to Nayríz, emphasizing that all expenses would be defrayed by the Assembly. The Brigadier-General agreed with the requested course of action and immediately sought and received by telegram Maḥmúd Ayrum's approval. The next day the Brigadier-General referred the execution of the task to Mr 'Aṭapúr. He in turn chose Captain Ḥusayn Áqá 'Azímí, whom he trusted, to carry out the work. The captain was given complete authority and instructions by Jináb-i Suhráb to deal severely with those who had caused the disturbance. The captain started off for Nayríz with two army trucks full of soldiers, accompanied by Mr Bahín'á'ín, the messenger. After explaining the details orally, Mr Bahín'á'ín presented the report of the Local Assembly of Shíráz, which confirmed the actions it had taken step by step.

Shortly after the arrival of the army detachment in Nayríz, the Assembly was informed that the Shaykh had been arrested. It also received a delegation consisting of four soldiers and the headman who was carrying a letter from the captain inviting all the members of the Assembly to visit him in his office at the local government headquarters in Maḥallih Bázár for consultation on certain matters. The Assembly members did as requested. When they met with the captain he read to them a letter outlining his mission. He then confirmed that the Shaykh had been arrested and asked for a list of the troublemakers and agitators. The Assembly needed time to carry out a thorough investigation, so it postponed the submission of the list until the next day.

That night the supporters of the Shaykh met and coerced a number of the inhabitants of Nayríz to sign their names to a scroll stating that they would sacrifice their lives for the Shaykh and would lie down on the route of his motorcade if he were expelled. The captain responded to their threat by saying that if a group of well-known and trusted citizens gave a written and signed guarantee that the Shaykh would not again attack the Bahá'ís from the pulpit, he would release him. Immediately a group of wealthy and influential people among the agitators signed a letter of guarantee and took it to the captain, who released the Shaykh. When the Local Spiritual Assembly members heard the news the next morning they became very concerned. Father went to see the captain and expressed the Assembly's misgivings. The captain responded, 'I am playing politics; later you will understand.'[40]

Whether or not the Shaykh ascended the pulpit again that day, whether or not he said something, the Bahá'ís never learned the details. However, that night the captain had him arrested and sent to Shíráz. It all happened very smoothly and nobody did anything to prevent it. Those who had signed the letter of guarantee, nearly 20 of them, were also arrested and imprisoned for a few days. Moreover, the captain arrested the people on the list prepared by the Assembly and they, too, were imprisoned and punished. He then made them promise that they would not engage in similar activities. After a few days, when calm was restored, the captain received a testimonial letter from the Assembly and returned to Shíráz.

The Local Assembly of Nayríz sent a letter of gratitude to the Local Assembly of Shíráz, and through it paid to the army's southern division the full cost of the deployment of the army detachment, which had successfully dealt with a grave threat to the lives and property of the Bahá'ís of Nayríz.

Thus ended the second of the two successive years of plotting against the Bahá'ís by troublemakers in Nayríz. Although these two episodes ended triumphantly for the Faith and the lives of the believers were spared, the Bahá'ís of Nayríz sustained tremendous financial loss; for the duration of the threat they could not continue their regular work. Many engaged in agricultural pursuits. Their inability to attend to the work at hand in a timely manner inflicted upon them irreparable loss. But the news of the end of the threat facing the Bahá'ís, of the success of the wise and timely actions taken by the Local Spiritual Assembly, of the assistance and support rendered by the Local Spiritual Assembly of Shíráz, of the united show of support by the Bahá'ís of Nayríz for the members of the Assembly and of their sacrificial efforts to root out the problem spread far and wide and induced interested souls to investigate the truth of the Cause of Bahá'u'lláh.

After this episode Jináb-i Fáḍil-i Yazdí was again invited to Nayríz. He responded positively and spent some time engaged in teaching activities in the town and its surrounding areas. As a result, a number of prominent people from different parts and various backgrounds embraced the Bahá'í Faith. The details are recorded in *Kháṭirát-i Talkh va Shírín*.[41]

The period of calm and tranquillity that ensued enabled the Bahá'ís to reestablish friendly relations with the non-Bahá'í population of the town and enjoy working together for the betterment of the lives of themselves and their neighbours. The wise politicians who held positions of power made sure that subversive elements did not get a chance to agitate the populace. As a result, people of all religious backgrounds associated with one another unafraid of the threat of punishment and reprisal. A secure environment provided peace of mind and made it possible for everyone to flourish and benefit from the blessings of life. Under those conditions father and mother built a comfortable life for themselves and their children and did what they could to serve the people among whom they lived.

## The Rebellion of Local Tribes in Fárs

The period of calm and tranquillity unfortunately did not last very long. Prolonged political unrest in the country threw many provinces into turmoil. Fárs was one of them. Aḥmad Sháh, the last of the Qájár monarchs, was deposed in a *coup d'état* in 1925 and the despotic Qájár dynasty finally came to an end. It took the new ruler, Riḍá Sháh, some time to establish full control over Iran. As a result of the prevailing chaos, the tribes in the province of Fárs raised the banner of rebellion and challenged the authority of the central government. The Bahárlú and Qashqá'í tribes occupied a large part of the province and the Kúhistání tribe, led by Shaykh Abu'l-Ḥasan and Shaykh Javád, the nephew of Shaykh Dhakaríyyá Kúhistání, occupied Nayríz and Iṣṭahbánát as far as the boundaries of Sírján in the province of Kirmán.

When Shaykh Javád's forces surrounded Nayríz, the Bahá'ís, with bitter memories of these inveterate and callous enemies from their previous attacks, abandoned their belongings and left the town. Not many remained. The most prominent of them was Mírzá Aḥmad (mother's father). He was an outstanding man, known for his fearlessness. He was a staunch believer with unflinching devotion and absolute loyalty to the tenets of the Bahá'í Faith. He encouraged the Bahá'ís, especially the younger ones who faced possible annihilation, to flee the town. Among them were his own daughter and son-in-law, Ṭúbá Khánum and Mírzá Muḥammad-Shafí'. They fled to Shíráz.

The forces of the Shaykh surrounded Nayríz and engaged in a battle with the armed forces of the local government, which were totally inadequate for the size of the onslaught. When the town's defences fell, the Shaykh ordered his men to plunder people's belongings. He also issued a verdict making it lawful for them to confiscate all agricultural produce and to take control of farms and orchards. His orders were carried out to the letter. He then made a list of the houses owned by the Bahá'ís and ordered them destroyed unless a certain sum was paid for each.

Grandfather had to act fast if anything belonging to the Bahá'ís was to be saved, for the transgressors had absolutely no notion of or respect for human life, let alone human rights. When the established system of law and order collapsed with the advent of a new victor, the Shaykh enjoyed full authority over the lives and belongings of the people he had conquered. Under such circumstances, human rights had little or no meaning. Thus people had to devise ways and means to protect themselves against such ruthless transgressors. Negotiating with them and complying with those demands that did not inflict harm upon other citizens was one way open to the defenceless Bahá'ís. Therefore grandfather went to see the Shaykh and told him candidly, 'If you have come to kill the Bahá'ís, here I am, a well-known Bahá'í. But if you are here to extort money, whatever others pay, I will pay proportionately the sum expected of the Bahá'ís.'[42] To show the sincerity of his pledge, he immediately paid the Shaykh the sum demanded for the house owned by his daughter and son-in-law. This sum father repaid at a later date.

The sojourn of my parents and their children in Shíráz prolonged as the chaotic situation in Nayríz steadily worsened, making it impossible for them to return and resume a normal life. It was also impossible to obtain news from home because all means of communication between Shíráz and most parts of the province were cut off and rebellious tribes controlled a considerable portion of Fárs. Three months elapsed and no news was exchanged between grandfather and parents. Shíráz itself was not immune from danger, for the rebels had reached a radius of twelve kilometres. The situation changed when the commander of the southern army, Maḥmud Ayrum, was dismissed and Major-General Shaybání was installed in his place.

The new commander had full authority to quell the rebellion and was provided with the necessary support and fighting equipment to do so. In a battle, which occurred in one of the suburbs of Shíráz, he defeated the rebel forces. His army then engaged the rebels in the surrounding areas and forced them to retreat.

The news of the victory of the government forces and General Shaybání's success in defeating the rebels reached those occupying Nayríz and caused Shaykh Javád great concern. To strengthen the base of his power in the town he devised a scheme. He sent for grandfather and Mírzá Aḥmad 'Irfán, a Bahá'í who worked as a secretary in the local government office. During the meeting he said to them:

> I have heard that Muḥammad-Shafí' Rouhani is related to the two of you. I have also heard from Shaykh Maḥmúd, who is in charge of keeping law and order in Maḥallih Pahlaví, that Muḥammad-Shafí' is a competent and intelligent man. I need such people in this area. I oppose the government and its forces. I have nothing against people's beliefs and am not vindictive. Be assured that henceforth you enjoy immunity regarding your lives and your possessions. Therefore, write to Rouhani and tell him to return to Nayríz immediately. Since he is a competent person, soon after his arrival, I will install him as the governor of Sírján.[43]

Grandfather and Mr 'Irfán tried hard to change the Shaykh's mind but he was adamant. He emphasized that the order had to be complied with immediately. Grandfather and Mr 'Irfán realized the gravity of the situation and saw that they had no alternative but to comply. The Shaykh told them what to write and demanded that the letter be written in his presence. He then asked them to appoint a messenger to take the letter to Shíráz. He wrote a letter himself, to help the messenger get past control posts and blockades on the way. As grandfather was illiterate, Mírzá Aḥmad 'Irfán had to write the letter according to the Shaykh's instructions. To make the letter more authentic, at the Shaykh's behest grandfather affixed his seal to it. When it was done they asked permission to provide the messenger, a Mr Muḥammad Báqir Imání, with the necessary funds for his trip. The Shaykh granted them permission. Grandfather and Mr 'Irfán knew that if the government forces around Shíráz intercepted the letter, they would try both the messenger and my father, to whom the letter was addressed, for treason and put them to death. So they wrote another letter whose contents were the opposite of what the Shaykh had dictated and gave it to the messenger. They told him that when required to present the letter, up to a distance of twelve kilometres from Shíráz he should present the one dictated by the Shaykh. After that point, they told him, he was to tear up that letter and to show the second letter to the government officers who had Shíráz and its vicinity under control. When everything was in order, the messenger was to find father and his family and tell them exactly what had happened.

The messenger was a good-hearted and sincere believer but illiterate. While traversing the area under the control of the rebels, he did as he was told and managed to get past them. When he reached the vicinity of Shíráz, he mistakenly destroyed the letter he was to keep and as he was tired and exhausted, he just walked to the control post and presented himself. He was questioned about his aim and purpose. He said that he was a messenger sent by Mírzá Aḥmad Vahídí and that he was carrying a letter for Mírzá Muḥammad Shafí' Rouhani. They read the letter, which implicated the messenger and the intended recipient in anti-government activities. He was arrested, tortured and chained. He was then taken on foot to Shíráz and delivered to the head of the military police, a man familiar with Mr 'Irfán's handwriting. He also knew grandfather and Mr 'Irfán personally, for he had met them during his trip to Nayríz previously. As soon as he read the letter and interrogated the messenger he realized what had happened, for he knew that grandfather was illiterate. He was also aware that Bahá'ís did not take part in political activities. He was thus eager to find an amicable solution. He called one of the high-ranking officers for consultation and together they decided to call father for questioning. As they had no home address for my parents, they sent two policemen to Mr Master's shop to look for father. Mr Master was a prominent and wealthy Bahá'í in Shíráz. His business premises were strategically positioned in the centre of the city and served as a meeting place for Bahá'ís who visited Shíráz.

To pass time and forget their ordeal temporarily, the Nayrízí refugees in Shíráz used to pack a picnic lunch every day and go a distance out of the city to spend their woeful days in the beauty of nature and uplift their burdened spirits. That day was no different except that on their way back in the evening they encountered Mr Muḥammad Ṣiddíq, who sought father out and said to him, 'I have been sent by Mr Suhráb to convey a message to you. He wants you to go immediately to Mr Ardishír Master's business premises and see him.'[44] Mr Ṣiddíq appeared very worried and briefly apprised father of what had happened. The precariousness of the situation was obvious and caused father great concern. If he was tried by a military court and found guilty of treason during wartime, he would be executed or imprisoned for life. Father's main concern was this: If found guilty, he would suffer a death sentence or life imprisonment for something that was against the Bahá'í principle of non-interference in politics. He was happy to die for his belief and for upholding the tenets of the Bahá'í Faith but dreaded the thought of being implicated in something so contrary to the teachings of the Faith, something that he had not done and would never contemplate doing.

Father, mother and the other refugees continued walking towards Mr Master's premises in the centre of the city but father was beside himself. He faced an unknown future and a serious problem, which nothing short of Bahá'u'lláh's bounty and grace could solve in his favour. When they reached Mr Master's premises, Mr Suhráb had left but had told Mr Master to tell father what he was to do. Mother, the children and a few friends who were with him that day stood a short distance away. Father went in. Mr Master explained in full what had happened. Father was advised to deny vehemently that the letter was genuine, for the alleged writer, i.e. grandfather, was illiterate and could not have written it. He was then told to introduce himself to the two policemen who were standing outside.

Mother knew something was terribly wrong but did not know exactly what. She was standing outside Mr Master's premises impatiently waiting to hear from father the full account. Father did not have the luxury of time and could not explain. So he approached her and hurriedly said, 'I am being arrested and taken to prison as a result of your father's fanciful ideas and lack of insight and proper understanding. My future is unknown. It is unlikely that we will see one another again.'[45] He then introduced himself to the two military policemen who were waiting. They took him away, fortunately without handcuffs.

Poor mother! Many things had crossed her mind but nothing like her husband going to prison because of something that her father had done. She knew very well how much her father loved and respected her husband. The more she thought about what father had told her, the more convinced she became that what she had heard did not make sense. Yet there was nothing she could do. She could not contact her father and find out the truth. She could not go with her husband to the military police and help him prove his innocence. Lack of accurate information and knowledge of the complexities involved made it impossible for her to figure out what she could do to help.

In those days women in Iran and in many parts of the world were not well informed of administrative procedures. They were often left in the dark because they were considered incapable of understanding the intricacies of schemes devised and enacted by men. They were also blamed for being emotional and irrational. The truth is that the treatment meted out to them made them behave in emotional and irrational ways. How could anyone be kept in the dark regarding things affecting her life and be expected to behave rationally? Indeed, a woman's worst trauma was being left in the dark. Mother was cool-headed and competent. She combined intelligence with practicality. Whenever presented with a problem, the first thing she considered was how she could help solve it in the best possible manner. Father knew this and appreciated what mother was capable of achieving under the most difficult circumstances. In this particular situation, however, he did not have the time to consult and seek her views, or perhaps he was angry that her father had done what appeared to be thoughtless and irresponsible. Also, compared with what is today considered the norm, even being the liberal and fair-minded man that father was, he had room to improve in this regard. Father did improve over the years to the point that there was nothing he did not share and talk over with mother.

The head of the military police received father warmly in his office. After dismissing the two policemen who had taken him there, he invited father to sit. This surprised father, who expected much worse treatment. Addressing him, the head of the military police said, 'A letter addressed to you has come to hand. The writer is Ḥájí Mírzá Aḥmad, your wife's father, and its contents indicate opposition to the government and cooperation with the rebels.' Father responded, 'I am a Bahá'í. I do not participate in politics. Ḥájí Mírzá Aḥmad is a captive in the hands of the rebels and is illiterate. He could not have written the letter.' The head of the military police replied, 'The letter is in the handwriting of Mírzá Aḥmad Khán 'Irfán. I am familiar with his handwriting and with Ḥájí Mírzá Aḥmad's seal. I met both of them in your house [in Nayríz]. I am sure that this letter has been written under duress; they had no alternative but to comply. It is your duty to deny the letter.'[46]

He then showed father the letter and read it to him. It said:

> My beloved son. It has been a long time since I have had any news of you and your wife, my dearly-loved daughter. Therefore, I am sending this letter with a messenger. Should you be interested in

> knowing how we are, sometime ago the forces of Kayván Shukúh Qulí, at the instruction of Shaykh Javád, conquered Nayríz. Shaykh Javád's aim is to do away with the government and its forces. He is not against the Bahá'ís. Your long time friend, Shaykh Maḥmúd, is the headman of Maḥallih Pahlaví and is living in our house. In view of your long time acquaintance with them, Shaykh Javád and Shaykh Maḥmúd favour you. If you return to Nayríz, they have promised to give you the governorship of Sírján. Delay not. Return soon. Write back and tell us how the situation is at your end.[47]

After he read the letter, the head of the military police told father, 'I know that your family is worried about you. Leave your address and immediately go home.'[48] Father left his address, profusely thanked the man, went home and explained the developments to mother and the children. The family spent a sleepless night and prayed for divine assistance, for the situation was still unclear. They feared that if General Shaybání learned about the letter and pursued it, father could still be tried and condemned. Four or five days elapsed. Finally, with the wise actions of the head of the military police, the messenger was freed and father exonerated. The refugees remained in Shíráz until the forces of the government established their control throughout the province of Fárs, then returned to Nayríz.

To quell the uprising in Nayríz, a battalion commanded by Colonel Síyáhpúsh was sent there. He defeated the Shaykh and his supporters and reestablished law and order. Father, mother and all the refugees gradually returned to Nayríz and started rebuilding their lives. Everyone, including my parents, had sustained terrible financial loss, for their houses, their orchards and farms had been plundered and everything taken. Father and several other Bahá'ís had to work so much harder to repay the money which had been paid to the Shaykh to spare their houses from destruction. However, everyone was happy that a frightening and chaotic period of tyrannical rule in Nayríz, which had turned many Bahá'ís into helpless refugees for several months, had finally ended.

Upon his return to Nayríz, father sent the report of the atrocities perpetrated against the Bahá'ís to Shoghi Effendi. At his instruction, his secretary wrote in response on 24 November 1929:

> That spiritual friend's letter has attained the glance of His Highness, the Guardian of the Faith, may my spirit be sacrificed for his friends. The account of the recent tragic events in Nayríz and the description of the calamities sustained by the loving friends there have become known in his presence and caused him sadness. He said: 'This Servant will, with tongue and heart, offer thanks at the Court of the Munificent Lord for having enabled His tested servants and trusted friends to appear, in the face of a deluge of trials and an onslaught of adversities and afflictions, with such firmness, steadfastness and integrity as to cause the Concourse on High to utter their praise and the dwellers of the Abhá Paradise to glorify them. Neither had the blade and shaft of the ungodly any effect on their glorious spirits, nor has the fatal poison and torture affected their illumined and attracted inner selves. Undoubtedly those sincere, detached and steadfast believers have, with their acceptance of various persecutions, caused the Blessed Tree to grow further throughout the world, have added to the splendours of the light of the brilliant truth of Bahá'u'lláh's Cause and the manifestation of the power and might of the Word of God.'
>
> He then said:
>
> This Servant, with a heart throbbing with love and a soul overflowing with affection for those gems of firmness and steadfastness, praises and extols the spirit of fidelity and sacrifice evinced by those chosen by the Almighty in the path of that Luminous Moon, and will continually pray in the Holy Shrine, beseeching God to protect and preserve those servants of His Sacred Threshold from the cruelty of tyrants and the oppression of the ungodly, and to cut off the hands of the transgressors. Assure all the persecuted and dear admirable friends of Nayríz of this Servant's loving-kindness. Impart to their hearts the hope that, God willing, soon will the ancient glory reveal the beauty of its countenance and the sun

of aspiration of the people of Bahá will shine on the highest peak. Patience and composure are essential, calmness and tranquillity needed. The evildoers will definitely pay for their evil deeds and will serve as a lesson to others.

The praise in his holy presence of the extraordinary steadfastness shown by Jináb-i Ḥáj Mírzá Aḥmad, the merchant, upon him be the glory of God, caused his bounteous favours to flow.

Convey loving-kindness and favours on behalf of Shoghi Effendi to your esteemed wife, Amatu'lláh Ṭúbá Khánum, your mother, Amatu'lláh Núríyyih Khánum, and your children, Áqá Mírzá 'Abdu'l-Ḥusayn, Áqá Mírzá Masíḥ and Shamsu'ḍ-Ḍuḥá.

Also gladden the hearts of Jináb-i Áqáy-i Tírandáz, Áqá Isfandyár-i Khursand, Jináb-i Áqá Khudádád, the Parsí merchants, upon them be the glory of God, with the glad-tidings of His favours.

Written at the instruction of his blessed person. Rajab 1348, 24 November 1929. Núru'd-Dín Zayn.

Postscript in the handwriting of Shoghi Effendi:

> This Servant will, in these holy precincts, remember that friend who hath endured patiently at times of calamity, affliction and adversity. I will also implore the Almighty to ease the affairs of those loved ones and to release them from tyranny. Be assured. The Servant of His Threshold, Shoghi.[49]

After the rebellion of the Kúhistání tribe in Nayríz, father engaged in trade, advanced rapidly and became one of the most trusted and successful businessmen and traders in the area. He owed his extraordinary success to the outpourings of Bahá'u'lláh's bounty and the prayers of Shoghi Effendi. He had business dealings with a number of renowned traders in Shíráz and through them exported several items to national and international markets.

Father's business success and the high respect shown him by different sectors of society enhanced his popularity. Soon he was elected to the board of governors of the town and served as its honorary secretary and treasurer for several years. By virtue of his responsibilities and social stature, father associated closely with the chairman of the board, Amír Ḥusayn Khán Fátiḥ, and other town dignitaries who served as members, and provided mother with the opportunity to associate with their families. Mother's natural charm and social skills played an important part in establishing and maintaining friendships on a family basis. She was what today is called a 'people person'. She loved to be with people and enjoyed helping them overcome their problems. Those who knew her loved her for who she was and enjoyed her company.

Association and fellowship between Bahá'ís and non-Bahá'ís laid the basis for enduring friendships and familiarized the authorities with Bahá'í tenets to the extent that they defended father openly when agitators tried to undermine him. During the month of the fast, if the meetings of the board prolonged beyond sunset, father was offered food to break his fast. Mr Fátiḥ was so attracted to the principles of the Faith and became such an intimate friend that he visited father in the Ḥaẓíratu'l-Quds of Shíráz, to return his visit at Naw-Rúz.[50] The ties of friendship between Mr Fátiḥ's family and my parents were so strong that when Mrs Keith Ransom-Kehler was scheduled to visit Nayríz, because my parents' house had been pillaged and stripped of its furniture during the rebellion of the Kúhistání tribe, father arranged to borrow from Mr Fátiḥ's house, for the duration of her stay in Nayríz, furniture befitting a distinguished Bahá'í from the West.[51]

The amicable relationship that existed between Bahá'ís and non-Bahá'ís enabled the Local Spiritual Assembly of Nayríz to enforce, without any objection, Shoghi Effendi's instructions regarding Bahá'í laws of burial and marriage.[52] The first Bahá'í to be buried according to the Bahá'í laws was Jináb-i Shaykh Áqá, Fáḍil-i Qaṣru'd-Dashtí. As he was teaching Arabic in the government school, the director of education ordered all schools in the town closed, enabling all teachers and students to attend his funeral. Other government officials were present as well. They all accompanied the body on foot for a distance of one kilometre to the Bahá'í cemetery in front of the fort of Khájih on the outskirts of the town and remained there until the prayer for the dead was recited, then dispersed. This was a great victory for the Faith, marking its relative emancipation which allowed its adherents to practise their own religious rites without hindrance.

The freedom enjoyed by the Bahá'ís of Nayríz made it possible for prominent Bahá'í teachers, such as Jináb-i Mírzá Ṭarázu'lláh Samandarí, later designated by Shoghi Effendi as the Hand of the Cause of God, Jináb-i Fáḍil-i Yazdí and Jináb-i Muṭlaq to visit Nayríz and witness the close relationship between Bahá'ís and non-Bahá'ís. This period of calm and tranquillity attracted to the Faith a number of prominent people. Among them was Shaykh 'Abdu'r-Raḥmán, son of Shaykh Dhakaríyyá who, as described above, had martyred 18 Bahá'ís in 1909. During the same period, Bahá'í youth gatherings and activities were open to non-Bahá'ís and many high government officials attended and enjoyed the programmes.

## Tragedy Strikes

About three years after their marriage, father and mother were blessed with their firstborn. A son was born to them in 1922, a year after father's return from the Holy Land. They named him Mírzá 'Abdu'l-Ḥusayn, after his paternal grandfather who had passed away several years earlier.[53] After 'Abdu'l-Ḥusayn, my parents had several other children. Mother was pregnant with the sixth child when tragedy struck and completely changed the course of her and father's life. The following is a brief account of what happened:

Father was keenly interested in the education of his children. When his father passed away, he had had to abandon his studies and become the breadwinner of the family. Having been deprived of the benefit of pursuing higher education when he was in the prime of his life, he was eager to provide his children with the best possible means for advancement in a rapidly changing world. When 'Abdu'l-Ḥusayn, a prodigy and the prize of the family, finished elementary school in Nayríz and was eager to continue his studies, father readily acceded to his request and made preparations for him to go to Shíráz for higher education. Mother was concerned about sending her young son so far away. Although the distance between Nayríz and Shíráz can nowadays be traversed by car in two to three hours, in those days, with the undeveloped and irregular means of transportation and bad roads, the likelihood of the mother and son seeing one another at regular intervals was negligible. Moreover, the rigours of travel and prevailing insecurity in the country made it most difficult for women to travel from place to place. Eventually, mother put the best interests of her son above all else and agreed to let him go. Her decision to separate from him was made easier when her own father also decided to send his youngest son, Mírzá 'Abbás, mother's youngest brother, to Shíráz for higher education. So, the uncle and nephew set out for Shíráz.

Father made all the necessary arrangements for 'Abdu'l-Ḥusayn's admission into the best secondary school in Shíráz. He also arranged for him and uncle 'Abbás to be accommodated in the house of a good and loving Bahá'í family in that city. 'Abdu'l-Ḥusayn's departure from Nayríz coincided with a time when father felt concerned that worldly affairs were preventing him from adequately serving the Bahá'í Faith. He longed to free himself from his responsibilities and focus more on spiritual pursuits but he found it impossible to disentangle himself from the burdensome chores of the material world.

'Abdu'l-Ḥusayn was a studious youth and studied until late into the night. In those days there was no electricity. Oil lamps were widely used for lighting. One night, after finishing his homework, 'Abdu'l-Ḥusayn tried to put the lamp in a niche high above the ground, before blowing it out. He had done this many times before but on that fateful night he was tired and sleepy. He lost his balance before the lamp had been properly placed in the niche, the lamp overturned, the oil poured over him and the flame quickly set his clothes on fire. Uncle 'Abbás, who was asleep, woke up and called the landlord to help. In their eagerness to extinguish the fire, they immersed 'Abdu'l-Ḥusayn in a pool of water in the centre of the courtyard. Almost all Persian homes in those days had a pool to provide water for domestic use. 'Abdu'l-Ḥusayn's deep burns became infected. He was taken to the Mursalín Hospital, set up by

Christian missionaries in Shíráz. His situation worsened steadily. Father writes in his memoirs:

> . . . My hope in life has always been service to the Cause of God and my highest aim the education of my children. I wanted them to be raised according to Bahá'í principles and become effective members of the community. So I was keenly interested in their studies. As Nayríz lacked the means – the standard of education there was low and its school did not offer more than the seventh grade – I sent my eldest child, Mírzá 'Abdu'l-Ḥusayn, to Shíráz for higher education . . . I arranged accommodation for him in the house of the late Mr Muḥammad-Riḍá Khán Vakhshúrí, a member of the Local Spiritual Assembly of Shíráz. He attended the Sháhpúr Secondary School. Six months elapsed. To free me from the whirlpool of the material world, which was threatening my spiritual growth, the hand of destiny designed for me a new plan which needed a worthy sacrifice.
>
> About this time Mr 'Abdu'lláh Muṭlaq, an erudite and well-known Bahá'í teacher, arrived in Nayríz and was a guest in my house. While talking about the news in Shíráz, he said, 'Your son, Mírzá 'Abdu'l-Ḥusayn, is suffering from burns in his leg, is receiving treatment in the home of the Vakhshúrís' and is improving. Mr Thábit Paymán asked me to inform you of this.' I became very worried. Although I knew that Mr Vakhshúrí would care for my son better than I, nevertheless I sent my brother, Mírzá Khalíl, to Shíráz to provide further care and assistance to 'Abdu'l-Ḥusayn.
>
> The home treatments administered by Dr Salmánpúr proved ineffective. They transferred him to the Mursalín Hospital. As several days elapsed and the news of his improvement did not arrive . . . I left everything and together with my wife, who was pregnant,[54] and our youngest child, Pourándukht, proceeded to Shíráz.
>
> About 36 kilometres from Shíráz in a place near Dudaj and Dáryún, the car in which we were travelling overturned. Several passengers, including my wife, were injured. I was so badly hurt that no one expected me to survive. Under the tremendous weight of the engine of the car and its cargo, my neck pressed

heavily against the rest of my body and made it almost impossible to breathe. The power to breathe, to talk or even moan was taken from me. I could hear my wife saying repeatedly, 'Mr Rouhani, say "Yá Bahá'u'l-Abhá!"' but I could not respond. Although I could not talk, in my heart I repeated 'Yá Bahá'u'l-Abhá' and asked Bahá'u'lláh to hasten the flight of my spirit and end the agony of the unbearable pain caused by the pressure of such a tremendous weight against my neck. Suddenly this thought crossed my mind: 'In this wilderness I breathe the last breath while I had hoped to attain the freedom of conscience and desired to find a new field for rendering service.' I was thus communing with God and repeating 'Yá Bahá'u'l-Abhá' when the pressure on my neck eased. The police arrived and pulled me out from under the weight of the car and its cargo. They moved me to a development near Dudaj. I received treatment overnight. Another car came the next morning and took my bruised and bloodstained body to Shíráz, to the same hospital where my son was, and I was placed in a bed next to him. The condition of my son worsened day by day, as mine improved steadily.

As the anniversary of the martyrdom of the Báb, i.e. 28 Sha'bán, approached,[55] I turned my face to that exalted Shrine, offered supplications and said the healing prayer. Then, with utter humility, I fixed my gaze on the sanctified court of the Ancient Beauty and said, 'If Thou desire my freedom from worldly affairs, if it is Thy will to use my son as a ransom for my spiritual growth, I am utterly resigned to Thy will. But if Thou has ordained the end of my own life, that, too, with open arms I embrace, especially if Thou make my end good. Whatever the pen of destiny has signed, I accept with gratitude; whatever Thy will is, make it manifest.' He accepted my son's sacrifice as the price for my freedom. 'Abdu'l-Ḥusayn died in the hospital before my eyes and before the eyes of his mother, as he was chanting prayers. He closed his eyes to this world and, like an eager bird, left behind the temporary cage. He ascended to the Abhá Kingdom and left his parents heartbroken and bereaved. This precious ransom changed the course of our lives. Upon him be God's mercy and pardon.[56]

'Abdu'l-Ḥusayn was about 13 years old when his spirit winged its flight to the world beyond. The members of the family and others who knew him testified to his spiritual and intellectual maturity, to his pleasing demeanour, his brightness, kind-heartedness and loving-kindness towards all.

My mother never wrote down her feelings about her son's tragic death but her eyes filled with tears every time his name was mentioned. Those sad eyes spoke volumes about the poignancy of the tragedy she had suffered. By the time I was born, some three years had elapsed from the date of 'Abdu'l-Ḥusayn's death. Even when I was old enough to understand these things, mother never spoke in detail about the effect of that agonizing experience in her life, surely because she did not want it to adversely affect our lives. Had she been able to write and trained to write her memoirs, had the society accepted the right of women to express and publicly discuss their feelings regarding things that deeply affected the course of their lives, most probably we would today have also her analysis of that tragic episode. In the absence of her own description of that woeful event, I have made enquiries from my older sister, S͟hamsu'ḍ-Ḍuḥá whom we call Rawḥanieh, the sibling old enough at that time to remember our mother's reaction to some extent and the one I was able to contact by telephone. I also made enquiries from other sources. What follows is based on the pieces I have patched together, to obtain as accurate a picture as possible of what mother went through in those days laden with sorrow.

Although mother understood the vital importance of providing the children with good education, she did not really want to separate from them. When the question of 'Abdu'l-Ḥusayn going to S͟híráz came up, she was not enthusiastic about it. She felt that he was too young to live far away from home. She was concerned that if he were unwell and needed help, she would not be able to provide motherly care. She did not know what to do. She could not stand in the way of his advancement and growth. Yet her heart told her 'don't let him go'. Finally she agreed when arrangements were made for her younger brother, 'Abbás, to go with 'Abdu'l-Ḥusayn. Both were being sent away to further their education, so her son was not going to be alone. Oh, how her heart pounded with the pangs of separation when he left! How often she raised her suppliant hands and asked Bahá'u'lláh to keep him safe!

Things seemed to be going well for 'Abdu'l-Ḥusayn and mother was so looking forward to the end of the year when he would come home for the holidays. Her heart leapt with joy at the thought of reunion. As she was rapt in her happy thoughts, the news arrived that 'Abdu'l-Ḥusayn was suffering from burns. However, details were kept from her since she was several months pregnant. On the whole, in those days it was customary for women not to be told everything. The plan was probably to wait until 'Abdu'l-Ḥusayn was better, then break the news to her. However, the hand of destiny drew a different design.

She was having disturbing dreams and wanted to know what was happening. As it became clear that 'Abdu'l-Ḥusayn's condition was not improving – in fact it was going from bad to worse – there was no alternative but to apprise mother of the incident. Once briefed, she had a strong urge to be with her child. She begged father and succeeded in convincing him to take her with him to Shíráz. They took the first available vehicle that was leaving Nayríz for that city, a truck loaded with cargo. Father and mother were to sit in front with the driver. At the last minute, the director of education and his wife decided to travel in the same truck. They were given the seats promised to my parents. Consequently, my parents had to sit up on the cargo together with a few other passengers. When the truck overturned near Shíráz, it turned over on the side that father was seated. The severe pressure against his head and neck crushed his teeth in his mouth and caused bleeding.[57] The sight of father's bloodstained body was a harrowing scene to behold at a time when mother was pregnant with one child and carried another in her arms. But that sight faded into insignificance when compared with watching her son die.

Heartbroken, grief-stricken and with souls weighed down with unbearable sorrow, my parents buried their beloved son in Shíráz, held befitting memorial gatherings in his honour, then returned to Nayríz. With them also was uncle Khalíl. When the inhabitants of Nayríz heard the news, they turned out *en masse* to receive the bereaved parents on the outskirts of the town. How friends and strangers unite in grief is an amazing phenomenon to behold. When calamity strikes, hard feelings and petty bickering disappear and all focus on the fundamental issue, which bonds everyone together. It is the realization of vulnerability in the face of calamitous events, from which no one remains immune, that connects the hearts and manifests the best of what human beings possess.

When the crowd came face to face with the grieving parents, all shed tears of anguish as though they felt the pangs of their sorrow and everyone had something loving and consoling to say. Oh, how poor mother and father must have felt! They had left Nayríz full of hope to rescue their son from the effects of his burns but returned heartbroken and bereaved, with no hope of seeing him again. The crowd accompanied the couple to their home in Maḥallih Pahlaví. Only God knows the depth of the feelings surging in everyone's heart and soul. When the weeping crowd reached the entrance to my parents' home, uncle Khalíl flung the two sides of the huge wooden door open and announced that it was the day of 'Abdu'l-Ḥusayn's wedding. With that announcement the sound of weeping and moaning reached the high heavens.

With my parents' arrival in Nayríz the official period of mourning began. From morning until nightfall well-wishers and sympathizers thronged the house. They remembered the kindness, gentleness and brightness of the youth whom they had lost, and prayed for the progress of his precious spirit in the world beyond. My sister Rawḥanieh remembers sitting on father's lap and watching his tears streaming down as he received the men of the town. In those days men and women did not assemble in the same part of the house. Father received the men in the outer section, mother stayed with the women in the inner quarters of the house. The children were free to move between the two sections.

## The Aftermath Effects of 'Abdu'l-Ḥusayn's Death

The death of 'Abdu'l-Ḥusayn so devastated mother that she fell ill. The child she was bearing was a girl born four or five months later. She was named Mahíndukht. When she was born, mother had no milk to breastfeed – the ordeal she had suffered caused her milk to dry up. To feed Mahíndukht, my parents searched and found a woman who was nursing her newly-born child. She was poor and in need of something to do to feed herself and another mouth. She was hired to live in the house and breastfeed not only her own child but Mahíndukht as well. The arrangement worked well. She became known as Naniy-i Mahín and developed a loving bond with the family, especially with Mahín. She stayed with the family until they moved to Shíráz about two years later.

Mother developed other health problems, which nearly claimed her life. She suffered from severe pain in her legs, which swelled to twice their normal size. In the description of my sister Rawḥanieh, they were as big and as hard as a tree trunk. Today, identifying the problem and administering treatment to relieve the pain would be a simple matter but in those days medical science was in its primitive stages and finding skilled doctors in Nayríz a rare phenomenon. So mother suffered with no relief in sight. Treatments were unsuccessful and hope for her recovery was fading fast. Her condition was a source of true concern to father, the children, grandparents, relatives and the inhabitants of the town, especially those living in Maḥallih Pahlaví. A search was made far and wide for someone who could suggest an effective and fast-working remedy. Then came someone from Shíráz who was trained in using alternative methods to cure certain ailments. He was brought to mother's bedside. He suggested the use of leeches. Fortunately they were plentiful in the streams of Nayríz that carried crystal clear water from deep wells dug outside the town for irrigation. He asked for several dozens of them. The treatment, as explained to me by my sister, was this: The doctor put the leeches in salty water. When they became thin, a sign that they were hungry, he put them on mother's legs. Apparently, leeches latch onto the skin when they are hungry and suck blood until they are full and heavy. At that point they automatically let go of the skin and fall off. When that happened, the doctor put them in salty water again and waited until they became thin. He put them back on mother's legs and repeated the procedure many times until mother's legs returned to their normal size. That treatment saved mother's life.

After the tragic death of her firstborn, one thing that mother made sure would not happen again was being separated from her other children before they were adults and could look after themselves. One of the repercussions of this was that in order to provide the children with good education, my parents had to leave Nayríz. The prospect of leaving Nayríz, although attractive, was nevertheless daunting. By then my parents had five children. Establishing oneself with a large family in an unfamiliar city is not an easy task. Added to the problem was the fact that after the death of his son, my father had lost interest in material pursuits. He neglected the demands of his business and consequently incurred substantial losses. It took much courage on his part to completely detach himself from his roots and all that he had worked for, uproot himself and his family and migrate to a new place. To ensure that what he was about to do would not run counter to the wishes of the Guardian of the Bahá'í Faith and also to beseech his prayers for the progress of the beloved son he and his wife had lost – the only consolation that could soothe their hearts – father turned to Shoghi Effendi. In a petition he explained the irreparable loss that he and mother had sustained and sought permission for himself and his family to leave Nayríz and settle in a place where the children could receive a good education. The response was written on behalf of Shoghi Effendi:

> Nayríz, Jináb-i Áqá Mírzá Muḥammad-Shafí' Rouhani, the pilgrim from Nayríz, upon him be the glory of God, the Most Glorious.
> The letter of that spiritual friend dated 5 Shahru'l-Masá'il 92 was presented to His Highness, the Guardian of the Cause of God, and its contents attained his blessed glance. The sincerity and luminosity of that spiritual friend made him happy and caused

him to express his loving kindness and compassion.

Your high praise of the sincerity, steadfastness, firmness and obedience of the Nayrízí friends in carrying out divine teachings and his own instructions, their frankness in fearlessly stating the truth, their valiance, as well as the integrity of those chargers in the field of understanding and certitude, particularly the Bahá'í youth, and most specially the actions of the Local Spiritual Assembly which have been the source of the glory of the Cause of God and exaltation of His Word, all of these have been hailed by the tongue of grandeur.

The Bahá'ís of Nayríz, ever since the rising of the Luminary of the world, have been self-sacrificing and self-effacing in the path of God, and are remembered for their valiance, bravery and high-mindedness. The activities of those ardent lovers are resplendent and brilliant like the morning star.

Praised be God! The spirit of His love still throbs in the veins and arteries of those believers standing firm in the Covenant and the glad-tidings of the Abhá Kingdom and outpourings of the Concourse on high keep them fresh, joyous and blithe.

The purpose is that Shoghi Effendi has not forgotten and will never forget the friends of that land. His loving glance and tender affections have been and will always be directed towards those true and faithful believers. At every moment he beseeches from the Kingdom of Splendours confirmations and success on their behalf. That spiritual friend has likewise been the recipient of his loving-kindness and favour. He was saddened by the news of the passing of your beloved young son, Mírzá 'Abdu'l-Ḥusayn. He expresses his condolences and sympathy to the survivors of the one who has soared to the Friend of the Most High. He will implore in the sacred Shrines pardon, forgiveness and an exalted station for him.

He acknowledges the contributions made towards the purchase of lands surrounding the Shrine of the Báb in your name and in the names of Amatu'lláh Ṭúbá Khánum Rouhani and your mother Nuríján Khánum Rouhani which have been received in the holy presence and accepted. He has issued separate receipts in the name of each individual.

You have requested permission to come on pilgrimage. He grants you permission. Your intention to leave Nayríz and settle elsewhere for the purpose of providing for the education and training of your children has met with his approval.

Those mentioned [in your letter], your children Jináb-i Áqá Mírzá Masíḥ and the handmaids of the Merciful Shamsu'ḍ-Ḍuḥá, Nayyirih Khánum, Pouràndukht Rouhani, your brothers Jináb-i Áqá Mírzá Khalíl, Jináb-i Áqá Mírzá 'Alí-Akbar and Jináb-i Áqá Mírzá Jalál Rouhani, also your father-in-law Ḥájí Mírzá Aḥmad Vaḥídí and brother-in-law Jináb-i Áqá Mírzá 'Abdu'l-Ḥusayn Vaḥídí and Amatu'lláh Fáṭimih Khánum 'Irfán, upon them, men and women alike, be Bahá'u'lláhu'l-Abhá, have been mentioned by the tongue of grandeur. From the court of the Most Glorious Lord he beseeches confirmations, success, bounty and favour on behalf of those spiritual friends. Convey his loving greetings to all.

Written in accordance with the instructions of his blessed person.

Núru'd-Dín Zayn
13 Shahru's-Sulṭán 92 – 30 January 1936

Postscript in the handwriting of Shoghi Effendi:

It was perused. Signed: The Servant of His Threshold, Shoghi.

Shoghi Effendi's message gave my parents the courage and assurance they needed to move ahead with the plans they had in mind. Father had to resign from those government agencies in which he served as an honorary member. He was particularly eager to relinquish his position as a member of the committee dealing with those eligible for conscription. He was also eager to hand over his responsibility as the treasurer of the board of governors of the town. Thus he was looking for an opportune time to tender his resignation. Such opportunity presented itself when the application of a Bahá'í for exemption from military service was being discussed. The applicant was a Mr Bahín'á'ín. In his application he had introduced himself as the son of Mírzá Ḥusayn and mentioned that since his father served as the custodian of the Bahá'í Centre and his salary was inadequate to take care of the needs of his large family, he had to work to supplement his father's salary. The guarantor of his application was father. When the chairman of the jurisdiction, Ḥájí Khán, known as Sarduzakí, heard the word 'Bahá'í', he was outraged. Attacking the applicant, he said, 'Bahá'í schools have been closed,[58] Bahá'ís have been pursued and annihilated everywhere, yet in Nayríz they still want a name and a position. They go so far as mentioning "Bahá'í" in an official government document.'

The tone of the objection raised by the chairman of the board caused father to arise in defence of the applicant and say:

> It is true that Bahá'í schools have been closed by the government owing to certain political considerations but Bahá'ís have not been pursued anywhere and they have certainly not been annihilated. This fire cannot be extinguished. The form for providing support must be filled according to what is true. The applicant cannot lie. Whatever he has put down is the truth. I am a trustee of the people. The governor, the honourable Mudíru'd-Dawlih, has appointed me to this post in full knowledge that I am a Bahá'í.

And addressing the attacker, he said:

> Jináb-i Captain Ḥájí Khán, chairman of the jurisdiction! We are meeting on behalf of the government for a lofty aim, which is supervising the affairs of those who are eligible for conscription. It is not a meeting for discussing religious matters and creating an arena for religious opposition. A spiritual leader is present in this committee. He knows that I am a Bahá'í, yet we are close friends. Since you agitated the meeting and insulted me, I will officially resign and will mention the reason for my resignation to the governor and chairman of the regional organization for conscription.

Immediately after his brief speech, father wrote a letter of resignation, placed it on the table and left the meeting.

When father left the meeting, the governor said to Ḥájí Khán:

> What you did was not good. I know this person. He will immediately send a complaint to the governor of the province of Fárs and to the regional head of the organization for conscription. As a result, this meeting, as well as you and I, will be called for questioning. It would be better to return him to the meeting and do everything possible to effect reconciliation between the two of you.[59]

All present agreed with the proposition tabled. The governor sent a message to father saying that the next day he (the governor) and members of the board would be father's guests for lunch and the venue would be father's orchard about a kilometre outside the town.[60] Father had no choice but to act as a gracious host. It was then mother's responsibility to ensure that a befitting meal was prepared at short notice and transported to the orchard, where the notables assembled. The chairmen of all jurisdictions in the area, as well as members of the board, except Ḥájí Khán, were present. During the luncheon meeting a friendly atmosphere prevailed and the governor succeeded in convincing father to withdraw his resignation.

One year elapsed from the receipt of Shoghi Effendi's message. My parents were seriously thinking of leaving Nayríz but did not know how to proceed. Father needed a secure job that would pay for the basic needs of the family. Suddenly doors of confirmation were flung wide open and an excellent opportunity presented itself.

One summer day in 1936 father received a telephone message from Mr Surúsh, president of Shirkat-i Rústá'í (a rural and agricultural development company)[61] in Shíráz saying that he and two high-ranking guests would visit Nayríz the next day. He asked father to prepare a luncheon in his orchard. Without knowing who Mr Surush's guests were, father complied with the request and spread a banquet in their honour. It was customary in those days in Iran for high-ranking guests to be accompanied by several others, so hosts always prepared enough food to feed a large number of people, lest lack of food become a cause of embarrassment. As usual, mother had the lion's share in making the occasion a success. It fell upon her to prepare for the banquet at short notice. Although she did not participate in the luncheon herself, behind the scenes she worked hard to ensure that everything was in good order and that the luncheon matched the stature of the guests. Considering that the memory of her son's death was still very fresh and that she had just recovered from a life-threatening illness, it was the strength of her indomitable spirit and character that enabled her to cope with the demands of her position as the wife of a prominent Bahá'í and a successful businessman with multiple responsibilities.

When the guests arrived, it became known that one of the high-ranking officials was the head of the Department of Justice, the other the prosecutor-general, and they were accompanied by a group of senior staff. After their arrival, they rested for a while then the head of the Department of Justice and the prosecutor summoned to their presence the governor of Nayríz, a Mr Naysárí, together with his secretary, Mírzá Aḥmad 'Irfán, a close friend of father's married to his aunt, Fáṭimih Khánum. After a brief conversation on different matters, the prosecutor asked the governor of Nayríz, 'What is the nature of the complaint that the Bahá'ís of Nayríz have lodged against the registrar's office? They have sent several complaints to the Department of Justice in the capital of the province.' The governor responded that the complaint concerned their marriages. He explained that they wanted the registrar's office to register Bahá'í marriages on their birth certificates. 'The registrar's office has refused, so they have been sending complaints to us, to you and to the capital of the province,' he said. The prosecutor asked, 'How many have had this kind of marriage?' Mr Naysárí responded, 'Mírzá Aḥmad Khán knows better, for he is both secretary and the man in charge of the files.' Mr 'Irfán said, 'Thus far five marriages have taken place. One of them is the marriage of Mírzá Jalál Míthaqí, brother of Muḥammad-Shafí' Rouhani, who is your host.' The prosecutor asked father if it were true. Father confirmed the accuracy of Mr 'Irfán's statement. The prosecutor said, 'You are not officially recognized. No punishment has yet been anticipated for this kind of offence. But the parliament may pass a severe punishment. What will you do then?' Father said, 'We will accept with heart and soul.' The prosecutor said, 'Dissimulation is permissible in every religion. Seek the advice of your leader. He will let you dissimulate.' Father said, 'His Highness Shoghi Effendi has issued emphatic instructions that Bahá'ís should consider frankness and truthfulness more praiseworthy than cajolery and dissimulation and has said that we should never deviate from the path of truth.' This response surprised the prosecutor, who became silent. Then the guests started whispering among themselves.[62]

The father-in-law of Mr Surú<u>sh</u>, who had accompanied him to Nayríz, was going to say something derogatory. Noticing his intentions, father used the ordering of tea for the guests as an excuse, got up immediately and left the gathering. The head of the Justice Department realized that the remark was to have been offensive and said, 'This man is our host and an honourable person. Do not say something that would hurt his feelings.'[63]

On that breezy summer day lunch was served in a beautiful and tranquil area shaded by the leaves of vine trees forming an arbour, on both sides of which flowed streams of crystal clear and cool water. Taking an afternoon nap was a formal part of luncheons, at least during long summer days in that part of the country. Guests were provided with pillows, sheets and mats. The air was dry and most guests opted to sleep under the shade of the trees. Almost all orchards in Nayríz served as summer resorts for owners and their families. As such each had a building structure with basic facilities. Mr Surú<u>sh</u> asked to sleep indoors. He occupied a bed in a room in the building and stayed awake until everyone was asleep. He then called father to himself and, after expressing gratitude for the luncheon, said,

> I am very happy and pleased with your work as the <u>Sh</u>irkat-i Rústá'í's agent in Nayríz. I go to various places to supervise and

> inspect the work of our agents but here I come to visit you, I don't bother to see the branch office. This is because I trust you completely. I have established about 50 branch offices in the area surrounding Shíráz. I have become a captive in the hands of a bunch of thieves. Come to Shíráz and rescue me from their hands. I will employ you, give you a good salary and appoint you as my deputy and director of the income section of the company. I know that here you have a business in addition to being the agent for the company. I also know that you have a brother and a brother-in-law who are very energetic. Leave your affairs to them. You can also keep the agency in your name but let one of them manage it. In Shíráz you will be better able to send them goods.[64]

Mr Surúsh went on explaining the advantages of father's move to Shíráz. As he was expounding on the merits of the move, father was thinking that only the outpourings of Bahá'u'lláh's bounties and the prayers of Shoghi Effendi in the holy Shrines on his behalf could have produced such results. He found the opportunity appealing and responded favourably to Mr Surúsh's proposal, provided that the salary was good, he was officially employed and he received a housing allowance. Mr Surúsh agreed and asked father to start packing.

Father left his responsibility as agent for Shirkat-i Rústá'í in Nayríz to his brother-in-law, 'Abdu'l-Ḥusayn Vaḥídí, and the one for Asafetida, as well as other trading affairs, to his brother, 'Alí-Akbar Rouhani. He relinquished his other business responsibilities and gave up the post of honorary treasurer of the board of governors of the town. He put 'Ali-Akbar Rouhani in charge of his pending affairs and left his other brother, Khalíl Rouhani, in charge of his farming and agricultural enterprises. When the official notification confirming his employment arrived, father and his family left their birthplace and moved to Shíráz, ending the first phase of their eventful life. Father was then 40 years old, mother about 30. They had already suffered the loss of their firstborn, whose tragic death had turned their lives upside down, for his death was the determining factor in their departure from Nayríz, a course of action which changed their future and the future of their children. 'Abdu'l-Ḥusayn's death was indeed catalyst for many developments and spiritual achievements that ensued.

## Departure for Shíráz

After receiving an official offer of employment, father wound up his business, settled all his financial affairs, sold some property to provide for the trip and, to the utter astonishment of the inhabitants, held the hands of his wife and five children and left his beloved birthplace. It was the first time someone in the Bahá'í community of Nayríz had taken such a drastic step. How could this be? What were they going to do? Why was he leaving and taking the whole family with him? Couldn't he go, if he had to, establish himself and call for the family to come later? These were the questions frequently asked and debated by everyone other than those directly involved. Such questions nowadays may sound rude and completely out of line. People today may argue that it was for the couple to decide in consultation with one another how they wanted to live their lives but that is not how things operated among the tradition-minded inhabitants of a conservative town. Friends and acquaintances showed their concern by speaking their minds, probing, asking questions and giving unsolicited advice. When the crowd had received the bereaved parents upon their return to Nayríz, they were welcoming them back and wanted them to stay. Besides, almost everybody was related to everyone else by blood or through marriage. As such, all felt the need to express an opinion, to show how much they cared. Poor parents! The loss of their beloved son weighed heavily on their hearts, yet they had to face the repeated questions everyone asked. Fortunately, they were determined to leave the town and for that they had the approval of the only person in the world that truly mattered. Shoghi Effendi had blessed their decision and that was all they needed to feel vindicated and justified.

Mother was happy to go as long as her children were with her but she was paying a high price for this pleasure. She was leav-

Grandfather Mírzá Aḥmad,
circa late 1940s

Father

Mother

Father is seated in the centre holding Rawḥanieh on his lap. Standing to his left is 'Abdu'l Ḥusayn, to his right Masíḥ. Behind him are three of his brothers, *left to right*: Mírzá Khalíl, Mírzá 'Alí Akbar and Mírzá Ismá'il, who is holding a child (not identified). Taken in Nayríz circa 1928.

*From left to right*: Grandmother Núríján, Pouran, mother, Hand of the Cause 'Alí Akbar Furútan, Rawḥanieh, who was visiting Shíráz, Mahín; *In front*: children of the family, circa 1954

*Left to right*: Father, Rawḥanieh and mother, in Italy, early April 1963, on their way to the first Bahá'í World Congress

Some members of the family attending the World Congress in London in April and May 1963. *Left to right*: Uncle Jalál, mother, father, Rawḥanieh, Baharieh, Pouran holding Sovaida in her arms, Knight of Bahá'u'lláh Ted Cardell, an early pioneer to Kenya (the man at the back is unknown).

Father, *centre*, is delivering a talk in Enugu, Nigeria, August 1977. To his right is Dr Mihdí Samandarí, who translated father's talk from Persian into English. To father's left is a Nigerian Bahá'í translating the talk from English into a Nigerian language.

*Left to right*: Dr Mihdí Samandarí, mother and father in the home of Firishtih and Massoud Samadi in Enugu, Nigeria, August 1977

Family members participating in the international Bahá'í conference at Enugu, Nigeria, August 1977. *Left to right*: Masíḥ, father holding Naseem (Firishtih and Massoud's daughter), Firishtih, Massoud, Parvín (Masíḥ's wife), mother and two of the friends. *Seated*: Gloria (Masíḥ and Parvín's daughter)

*Left to right*: Mrs V. Farahmand, mother, Mr B. Afshin, father, Mr Bahá'í Poostchi, in Panchgani, India, circa 1982

Father, *centre*, and mother, *second from right*, with a group of Bahá'í women in Panchgani, India, circa 1981

ing behind her own parents and siblings, as well her relatives and friends she had known all her life. She was a strong and courageous woman with an unshakable sense of commitment. She had confidence in the ability of her husband to provide for the family, no matter where they happened to be. Although she had enjoyed ease and comfort growing up and more recently in her life, she could easily adjust to changing requirements and meet harsher conditions if the circumstances required.

The new challenges that my parents had to meet in a foreign place were many. They no longer lived in a house of their own and did not enjoy vast space or an abundance of provisions for their daily needs. The family lived in rented quarters and tasted for the first time the agony of separation from loved ones. Mother had to adjust to life in the city and raise without help several children who were from one to twelve years old. At the same time, she had to be flexible enough to move to yet another place, for father was no longer self-employed and might well be transferred to another post.

Father started work in the Shirkat-i Rúst'í as the president's deputy in charge of buying and selling. He also planned and carried out Bahá'í activities, such as teaching the Faith. He served on the teaching committee, established a regular fireside and was happy that his school-aged children could receive a good education. All these he owed to the prayers of Shoghi Effendi. He was very careful to maintain a good balance between work and worldly affairs on the one hand, and Bahá'í activities and spiritual development on the other. This state of affairs continued for a while. When Shoghi Effendi encouraged the Iranian Bahá'ís to arise and fulfil the goals of the Forty-Five Month Plan for spreading the Faith throughout the country, father felt unhappy about living in a city. After all, he owed everything that he had to the prayers of Shoghi Effendi. Therefore, he could not ignore his pleas to the friends to pioneer on the home front. His initial unhappiness gradually turned into dissatisfaction with the kind of life he was leading. He talked with the family about it. Everyone was acutely aware that with a large family he could not leave without proper preparations and the assurance of a job. He consulted a trusted friend and a renowned

Bahá'í teacher, Mr Ḥasan Núshábádí, who came up with an instant solution. He said that Mr 'Azízu'lláh Khaḍrá'í, son of the martyr Mullá 'Alíy-i Sabzavárí, a close friend of his, was in Shíráz. The purpose of his visit was to establish a cotton-processing factory, called Shirkat-i Jean, in Shíráz and other parts of the province of Fárs. He was looking for hardworking and reliable Bahá'ís who could take over responsibility for and serve as presidents of the subsidiary factories. Mr Núshábádí had introduced to Mr Khaḍrá'í four Bahá'ís, one for the factory in Shíráz and three for other places. One of the three was father. Mr Núshábádí told father to go and see Mr Manúchihr Munajjim, the president of the main office in Shíráz, and through him get in touch with Mr Khaḍrá'í. Father did as advised. The next day he met Mr Khaḍrá'í, who offered him the presidency of the Dáráb branch with twice the salary he was receiving in Shirkat-i Rústá'í. He was also entitled to all administrative privileges.

Father accepted the offer pending the acceptance of his resignation by the president of Shirkat-i Rústá'í. Mr Munajjim was a close friend of the president of the board of directors of that company and promised to help to get father's resignation accepted. Father turned over his responsibilities to another person, submitted his resignation and left for Dáráb to install a cotton-processing factory and serve as the president of that branch office.[65]

## Life in Dáráb

As it was in the middle of the school year, so as not to interrupt the children's education, father went to Dáráb alone. Mother stayed with the children. Life was not easy. This was the first time in her life that she had had to take sole responsibility for herself and her children. But she preferred this to being separated from them. However, she had to reduce her family's living standard and make plans to settle in yet another unknown town.

Immediately upon arrival in Dáráb, father began work on building the cotton-processing factory and invited several Bahá'ís from Nayríz to work as builders and staff of the newly-established branch office. Soon after the arrival of the new Bahá'ís, the Local Spiritual Assemly of Dáráb was formed and 19 Day Feasts held regularly. The friends enjoyed each other's company and attracted those who had drifted away. The resumption of Bahá'í activities did not please the fanatic Muslims in the town. They started plotting in secret and got some of the town officials to cooperate with them. The first plot concerned the murder of a factory worker. They accused some of the Bahá'ís and non-Bahá'ís from Nayríz, who were working for father, of being the murderers. They spread rumours that because the victim had abused and cursed the Bahá'ís, the president of the Shirkat had persuaded the workers to murder him.

Father was interrogated. His opponents incited the subversive elements of the town to form groups, demonstrate and ask that he be tried. To keep everything under control, the Local Spiritual Assembly asked father to stay home for a few days and advise his staff and the workers in his employ to do the same. He fully complied with the Assembly's decision. One of the members of the Assembly, an influential man from Dáráb by the name of Mr Adab, played a very important role in repelling the uprising. He sent a message to the wealthy leaders of the town who were fuelling the fire saying:

> You all know that Mr Rouhani has had no part in the activities of which he is accused. If he is indicted and tried, he will be exonerated in no time. However, if we expose your long record of subversive activities against the government and make certain facts known to the highest authority in the land, surely several of you will be completely annihilated. If you persist in falsely accusing Mr Rouhani and inflict the slightest harm on him, you may be sure that this course of action will be followed.[66]

As the agitators were among the subversive elements of the area and despised by the government of the day, they took the threat seriously and withdrew the charges against father. Thus the conspiracy came to a halt. Others falsely accused of the crime were arrested, indicted, tried and sent to Shíráz, where they suffered imprisonment for some time.

At this juncture father sent for his family who were living in Shíráz to join him in Dáráb. Mother packed up everything and left Shíráz together with the children. The arrival of mother and the children eased the burden on father in some ways but did not check the enemy's plotting against him. Those who wanted him harmed continued their secret plans. One such person was Mr Sájidí, the director of the Department of Education in Dáráb. He had an insatiable thirst to drive father and his family out and had many supporters among the 'ulamá. To accomplish his design, he needed a pretext. When the wedding ceremony of Crown Prince Muḥammad Riḍá Pahlaví with Princess Fawḍíyih was being celebrated throughout Iran, father, as the president of Shirkat-i Jean, held a banquet in their honour. Ironically, it coincided with the first day of the Riḍván festival. A huge crowd consisting of presidents of various offices and dignitaries of the town were present. One of the Bahá'ís who had recently become active and served as gate-keeper of one of the government offices in Dáráb composed a piece of poetry extolling the Feast of Riḍván and the Crown Prince's wedding celebrations. In his poem he referred to the two celebrations thus:

> Two Feasts have been joined together
> Stop moaning, O heart, from disunity
> The one is the feast of the sovereign
> The other reunion with the King.[67]

Underneath the poem he penned a note congratulating father in honour of the auspicious occasion.

The poet was applauded for his poem. Mr Bahá'ul-Mulk, the governor of Dáráb, a friend of the Bahá'ís who also liked the Bahá'í Faith, took the text of the poem to forward to the Sháh. As the poet had not read out his note at the foot of the poem, no one noticed his intentions. Mr Sájidí, who was sitting next to the governor, saw the note and was outraged. His face betrayed his inner rage. He decided that the time had come for him to carry out his hitherto hidden plan. He immediately announced that the Department of Education was hosting a banquet in honour of the wedding of the royal couple and extended an invitation to everyone present to attend the celebration the following night.

Knowing Mr Sájidí's background and his animosity towards the Bahá'í Faith, all the friends, especially members of the Local Spiritual Assembly, were certain that he was laying a plot and had in mind attacking the Bahá'í Faith in the speech he was going to deliver during the celebration. Therefore, several members of the Assembly, who held prestigious positions in the town, decided that as soon as Mr Sájidí began to say anything abusive, they would all rise and leave. They advised other Bahá'ís who were present to do likewise. The following night, as soon as Mr Sájidí began his verbal attack, the Bahá'ís stood up and left. With their departure the celebratory gathering broke up. Since Mr Sájidí was unable to finish his speech that night, he decided to retaliate. He sent a detailed letter of complaint about the Bahá'ís to the provincial director of education in Shíráz, capital of Fárs. In his report he said:

> At this time when, according to instructions of His Majesty the Sháh,[68] all gatherings, including Muslim religious sermons, are cancelled, a group of people in Dáráb are constantly meeting and planning sedition.[69]

The provincial director of education referred the report to the governor (*ustándár*) of the province of Fárs for action. The provincial governor forwarded the report to Mr Bahá'u'l-Mulk, the local governor (*farmándár*) of Dáráb, asking him to investigate the matter and report back the nature of the meetings and the ideology of those involved. Mr Bahá'u'l-Mulk, who knew what the motivating force behind the report was, sent a letter to Mr Sájidí. The letter said that according to a report he had sent to Shíráz, meetings were taking place in Dáráb and certain individuals were planning to stir up sedition and to arise in opposition. He was asked to explain the place of such secret meetings and their purpose. Mr Sájidí responded that he would meet the governor in person and submit an oral report. Bahá'u'l-Mulk took advantage of the response and reported to the governor of Fárs that the motivating force behind the report was personal feelings based on religious prejudice. He added that since the allegations were baseless, he had got them to reconcile with a hug. He sent with his response the short letter he had received from Mr Sájidí on the subject.

Mr Sájidí's schemes did not end with the above episode. He waited for another chance to bring trumped-up charges against father. The opportunity presented itself when a Mr Mustaqímí, an employee of the provincial Department of Agriculture, was transferred to Dáráb and put in charge of acquiring cottonseeds for the plantation. His job also involved the task of sifting and cleaning the seeds, so he had to work in the Shirkat-i Jean and deal with labourers hired for the job. One of the labourers was a woman who had had several miscarriages. One day Mr Mustaqímí saw that she was not doing her work properly. He protested. Later that day the woman had a miscarriage. Mr Sájidí and his supporters incited her husband to lodge a complaint with the police. The complaint said, 'Mr Mustaqímí kicked my wife in the stomach and caused her to lose the baby.'[70]

The police officially asked the office where Mr Mustaqímí worked to deliver him for interrogation regarding the woman who had had a miscarriage. Before going to the police, Mr Mustaqímí went to see father and explained the circumstances. Father encouraged him to be brave and, when asked, state his religion without fear. When Mr Mustaqímí went for interrogation, father sent for the husband of the woman who had lodged the complaint. The man was advised not to be an instrument in the hand of others and told that the head of the health services would examine her. Since there was no sign of kicking, father explained, the complainant would be exposed and charged with perjury. Since he was poor and needy, he received ten túmáns and withdrew his complaint.

That afternoon the Assembly met in an extraordinary session to prepare a report to be sent to Shíráz. During the meeting news was received that Mr Madaní, the provincial director of agriculture for the province of Fárs, had arrived in Dáráb. When he had arrived at the Department of Agriculture, he had seen a letter from the police and asked Mr 'Iráqí, president of the office, what it was about. Mr 'Iráqí had explained that it was about Mr Mustaqímí. Mr Madaní opened the letter and read the contents, which reported that during interrogation Mr Mustaqímí had introduced himself as a Bahá'í and signed the form specifying his religion. It further indicated that since this was against the laws of the country, he had to be dismissed from his post. Mr Madaní was outraged. He immediately drafted a letter to the Police Department saying that Mr Mustaqímí was an employee of the Department of Agriculture with an excellent record of honesty and trustworthiness, that the Department had full confidence in him and that it had employed him in the full knowledge that he was a Bahá'í. He further indicated that the police had overstepped their boundaries by entering into such questions. The draft was transcribed and sent to the police. When the Bahá'ís visited Mr Madaní he confirmed the details.

The chief of police, in the meantime, was overtaken by the fear that a negative report would be sent to Shíráz and adversely affect his service record. He consulted with the heads of those offices that conspired to undermine the Bahá'ís. They concluded that it was necessary to find a way to effect a reconciliation between Mr Madaní and the chief of police and decided to do their best to remove all traces of the incident.

The next day Mr Madaní was invited to a luncheon in the home of the head of the local branch of the treasury. The chief of police and those who opposed the Bahá'ís were all there. After lunch, the chief of police complained to Mr Madaní regarding the way he had handled the situation concerning Mr Mustaqímí, which he had found derogatory. Mr Madaní said in response that the police chief needed to familiarize himself with what was unacceptable administrative procedure. Bahá'ís, he said, were serving in all departments of government and the military and no one was bothering them. 'You have just left university and are inexperienced,' he added. 'You need to learn all administrative procedures.' Others tried to mediate. Mr Madaní said, 'You must respect the rights of all citizens' and referred them to the constitution of the country. He then announced to those present, 'I want you to know that I am a Bahá'í and my wife and children are also Bahá'ís. Now what have you got to say?'[71] Mr Madaní was married to a Bahá'í and his brother-in-law was a well-known believer. The incident prompted Mr Madaní to proclaim that he was a Bahá'í as well. When the audience heard his declaration, they all became silent, apologized and asked that the records regarding the episode in both offices be destroyed.

When the opponents of the Faith failed in their attempts to discredit the Bahá'ís of Dáráb, all the inhabitants of the town lived in peace and tranquillity for a considerable time. The Bahá'í work progressed steadily and father climbed the ladder of success and fame. He and mother associated with the notables of the town and their families and enjoyed their respect and trust. Among the people with whom they had close ties of friendship were the heads of the Bahárlú tribe.[72] When the new government installed by Riḍá Sháh Pahlaví began disarming members of the public, the Bahárlú leaders opposed the order but were forced to comply and three of them were sent into exile. Others found it difficult to stay and decided to leave. Two of them who were impressed with father's honesty, integrity and reliability rented their properties to him on easy terms and left Dáráb. One of the Bahá'ís of Shíráz, whose initials were F. B., joined father in forming a partnership. Together they rented the farms for cultivation. The first year's yield was wonderful and the profit very good. When World War II broke out, Mr F. B., fearful of the instability that the war was going to cause, refused to continue with the pact he had made. Father was left alone. He was a shareholder in another company. His partner in that company also followed the example of Mr F. B. At the same time, leaders of the Bahárlú tribe took advantage of the weakening position of the central government as a result of the war, breached the terms of their contract and forcibly took their farms back. Being a Bahá'í, and a prominent one, worked to father's disadvantage, for he stood no chance of achieving justice when lawlessness and the use of force prevailed across the land. Father lost whatever he had spent on purchasing seeds, paying for cultivation, paying labourers, etc. As his partners refused to pay their share of the expenses, he incurred a tremendous loss. He felt terribly lonely and helpless in the face of gross injustice and cruelty. The weight of betrayal by friend and foe and the dynamics of the impossible situation in which he found himself were overwhelming. So he left to his brother, Mírzá Khalíl, the other agricultural enterprises he was involved in and returned to Shíráz. With the sale of some property in Nayríz, he paid all his debts. However, he felt betrayed and was heartbroken and hurt. He did not want to go back to Dáráb. He resigned from Shirkat-i Jean, took his family back to Shíráz and alone went to Ṭihrán to look for a job in a place far away from the province of Fárs and its people.

When father committed himself to doing a job, he gave it his all and worked very hard to make it a success. His honesty was impeccable, his integrity second to none. He was highly motivated, responsible, absolutely trustworthy and also very sensitive. Betrayal was something he abhorred and could not stand, especially from a friend, and fighting was against the principles he held dear. For these reasons we see him more than once in his life, and usually at a time when he was at the height of his career, leaving everything behind, moving away and starting all over again. By so doing, he suffered tremendously and with him also his family, especially mother, who had to make drastic adjustments to cope with new and unpredictable circumstances. However, his and the family's spiritual joy was that wherever they lived, they shunned discord and did not become the cause of disunity in the community.

For consolation and to regain his confidence and tranquillity, father again turned to Shoghi Effendi. The purpose was not to complain about those who had betrayed him. He rather reported his lack of success in Dáráb and beseeched fresh confirmations to succeed in rendering befitting service to the Cause of Bahá'u'lláh. After a short while, he received the following response:

> Dáráb, Jináb-i Áqá Mírzá Muḥammad-Shafí' Rouhani, the pilgrim from Nayríz, upon him be Bahá'u'lláhu'l-Abhá
> The letter of that dear spiritual friend dated 10 Shahru'l-Bahá

attained the loving glance of His Highness, the Guardian of the Cause of God, may our spirits be sacrificed for him, and the details of the circumstances you have described became known in his illumined and spotless presence. He beseeches divine favours and hopes that the resultant difficulties may be vanquished, that your affairs may improve, that God's mercy, blessings and bestowals may surround you, that you may be successful in rendering service to the Cause of God and that you are able to manage your affairs with absolute confidence and reliance [on God], directing your full attention to Him.

It is hoped that heavenly assistance may come to your aid and that all the troubles and hardships you have endured may not be wasted and may produce the desired result. In all circumstances the glance of his loving-kindness and generosity has been and will continue to be directed towards you. Be assured and joyous.

Your esteemed wife Amatu'lláh Ṭúbá Khánum, your honourable mother Amatu'lláh Núríyyih Khánum, your brothers Áqá Mírzá Khaíl, Áqá Mírzá Jalál and Áqá Mírzá 'Alí-Akbar, and your dear children, Mírzá Masíḥ Rouhani, Shamsu'ḍ-Ḍuḥá, Nayyirih, Pourán-dukht, Mahíndukht and Baharieh, were all mentioned by the tongue of compassion and loving-kindness. He beseeches on behalf of all divine assistance, confirmation, success and easing of affairs.

Written at the instruction of his blessed self. 11 Shahru'l-'Aẓamat 97 BE, 27 May 1940. Núru'd-Dín Zayn.

Postscript in the handwriting of Shoghi Effendi:

Was seen. The Servant of His Threshold, Shoghi.[73]

## The Family in Shíráz

During the stay in Dáráb the family had expanded further: the sixth child and fifth girl, named Baharieh (the writer), had been added to my parents' surviving offspring. I was an infant when the family returned to Shíráz, and by the time father went to Ṭihrán in search of a job, mother was pregnant with yet another child. Being pregnant, having to look after several children, living under very stringent financial conditions and having her husband unemployed and living away from home weighed heavily on mother's heart. In Dáráb she and father had lost almost everything they possessed. Additionally, they had sold some of their property in Nayríz and paid off debtors. For the first time in her life mother had a problem making ends meet and realized what it meant for the children to need something she could not provide.

The cultural norms of the time and my parents' affluent background made circumstances even harsher than they appeared. Although poverty had visited them at the worst possible time, they had to maintain a certain standard of living and keep up appearances to ward off pity and unsolicited advice from those who had considered their departure from Nayríz unwise. Four of the children were going to school and their educational expenses had to be met. The eldest son, Mírzá Masíḥ, was in secondary school. The eldest daughter, Shamsu'ḍ-Ḍuḥá (Rawḥanieh) was in the last year of primary school. When the time for the final exams arrived, she needed a piece of fabric to make a dress for her sewing exam.[74] Mother did not have sufficient cash on hand to pay for the fabric. Rawḥanieh wept bitterly over the possibility of failing the final exams and having to repeat them at a later time. Mother was bewildered. The sight of her child crying made her wonder how she could solve the problem. She did not want to borrow money from a friend or relative. She looked around and her eyes fell on a copper pot, probably a part of her dowry, which had thus far survived. This was the pot in which she cooked rice for the family. She picked it up, put on her *chádur* and dashed out of the house. She returned after a short while without the pot but with sufficient money to pay for two metres of cheap fabric for her daughter's sewing project. She had gone to the man from whom she had rented the two rooms and offered the pot for sale. The man bought it for a paltry sum, sufficient only to pay for the needed fabric. Rawḥanieh did extremely well and passed her exams with flying colours. She had the highest passing marks in her class. Her outstanding success warmed the heart of a mother surrounded by adversity on all sides. Her daughter's impressive achievement was the best reward she could have had.

Another incident occurred in those difficult times. Although seemingly insignificant, it nearly cost my sister Pouran the continuation of her education a few years later. She was in grade three and needed a notebook for her class work. Mother had no money to spare. Pouran decided to make herself a notebook. She needed heavy cardboard for the cover. Her second grade certificate looked right for the purpose. In those days school certificates were made of good cardboard and looked impressive. Pouran cut up her certificate, pasted the pieces together and, to avoid attracting unwanted attention, used glue to cover it with white paper. Pouran produced a nice notebook and was proud of her handiwork. However, her innocent mistake created a huge headache for mother about three years later, as we shall see.

Meanwhile, mother spent the last months of her latest pregnancy struggling to meet the needs of her children with the meagre financial resources she could obtain through the sale of fruit and agricultural produce from the property she and father still owned in Nayríz. And all this at a time when she herself needed as much attention and care as she could get. By then mother was in her mid-thirties. She had seen many ups and downs in the years she had been married. She and father had several times lost everything they had worked for and had been divinely assisted to obtain things that were better than the old ones. She was a strong woman and did not give up easily. She had full confidence in the outpourings of Bahá'u'lláh's bounty and grace and was certain that this time would be no different. One thing she did not know was how long the ordeal was going to last. Her concern was not for herself and not so much for the children who were managing somehow but for the baby she was carrying under those hard conditions. And when the time of delivery came, she had no experienced help around. In those days in Iran women gave birth at home. Traditional midwives were called in when the delivery time seemed near. Such midwives could handle normal deliveries but any complication was beyond their expertise and not infrequently women died at childbirth or babies lost their lives because of midwives' lack of competence. So mother's concerns were immense, especially with father being so far away. Praised be God, a healthy baby was born and survived. It was the first boy my parents had had since their firstborn had died.

## Father's Search for Work in Ṭihrán and Short Stay in Khurásán

Father was unemployed for three months. During that time he could not send help to the family in Shíráz. He stayed in Ṭihrán and tried every possible avenue to secure a job. One day a friend suggested to him to contact a certain Bahá'í, who was Mr Khaḍrá'í's uncle and a grandson of Mullá 'Alíy-i Sabzivárí, one of the martyrs of the Faith. This man was a very influential person in the country. A favourable recommendation from him would have got father any job he wanted in any of the ministries. When father discussed with Mr Ḥasan Núshábádí, who had just been released from prison,[75] the prospect of getting a job through this man, he was told that it did not befit him to even mention his name. Father was startled and asked Mr Núshábádí whether the man had broken the Covenant. Mr Núshábádí responded, 'He has not broken the Covenant but has drifted away, and His Highness the Guardian of the Faith has said that he should be left alone.'[76] So father dropped the idea of seeking assistance from him. After a while, he found a job in the Ministry of Finance. He was offered a position as the head of the accounting section in the Department of Finance in Bandar 'Abbás.[77] He was about to confirm his acceptance when Mr Muḥsin Asásí, a member of the National Spiritual Assembly of Iran, advised him against taking up the job. He said that with a large family and the harsh living conditions in Bandar 'Abbás, life would be extremely difficult there.

Father felt absolutely helpless. He had run out of money and his family in Shíráz was hard pressed for lack of finances. He was willing to accept a job even if the place was a burning hell. Although he was willing to undergo all kinds of hardship, he did not know how his children would be able to cope. Should he or should he not accept the job, that was the question. What if he refused the offer and nothing further appeared on the horizon? On the other hand, he could accept the job and put his family's health in jeopardy. He was at the end of his tether. He had no choice but to completely rely on divine assistance. It was during the month of the fast. He needed a quiet place to pray, meditate and commune privately with God. He entered one of the vacant rooms of the Ḥaẓíratu'l-Quds, turned to Bahá'u'lláh, raised his hands in supplication and implored Him to show him the right course of action. He then put his forehead down and, in a state between wakefulness and sleep, heard the words 'patience and resignation'. When he opened his eyes, it was dark. He went to the dining room and saw everyone seated at the table waiting to break the fast. They were waiting for him and asked the reason for his untimely nap. He described what had happened and asked Mr Núshábádí to elaborate on the meaning of 'patience and resignation' and to interpret the significance of what he had heard. Mr Núshábádí said, 'Give up the idea of going to Bandar 'Abbás. Adopt patience, submit to God's decree and leave your affairs to Him. Surely will God do that which is praiseworthy.' Father responded, 'Tomorrow I am supposed to go and receive the official notification of the job offer.' Mr Núshábádí said, 'Do not go to the Ministry tomorrow. It is close to Naw-Rúz, after Naw-Rúz all government offices are closed for several days. Make a decision after the New Year holidays.' Father followed Mr Núshábádí's loving advice.[78]

Naw-Rúz arrived. As Mr Núshábádí had just been released from prison, most of the Bahá'ís of Ṭihrán paid him a visit on the occasion of the New Year. Since he and father were room-mates, father got to meet a large number of the Bahá'ís of Ṭihrán during the Naw-Rúz holidays. The day after Naw-Rúz, Mr Maḥbúbí, the chief credit officer of Bank-i Millí (National Bank) of Ṭihrán, came to see Mr Núshábádí. After being introduced, he recognized father, who had been among the Bahá'ís who had welcomed Martha Root upon her arrival in Ta<u>kh</u>t-i Jam<u>sh</u>íd (Persepolis) and had attended the meetings held in her honour in <u>Sh</u>íráz. Mr Maḥbúbí asked why father was in Ṭihrán. Mr Nú<u>sh</u>ábádí briefly explained father's situation. Mr Maḥbúbí was saddened to hear his plight and said:

> If you are happy to remain in Ṭihrán with a salary of 800 riyáls, I can offer you a job in the National Bank. But if you are looking for a better paid job away from <u>Sh</u>íráz, and are willing to go to <u>Kh</u>urásán, somewhere around Sabzivár and other places in that province, I will straightway make recommendation that you be employed in the railways there.[79]

Father chose the second option. Mr Maḥbúbí immediately wrote a note, which secured father a job as an accountant for section 13 of the railways between Sabzivár and Ju<u>gh</u>táy. After a stay of three months in Ṭihrán, father left for <u>Kh</u>urásán and, at Mr Nú<u>sh</u>ábádí's advice, visited the friends in <u>Sh</u>áhrúd, Ní<u>sh</u>ábúr, Sabzivár, Niqáb and Ju<u>gh</u>táy before reaching railway section 13, situated about four kilometres from Ju<u>gh</u>táy, where he started his new job.

Father was paid well for the job he was doing and managed to send money to <u>Sh</u>íráz for the family, which eased his mind considerably. The money arrived in good time and brought relief to his hard-pressed family. It helped with some preparations that needed to be made for the birth of the child my parents were expecting. The circumstances of father's life and work in Ju<u>gh</u>táy, however, began to deteriorate with the prolongation and spread of World War II. As the general situation worsened, animosity increased between German and Russian engineers who were building the railway in that part of Iran and conditions of life became more precarious. Arguments between engineers from the two opposing nations in the war were commonplace. At times they would develop into open hostility and fights. The area where father worked was close to the border of the Soviet Union and emotions on both sides were hard to control. As a Bahá'í, father stayed clear of all partisan politics. He continued doing his work and conveying Bahá'u'lláh's redeeming message to those he found receptive.

On the first day of Riḍván father suspended work and went to Jughtáy to celebrate the Feast with the Bahá'ís there. In the evening he returned. The weather was rainy and cold. He spent the evening remembering the wonderful Bahá'í Feasts he had celebrated in the Holy Land, Ṭihrán, Shíráz and Nayríz. He spent the night alone in his tent, which was guarded by a watchman, because the situation was tense. Although alone, he was happy with his pleasant memories of the past. After prayers, he went to bed and had a wonderful dream. In his dream he saw himself in Nayríz. His financial situation was poor, his house and furniture were not as good and comfortable as in the past. However, this did not bother or sadden him. He had just returned home from his work. When he entered he received news that 'Abdu'l-Bahá had arrived in Nayríz and was going to bless his house with His presence. On the one hand father was ecstatic for so great an honour; on the other he was embarrassed that the house was small and the furniture unfit for so distinguished a guest. He was rapt in thought when 'Abdu'l-Bahá arrived. With his mixed feelings he did not know what to do and became speechless. He threw himself at 'Abdu'l-Bahá's feet and wept loudly. He thought to himself, 'When things are conspicuously evident, there is no need for explanation.'[80] In his heart he communed with 'Abdu'l-Bahá, saying, 'O Master! You are aware of my heart's agony. You know that I have been reduced to this because of the tribulations and afflictions I have suffered at the hands of strangers and friends. I have endured it all and have not uttered a word. I have left my affairs to God. You are my Master. I beg you to intercede on my behalf. From the beginning I have left you the control of my life.' As these thoughts crossed father's mind in his dream, he felt that 'Abdu'l-Bahá raised him up with His own hand. He then went to the side of the room where bedding had been stacked and sat on top of it.[81] Father's mother presented to 'Abdu'l-Bahá a baby who looked about three months old. 'Abdu'l-Bahá took the baby from grandmother's hand, held him up in His hand and started talking with him. He then addressed father, mother and every member of the family with loving words. At that moment, one of the friends, who had treated father unfairly, passed by. ‘Abdu’l-Bahá turned His face away from him. At that point father woke up and with great excitement put on the lamp in his tent and looked at the clock, which registered 2:00 a.m. He looked outside and saw that it was snowing. He turned his heart to ‘Abdu’l-Bahá for the interpretation of the dream. He recited three prayers then interpreted the dream thus:

> My Master and Intercessor ‘Abdu’l-Bahá has turned His loving glance to me. The tree of my forbearance is yielding the fruit of reunion. Ever since the passing away of my son ‘Abdu’l-Ḥusayn I was yearning for another male offspring to replace him and mitigate, to some degree, my grief. Now that my wife is pregnant, this night that male child is being born. His birth is an absolute bounty from God. The fact that ‘Abdu’l-Bahá talked with him in my dream is an indication of His special favour and grace. Therefore, he shall be called Mawhibatu’lláh (God’s bounty). In my dream he was three months old and although my return to Shíráz is nothing but a dream, through God’s absolute bounty it will be possible for me to see him when he is three months old. The formidable enemy who is still continuing his animosity is despised by ‘Abdu’l-Bahá and he shall be ashamed. God’s decisive decree will enable me to live once again with my family . . .[82]

The next day father sent a letter to mother in Shíráz explaining the dream and his interpretation of it. In that letter he expressed the hope to see the child in Nayríz when he was three months old.

## The Family Reunited

A few days elapsed from the date of the dream. Father received a telegram from Mr ‘Azízu’lláh Khaḍrá’í, who had previously offered him a job in Dáráb. It read: ‘Jughtáy, Railway Section 13, Muḥammad-Shafí‘ Rouhani. Present yourself in Mashhad. Suitable job available for you.’[83] Father resigned his job with the railways and set out for Mashhad via Sabzivár. Mr Khaḍrá’í put father in charge of his properties in the Sávujbalágh block near Karaj. He offered father a good salary and asked him to go to Nayríz in the company of his son, Mr Firaydún Khaḍrá'í, to employ a number of farm workers and take them to his farms in Mishkínábád and Shahnám, two small villages near Karaj. Father did as he had been asked and succeeded in reuniting with his family when the newly-born son, Mawhibatu'lláh, was three months old. Father took with him to work on Mr Khaḍrá'í's farms sufficient number of adult male Bahá'ís from Nayríz to form a Local Spiritual Assembly. Thus an Assembly was for the first time established in Mishkínábád.

Moving the family to a small village in the suburbs of Ṭihrán would deprive the school-aged children from receiving proper education. This my parents could not do. After all, they had left Nayríz for the purpose of providing their children with a good education. Leaving the older children in Ṭihrán was one option but mother would not consent and commuting was out of the question, since in those days regular public transportation did not exist.[84] To solve the problem, father consulted the secretary of the National Spiritual Assembly of Iran, Mr 'Alí-Akbar Furútan, who was later appointed by the Guardian of the Faith a Hand of the Cause of God. He suggested that my parents employ a private teacher to tutor the children in Mishkínábád. Father liked the idea and mother agreed with the proposal. Mr Furútan introduced a Mr Ḍíyá'í, originally from Mashhad, for the purpose. His salary and terms of service were agreed upon and he accompanied the family to their new pioneering place.

## Life in Mishkínábád and the Success of Development Projects

During the two years that the family spent in Mishkínábád and Shahnám, at father's initiative and with the cooperation of mother, striking improvements were made in all aspects of the life of the inhabitants.

The most outstanding success was the eradication of malaria from the area. In those days the agency for the eradication of malaria had either not formed or was not active in the region. To free the residents of the two villages under father's control from this debilitating disease, he started draining lagoons and marshlands and created canals channelling the water for irrigation. As a result, the wastelands were cultivated and yielded wonderful produce. Medicine for the treatment of malaria was placed freely at the disposal of the inhabitants. With the landlord's blessing, a doctor was hired who visited the area every week and freely treated those who were in need of medical care.

A rural trading company was set up under the directorship of my eldest brother, Masíḥu'lláh. The company made it possible for the peasants to purchase their daily needs at a reasonable fixed rate.

The living conditions improved tremendously when a proper structure was built to accommodate the farm labourers and their families. Their accommodation prior to this consisted of shacks utterly inadequate for living and hazardous in terms of hygiene.

Illiteracy was in those days widespread among the peasants. As a result, they were unable to improve their lot and the lot of their children. Under father's regime, those who had never before had the possibility to benefit from the blessing of literacy were provided with the opportunity to send their children to literacy classes. Some took advantage of the opportunity and sent their children to Mr Ḍíyá'í, the contracted teacher, who tutored them free of charge.

World War II was raging and some items, such as sugar, were rationed. Villagers had to go at regular intervals to Ṭihrán or to a distribution centre to collect their rations. In addition to the inconvenience, they had to incur the cost of transportation. The headmen of the two villages were directed to collect everyone's coupons, take them to Ṭihrán for collection and distribute the items to the peasants without charging them for the service. Father paid the transportation expense on behalf of the landlord and was reimbursed.

The public bath in the village, like most public baths in those days, had a common water reservoir in which the villagers bathed. The reservoir was replaced with showers and the hazard of contracting contagious diseases was eliminated.

Animal husbandry was established according to the best techniques available at that time. An incubation machine for mass-producing chickens was imported and started working.

As World War II continued the economic situation worsened, the cost of food became unaffordable to lower income people and famine threatened the land. To provide people with some source of income, the owner of the land started construction work on a wide scale. As a result, many unemployed found work and in lieu of their wages received food.

As food in the country became scarcer, father's wise use of water resources made cultivation of additional fertile land possible and the agricultural yield of the two villages under his control was marvellous. The volume of legumes and grain produced exceeded the amount promised to the government. The surplus was made available to the Bahá'ís of Ṭihrán at a reduced rate. Since the National Spiritual Assembly of Iran was concerned about the survival of Bahá'ís who were poor, it decided to buy wheat and distribute it among them. Jináb-i Ḍargh̲ám and Jináb-i Na'ím were in charge of this service. When they approached father, he consulted the owner of the land and with his agreement sold one hundred donkey loads of wheat to them at a very reasonable price. The wheat was milled in the village and the flour packaged and sent to Ṭihrán.

The first Local Spiritual Assembly of Mish̲kínábád was established and teaching activities resulted in the registration of one local believer, who became a member of the Assembly. Many others heard about the Faith, some investigated and several were very close to becoming registered Bahá'ís by the time father and his family left.

As the farms prospered, the villages developed, the economic situation of the peasants improved and the news of the outstanding success achieved became well known, many landowners showed an interest and bid high to buy the farms. Finally, the owner sold them to a Mr Kásh̲ání for 1,200,000 túmáns, a lot of money in those days. Consequently, father was transferred to Ṭihrán and started working in the trading chambers of Mr Kh̲aḍrá'í who was to buy another farm and put father in charge of its development.

Mother's life during the two years the family spent in Mishkínábád was very different from what she had known earlier and was familiar with. In Dáráb she had the opportunity to associate with the wives of the heads of government departments and prominent influential people. She also had the advantage of being geographically close to Nayríz and was therefore able to visit her parents and relatives frequently. During the family's stay in Shíráz, she experienced good and bad times but was still close to Nayríz and her family. Mishkínábád was an entirely different story. In addition to the family, her work most of the time involved dealing with peasants and their families, yet she adjusted well. But every now and then she felt the need to get away from the daily chores, which at times became overwhelming. Going to Ṭihrán was a welcome change. She enjoyed visiting the city and often joined father on his business trips there.

Another welcome break mother had from the otherwise routine life of the countryside was when Mr Khaḍrá'í's family visited Mishkínábád. To escape the intense heat of the summer months in Ṭihrán, his wife and children spent some time in Mishkínábád, where they had a summer house.

The harsh conditions of life in Iran deteriorated further during World War II. Although Mishkínábád and Shahnám had good harvest years, a major portion of the agricultural produce of the two villages had to be made available at reduced rate to the government. The peasants' ration was given to them daily. Mother was in charge of the distribution of wheat flour to them. She spent a good part of every morning filling up the peasants' receptacles with flour. To ensure that justice was observed, she had to use a special measuring bowl for the purpose. This work she found exhausting, especially since she had to care for her infant son and several other children. Of course she had help. The Bahá'í farmers that father had brought from Nayríz, their families and the older children all lent a helping hand to make the experience as enjoyable and successful as possible. Moreover, grandmother Núríján and uncle Jalál, mother's younger brother, had joined us in Mishkínábád. Therefore the family circle had widened and mother was not as homesick for her family as before. Nevertheless, being the highly sociable person that mother was, she found life away from the city's many activities somewhat boring and at times unbearable. So the frequent trips to Ṭihrán helped a lot. On such trips, in addition to her infant son, she took one or two of the older children. My eldest brother, who was then in his teens and an able helper to father, and my older sisters, Rawḥanieh and Nayyirih, accompanied my parents to the capital more often. The younger children stayed with grandmother, who was very loving and gentle. She often related stories of her younger years when her husband was away on pilgrimage. She described with pride and spiritual ecstasy how the Bahá'ís of Nayríz had stood firm in the face of fierce persecution in 1909, which culminated in the martyrdom of 18 of them. As she spoke with emotion and enthusiasm, we listened spellbound to the accounts of heroism and self-sacrifice marking their lives. When talking she would look around to see when we were tired. As soon as she saw droopy eyes, she would stop and promise to continue the next night. With her stories she instilled in us the love of the Faith and taught us about Bahá'u'lláh and His principles, which prohibited His followers from taking up arms against their persecutors. She told us the purpose of religion was to unite people, not to cause bloodshed. Thus we learned at a very early age why the Báb and Bahá'u'lláh had suffered at the hand of those who arose against them, what the purpose of Bahá'u'lláh's Revelation was and how we could help to establish His new world order, which would bring about universal peace and the unity of all people.

I faintly remember life in Mis͟hkínábád. From what I remember, life was good; there were more happy times than bad for everyone who shared the experience. Father was keenly interested in farming, something most Nayrízís did well. It was the main source of income for them. He also had a good instinct for development, which he followed to turn barren lands into a corner of paradise. Moreover, he had wonderful human and public relations skills. He knew how to inspire the peasants to work hard for the good of all. He was keenly interested in improving their lives and helping them to better their lot. He had a genuine love for the job and respect for those who worked for him. He had been a successful farmer in Nayríz, in Dáráb and now in Mishkínábád, though farming was not the only thing he did. He was a resourceful person and a man of many trades. He was a good businessman, a good administrator, a good accountant, a good teacher and, because of his impeccable honesty, a person very much in demand. After the tragic death of his son he was very careful not to focus too much energy and attention on worldly pursuits. Instead, he was constantly mindful of creating and maintaining a good balance between the spiritual and material aspects of life.

When the period of stay in Mishkínábád came to an end after two years, the family packed its belongings and moved back to Ṭihrán. By then I was three or four years old, hence I have retained some memory of that time. One of the things I distinctly remember is how frightened everyone was when, on a cold winter night during my parents' absence, a bat entered the house. It looked like a flying beast completely out of control. It kept hitting itself against the windows and walls and could not find its way out. The more it was chased, the fiercer it became until at someone's suggestion all lights were put out and the entrance door and windows left open. When the place was dark, the bat calmed down and found a way out. It was incredible! The light through which we see everything makes the bat blind. For that reason it comes out when it is dark, we were told. When I grew older and read in the writings about the Covenant-breakers being like bats who work in the darkness of the night, I could well understand the meaning of the analogy.

Another vivid memory I have of those days is that in his infancy and childhood Mawhibatu'lláh, my little brother, was the focus of mother's undivided attention. Any illness that he suffered worried her no end. Ironically, he seemed more prone to illness than other children. Father, too, was very concerned but he had to attend to a myriad other things, so his concern was not as obvious as mother's. Besides, to strike the desirable balance, he tried to make up for mother's lack of time and spent quality time with us whenever his busy schedule allowed. The wonderful thing was that we all felt loved and had a strong sense of belonging. Furthermore, we all understood and appreciated the fact that mother was so occupied with and attached to Mawhibat, therefore, the special treatment afforded him did not bother us. When he was ill, everyone was genuinely concerned and joined in prayers for his recovery. After 'Abdu'l-Ḥusayn's passing, my parents had hoped to have another son and their wish was fulfilled when Mawhibat was born. I was then too young to know what was going on but from what I have heard, also from what I gathered as I grew older, he needed and received special care.

## Departure from Mishkínábád

The return to Ṭihrán would have provided my parents with an excellent opportunity to settle in the capital, to establish a home there and to live a reasonably secure and prosperous life. However, they were not as interested in material success as they were in spiritual health and development.

Upon returning to Ṭihrán father started work in the business firm of Mr Khaḍrá'í, who put at father's disposal one of his magnificent buildings to serve as a temporary dwelling for the family. The school-aged children went to school and life began to take shape and assume a new glamour. The return to Ṭihrán coincided with the approach of the centenary celebrations of the declaration of the Báb in Shíráz. Shoghi Effendi's messages encouraged the believers to settle in areas where the Faith had not yet penetrated and to establish new Local Spiritual Assemblies. One of the families responding to the call for home front pioneers was the family of Mr Kalímu'lláh Ma'ání. They were looking for a reliable person to buy their belongings and look after their property in their absence from the capital. They had heard that father would be a good candidate. Mr Ma'ání contacted father and explained his reason for leaving Ṭihrán. Before father gave a definite answer, he consulted with mother and the older children, who agreed with him that instead of weighing themselves down with worldly chores and financial obligations, it would be better for them to seriously consider responding to the call of the beloved Guardian regarding home front pioneering. As a first step they decided that rather than buy more things, they would start selling what they had. They therefore turned down the proposed deal with Mr Ma'ání, informed the Pioneering Committee of their willingness to pioneer and asked to be assigned a place in which to settle.

The next day, to Mr Khaḍrá'í's regret, father resigned from his job. No amount of advice and encouragement on the part of Mr Khaḍrá'í had any effect on father's determination to leave the capital and go pioneering. Finally, Mr Khaḍrá'í made father promise that whenever he found himself financially straitened and needed a job, he would let Mr Khaḍrá'í know. Father then informed Mr Ma'ání that he and his family would be pioneering soon and were therefore unable to take on a responsibility for anything in Ṭihrán.

The Pioneering Committee, realizing that such a large family could not go to Tákur, which was a priority goal, asked them instead to go to Bábul, a town in Mázandarán. The committee told them to seek the advice of the Local Spiritual Assembly, which would assign them a pioneering place in that province. My parents did as advised. The Local Assembly of Bábul asked them to go to Maḥmúdábád.

## Home Front Pioneering – The Maḥmúdábád Experience

Before Riḍván 1954 the Bahá'í women of Iran did not enjoy the right of election to Bahá'í institutions. Up to then they could vote but could not be elected. To form a Local Spiritual Assembly in a goal area, it often happened that nine families had to pioneer there. Some such families had several children. Our family was a case in point. It comprised ten people: father, mother, grandmother and seven children. My eldest brother was not yet 21 and so ineligible for membership on the Assembly. The Ma'ání family was another example. It consisted of parents and seven sons below the age of administrative maturity.

As father intended to acquire land and engage in farming in Maḥmúdábád, he took with him an agricultural worker from Nayríz. Mr Báqir Ittiḥád lived with the family and helped to carry out chores. The family stayed in Bábul for 20 days, then moved to Maḥmúdábád, which needed two more adult male Bahá'ís to form an Assembly. With the arrival of our family and Mr Ittiḥád in the summer of 1943, the establishment of the Local Assembly at Riḍván 1944 was assured.

Finding accommodation in Maḥmúdábád proved challenging. At one point six families lived in one house belonging to the royal family. It was called Cháykhurán, literally meaning the place where tea is drunk. Mr Khudábandih Dastán had rented the house for his and another pioneer family but shared it with several other families until they found their own accommodation.

With the arrival of the pioneers and establishment of the Local Spiritual Assembly a vibrant community started functioning in Maḥmúdábád. Teaching work began in earnest and Bahá'í activities were conducted on a regular basis. The pioneers engaged in agricultural, trading and business pursuits. An agricultural company was formed under the directorship of father. It was called Shirkat-i Núr. Masíḥ, my eldest brother, established a provision store in partnership with a local man. As the local school had only four classes, the older children could not attend.

The centenary celebrations were held with pomp and glory, awakening the inhabitants of the town to the advent of Bahá'u'lláh and to the existence of Bahá'ís in their midst. Some resented the activities of the Bahá'ís and the developments that were taking place in their town but could do little to stop them.

A year and a few months elapsed. During this time my parents had another son, named Cyrus. The poor baby was born at the worst possible time and did not stand a chance of survival. I remember murmurs among family members about how beautiful the child was. He had green-grey eyes and a fair complexion like grandfather Aḥmad (mother's father), everyone said. None of us had inherited those features. The irony is that this precious child opened his eyes to the world just when the family was working against numerous odds and had to struggle to survive.

I asked my sister Pouran, who was old enough to remember vividly how the family was evacuated from its premises in Maḥmúdábád, to relate the experience. This is an extract from her account:

> Late one night we heard a knock on the window of the room where we were sleeping. We noticed strange-looking soldiers with cone-shaped hats pointing to us to get out. When we got out, we saw some foreign military officers [Russian] with their Mongolian soldiers talking to my father and brother through an interpreter. They ordered my father to evacuate the place and gave him several hours to do it. The soldiers had boxes ready to pack our belongings. They threw everything into the boxes, nailed them and put them on the pavement of the main street, in front of our residence. My father and brother were looking for a shelter or a house to live in but, alas, the only thing they could get was an old wooden, uninhabited cabin in the forest.
>
> My mother had to care for her seven children and my grandmother (my father's mother). We all lived in one room in the cabin, which was infested with worms and bugs. A room next to us was used to store sheepskins, which stank terribly. The time for the fast approached. As a nine year old child I remember watching my father, mother, brother Masíḥu'lláh and sister Rawḥanieh sitting in the middle of a bed, saying prayers, and having their dawn meal . . .
>
> My mother was pregnant with my younger brother, Cyrus. He died soon after he was born.[85]

The fire of World War II, which had engulfed Europe, was raging in Russia. America had entered the war. The allied forces were looking for a safe route to assist Russia in its war against Germany. The north of Iran met the criteria. The strategic position of Maḥmúdábád with its royal palaces and vast adjoining lands was indisputable. Russia started expanding its operation in the area, landed a large force there and demarcated a major part of the town with barbed wire. The appropriated area included the two royal palaces, the Cháykhurán and the surrounding lands, which the Bahá'ís had rented for accommodation and cultivation. After appropriation, the developed lands and their produce were completely lost. As the war became protracted, the circle of hardship around the residents tightened until one day the commander in charge of the Russian army issued an order giving people living in the area 24 hours to vacate their residences. The Local Assembly met and decided to inform Mr Fírúz Samandarí, the head of the military police in Bábul. He immediately visited Maḥmúdábád and tried in vain to change the order. To help the Bahá'ís, he requested those gendarmes who were able to assist to place one room in each of their residences at Mr Samandarí's disposal. He assigned each room thus obtained to one Bahá'í family. With the loss of property and produce, Shirkat-i Núr was unable to function. It was therefore dismantled and its capital lost. Father and other shareholders lost everything they had invested in the firm.

Masíḥu'lláh's business venture was also threatened. The Muslims considered the Bahá'ís to be ritually unclean and the inhabitants of the town at the instigation of the clergy refused to buy provisions from a Bahá'í-owned store. The fear of ostracism kept potential customers away. At the same time, invaders demanded things free of charge. These and other problems combined and forced Masíḥ to close down his provision store. Shortly thereafter he contracted typhoid and had to be taken to Ámul for treatment. Mother, remembering the tragic circumstances surrounding the passing of her firstborn, was terribly worried. She could not let Masíḥ, so ill, out of her sight. She accompanied him to Ámul to provide whatever care she could. She left the newly-born son Cyrus with grandmother and her older daughters and left with father, Masíḥ and Mawhibat for Ámul. Masíḥ's illness was prolonged and the treatments went on for some time. Fortunately, Masíḥ survived but Cyrus succumbed to the inhospitable conditions surrounding his tender life. He was three months old when he died. There was no Bahá'í cemetery in Maḥmúdábád. He was buried in the only cemetery in the town. Some years later, the poor child's grave was opened and his remains removed and burned. The reason for this inhuman atrocity was that he was a Bahá'í infant. Cyrus's death added to the family's grief, which was surrounded on every side by seemingly insurmountable difficulties.

The unbearable living conditions forcing a family of ten to live in a small damp room, suffering illness and death, could not be sustained for long, especially when a new problem with far-reaching consequences showed its face. That problem was a cataract in father's good eye. Ordinarily, a cataract in one eye is not a devastating development in one's life but in father's case it was. In childhood he had contracted chickenpox. One pimple was near the pupil of an eye and left pockmarks on it. As a result, 90 per cent of his vision in that eye was lost in childhood, causing him to depend almost entirely on the good eye for vision. So a cataract in the good eye was a serious problem for a man who had responsibility for a large family and who had an insatiable love for acquiring knowledge and a deep desire to work hard to serve humanity through Bahá'í activities and engaging in agricultural pursuits.

Father's eye problem affected all aspects of the life of each and every member of the family, especially mother, whose colossal responsibilities multiplied, as will be seen later. Other ordeals continued unabated but first he had to establish himself in a place where prospects for earning a living existed.

For the fourth time in their lives my parents had lost everything they had. But this time it was different. Father was older, less well and had responsibility for a larger family. It became untenable for a family of that size to continue to live in Maḥmúdábád under those dreadful conditions. With the approval of the Local Spiritual Assembly, my parents sold their carpets and whatever was of value in order to pay their way back to Nayríz via Ṭihrán and Shíráz. They had in mind selling more of their estate in Nayríz and using the money to settle in another pioneering post in the province of Fárs. Some of the friends in Ṭihrán and Shíráz encouraged them to make Nayríz their home again.

## Return to Nayríz

My parents' return to Nayríz after about seven years' absence was met with happiness and joy by the family, friends and acquaintances. Father's previous excellent record of service and the valuable experiences he had gained in the meantime provided him with splendid opportunities to reestablish himself as a businessman. Moreover, he knew influential people in the local government, people who were familiar with his absolute honesty and good work, who were willing to help him in any way they could. So, father regained some of the agencies he had before and began a new life in the town of his birth.

The eldest son, Masíḥu'lláh, was then about 20, old enough in those days to think of getting married and having his own family. After staying in Nayríz for a while, he became engaged to Parvín Khánum, a maternal cousin. They were married in Shíráz. Their Bahá'í marriage took place in the house adjacent to the House of the Báb in a quiet and rarefied atmosphere, followed by a visit to the blessed House. I was very young then but remember vividly when my parents made preparations for the journey to Shíráz, together with Mawhibatu'lláh, to attend the wedding. I missed mother terribly and cried a lot. Finally, my older siblings decided to send me to Shíráz with uncle 'Alí Akbar, who was going there a few days later. By the time I got there, the wedding was over. After his marriage, Masíḥ settled in Shíráz.

Rawḥanieh could not continue her studies in Nayríz beyond what she had accomplished in Shíráz and Mishkínábád, for the town had no secondary school for girls. Nayyirih, Pouran and Mahín went to the only girls' school, which was in Maḥallih Bázár. It was quite a hassle for them and the other Bahá'ís from Maḥallih Pahlaví to attend school in that section of the town. Fortunately, one of the teachers of the school was a Bahá'í woman, Mrs Nuṣrat Míthágí (Jahánpúr). She accompanied the students to and from the school, yet they had a hard time coping with the insults and humiliation heaped upon them by fanatic Muslims as they passed.

Life in Nayríz held new challenges. In addition to opposition from certain hostile elements in the larger community, which was always there, those who lost their jobs because of father's return were not happy about the way things had turned out for them. Petty jealousies started showing their ugly face. Father's indisputable standing in the town, the respect he enjoyed in the Bahá'í community and his success in business unsettled some insecure elements, who felt threatened by his return. Their offensive behaviour was not only hurtful to father but also injurious to the interests of the community. Father could not let his presence in Nayríz threaten the unity of the community, neither could he go against the principles he believed in by contending with those who wanted him out of the way. He did the only thing he could under the circumstances. He decided that Nayríz was not the right place for him and his family. After all, he argued, Shoghi Effendi had approved his request to leave Nayríz for good reasons. So he wrote to Mr Khaḍrá'í, explained his situation and declared his readiness and willingness to work for him anywhere in the province of Fárs. Mr Khaḍrá'í instructed the provincial director of Shirkat-i Jean va Panbih, a cotton processing and trading firm based in Shíráz, to give father the directorship of any branch office that he desired. He was immediately installed as the director of the Kázirún branch. Thus came to an end a 14-month stay in Nayríz.

## The Kázirún Experience

Father went to Kázirún alone to establish himself. After about a year he was able to take his family there. Moving the family to Kázirún and arranging for Rawḥanieh and Nayyirih to continue their studies in Shíráz needed additional funds, which my parents provided by selling more property in Nayríz. The more property they sold in that town, the more detached they became from the place and the less frequent were their visits there. To address mother's concerns about separating from her two older daughters, it was arranged for grandmother Núríján to move to Shíráz and stay with them. The rest of the family, comprising father, mother and four smaller children, moved to Kázirún, another place in need of pioneers. My parents intended to make it their home for the rest of their lives. Therefore, they took all their belongings with them.

Our residence was a nice and spacious house in a delightful area adjacent to the premises of Shirkat-i Jean. Life seemed good. My parents started associating with the inhabitants of the town and the teaching work gathered pace. There was considerable social activity. With the presence of father in the community, Bahá'í activities began in earnest. The Local Spiritual Assembly was formed and a site for a Ḥaẓíratu'l-Quds purchased and fenced. A short while after our arrival, the school year began. I was registered in grade one. Pouran and Mahín attended the same school and were in higher classes. Pouran's status was unclear, for reasons that will be discussed later.

As we were getting used to the rhythm of an entirely new way of life, the situation changed suddenly. The members of the Turk and Lur tribes in Fárs arose against the government. Their forces besieged Kázirún and war broke out between government forces and the rebels. The inhabitants of the town supported the government forces. The rebels cut off telephone and telegram lines and soon all communication with the outside stopped. The government forces lacked a proper base and strong defences. When the commanders looked for a suitable place to establish an army headquarters for the duration of the war, they set their heart on the premises of Shirkat-i Jean, a strong, spacious and secure building with a vast courtyard. In those days, as is the case today, when the government wanted something, nothing could stand in its way. To question or oppose the government's demand was both futile and dangerous. So father had no choice but to agree. The army moved in with all its equipment.

As the fighting intensified between the government forces and the rebels, our daily life became a living hell. Father decided to move the family to temporary accommodation in the town. He placed everything we owned, as well as the goods belonging to Masíḥu'lláh who had a trading business in Shíráz and Kázirún, in one large room, sealed it, obtained a receipt from the commander-in-chief of the army regiment, and moved us to the house of a Siyyid who liked the Bahá'ís and with whom father had business dealings. The Turks and Lurs respected the Siyyids and treated them with kindness. So if there were a safe place in the town, that was it.

The fierce fighting continued for 13 days from 28 Shahrívar to 9 Mihr 1325 (19 September to 1 October 1946). As our temporary residence was situated between the two opposing forces, bullets often hit the house and made holes in its columns and walls. I do not know about the grown-ups but we children were absolutely terrified. Numerous were the times when we had to take refuge in the unsightly basement of the house and stay there for a considerable time. After the lapse of several decades, I still remember that underground cell and can hear the voice of mother murmuring, 'O Bahá, protect us from all calamities'. She repeated that one sentence over and over again until the shooting stopped. I also remember the foul air in that basement which made breathing very difficult. My sister Pouran once had a severe asthmatic attack and nearly died. She was gasping for air, her eyes were red and she could not talk. My parents had to take her out amidst the shooting. My siblings and I were scared that they would get killed. It was a frightening experience.

In the meantime, water became scarce, food unavailable and my parents' cash flow was drying up. We faced annihilation. Father told the owner of the house, the kind Siyyid, that all our belongings were left in the premises of the Shirkat-i Jean and would probably be plundered. However, he said, we had several pieces of carpet with us which would be offered to him as a ransom for our safety. The Siyyid promised to help in whatever way he could. And mother exercised stringent economy. We lived on the barest minimum, just enough to survive until the ordeal was over. The quick way we humans adapt to new circumstances when faced with annihilation is a strange phenomenon. Ordinarily, children make demands for more and are rarely happy with what they get but when danger is imminent, they are happy to forgo all that and do whatever it takes to survive.

To everyone's utter disbelief the rebels won the war and took over the defences of the army and all military equipment. Then they focused on finding my father, who was in charge of the company whose premises had become the headquarters of the army. They went from house to house looking for him. When they came to the house where we were staying, the angelic Siyyid, with a copy of the Qur'án in his hand, swore from his rooftop that no president of any government department lived in his house, which was absolutely true. Father did not work for the government; Shirkat-i Jean was a private enterprise. The victors respected the Siyyid's word and moved on. The premises of the Shirkat, however, after the humiliating defeat of the government forces, were plundered and the building set on fire. Thus whatever my parents owned was once again lost.

When the war ended a coalition of the victorious tribes ruled the area. As that region was under the rule of Ilyás Khán-i Kashkúlí, whose wife was a Bahá'í, father went to see him with great difficulty, introduced himself and described his plight. Ilyás Khán apologized and expressed sympathy but said, 'At that time the Turks would not listen even to me.'[86] However, he offered to help in any way he could. Father said,

> Whatever the company owned, as well as my own belongings, have been plundered. The premises are in ruins, fire is still raging in the company's warehouses, only a skeleton of the buildings is left. That, too, they are trying to raze to the ground. Kindly issue orders that the fire be put out, that no one prevent me from entering the area, and assign two armed guards to guard the place. Their wages will be paid.[87]

Father's real intention in taking this course of action was to be able to search under the debris and rescue the Bahá'í books and Tablets, some original, which he had taken with him to Kázirún. However, he was unsuccessful. The feeling of deep regret caused by this irreparable loss stayed with him to the end of his life.

For one month all communication with Shíráz was cut off.

During that time we lived under precarious conditions in the house of the Siyyid, for although the Siyyid himself did not interfere with how we lived our life, his elderly wife had a lot to say about almost everything that we did or did not do. She took issue with a range of things from not going to the mosque to the way we washed our clothes. To her and many Shí'í Muslims of the time, no matter how well clothes had been washed, unless rinsed in water that was *kurr*,[88] were not clean. The pond she used for the purpose was in a mosque close to her home. The water it contained was dark green and did not seem clean. To please her, mother had to find a solution, otherwise these petty things could turn into huge problems and endanger our lives. Mother's solution was this: We had a servant called Akbar. Mother had him carry the washed clothes in a large copper tray over his head to the mosque. He was instructed to spend a while in and around the mosque at a time when the place had none or few visitors, then return the clothes to the house without rinsing them in the mosque's pond, and hang them to dry. Once I accompanied Akbar on this errand. While he was holding my hand, he entered the mosque, looked around, circumambulated the pond, lingered a while and left. My little mind failed to fathom the wisdom of the exercise. When I asked mother, she explained the reason and told me not to divulge the secret, for it could be very dangerous for us all. At that tender age I was made aware of how important some seemingly mundane things could become and what it meant to be wise. I respected mother's admonition and breathed not a word regarding the exercise to anyone. After a lapse of 57 years this is the first time I am talking about that incident!

Regarding visiting the mosque, mother's most acceptable excuse was the number of her children. She argued that she could not leave them unattended at home and taking them to the mosque would be inappropriate, for they were likely to make noise and misbehave when bored. Mother had an answer for everything, and since members of her parents' immediate family were Muslims, she knew exactly how to deal with everything with which our Muslim landlady took issue.

After one month, the managing director of the provincial headquarters of Shirkat-i Jean in Shíráz, a Mr Pizishkí, obtained a letter of recommendation from the coalition of tribes and clans who had arisen against the government, and accompanied by my brother, Masíḥu'lláh, came to Kázirún to rescue us from the deplorable circumstances under which we lived. I well remember the joy of seeing Masíḥ and the relief that their visit brought. My parents gave the Siyyid the valuable carpets they had and left Kázirún divested of earthly possessions. Our trip to Shíráz was fraught with danger, for roads were unsafe. We travelled overnight. When we reached Dasht-i Arjen near Shíráz, for some reason we had to wait until dawn to continue our trip to Shíráz. We were taken to a rundown roadside coffee house called Qahvih Khánih and were offered a wet rug to sit on. It was a cold night and the wet rug made it feel much colder. I shivered until the dawn and clung to mother to feel warm. I still feel cold and miserable when I remember that night.

## Return to Shíráz and the Struggle for Survival

Empty-handed, exhausted and bewildered, with failing eyesight and dashed hopes, father accompanied the rest of the family from Kázirún to Shíráz. We were destitute but joyous to be alive and out of danger. We were ecstatic to be reunited with other members of the family who lived in Shíráz. Father started working in the offices of Shirkat-i Jean in that city and a hard, long drawn-out period fraught with numerous difficulties began.

Soon it became evident that father's salary was not sufficient to pay the educational expenses of all the children. Therefore Rawḥanieh and Nayyirih decided to do something that would earn a living. About that same time the Ministry of Health introduced a scheme for training midwives to serve in the rural areas of each province. Rawḥanieh and Nayyirih opted for that. Rawḥanieh decided to continue her education while attending the midwifery school. She and two other Bahá'í girls studied with a private tutor. She finished three grades in one year. She also passed the final midwifery exams with great success and received the highest honour for that achievement. Nayyirih followed in her footsteps and finished the midwifery school the following year.

What Pouran had done with her school certificate a few years earlier came back to haunt her and caused a huge headache for my parents at a time when difficulties surrounded them from every direction. She could not register and study in the fifth grade because she had torn up her second grade certificate and after that she had been tutored at home, for which she had no certificate to show. Mahín and I had no problem. I was in the first grade and Mahín in the second. To get Pouran registered in a primary school in Shíráz proved much more problematic than anyone had thought. Father had enough on his hands and could not handle the burden of dealing with bureaucrats, who had a 'legitimate' excuse to deprive a Bahá'í child of the blessing of education. Mother, too, had more than she could deal with. However, she could not let her daughter go without an education, notwithstanding all the odds stacked against her. Pouran has sent me an account of the efforts mother exerted to reinstate her in school:

> When we returned to Shíráz everyone was able to resume school except me as I had torn up my certificate and made it into a notebook. Therefore, I had no record of previous schooling and were it not for my mother's efforts and perseverance, I would have been left without education. I remember my mother used to put on her veil every day and go to the Department of Education in Shíráz. She would spend hours in the hallway waiting to see Mr Fiqáhat, the person in charge of elementary schools. He was a fanatical Muslim who knew we were Bahá'ís and enjoyed seeing mother standing at the door of his office, waiting to be let in. When she finally had an audience with him, she would present the case. He would listen to her reasoning and pleas, then, unmoved, would use every conceivable excuse in the book to reject her pleas. Utterly exhausted, mother would come home and think of new ways she could pursue the case. It was through the power of prayer, Bahá'u'lláh's blessings and mother's perseverance that I was admitted to school again and, after an entry exam, I was admitted to the fifth grade.[89]

In the meantime, father continued grappling with the consequences of his failing eyesight. Several months elapsed. The managing director of Shirkat-i Jean realized how hard father struggled to cope with the demands of his job. He sent father a message which said that since father's eyesight was failing, it was better for him to stop going to the office and advised him to seek medical treatment. Father stayed home for five months and underwent various treatments. Nothing helped. The company's board of directors in its annual meeting decided that since father was unable to work and the treatments were unsuccessful, his employment with the company was to be terminated. The decision was conveyed to father orally through his brother Mírzá Jalál and was later confirmed in writing. Without a regular source of income, the family would have been completely stranded. I do not know how it is in Iran today but then there was no health or any other kind of insurance and the government had no responsibility towards the welfare of its citizens. I must add here that even if it had had such a responsibility, father would not have acceded to live on welfare.

When father heard that he was to be dismissed as of 21 April 1947, he decided to meet with Mr Pizishkí, discuss with him his situation and seek solutions. Assisted by mother, who held his hand, they went to see Mr Pizishkí in his house. Mr Pizishkí said that since the decision had been made by the board of directors, there was nothing he could do. However, he said that there was one possible solution and that was referring the matter to Mr Maḥmúd Dihqán, an influential member of the board who was empowered to reinstate him. Maḥmúd Dihqán was a member of a prominent and wealthy Bahá'í family in Shíráz. He disregarded Bahá'í marriage laws and broke the Covenant by opposing Shoghi Effendi. Father said he preferred to die of hunger than seek the assistance of a Covenant-breaker. He added that he had always sought his daily bread from God's hidden treasury and had never been disappointed. He then got up, said goodbye and, with the help of mother, started off. As they were exiting the house, Mr Pizishkí said, 'I can think of another solution and that is referring the matter to Mr 'Azízu'lláh Khaḍrá'í, the president of the board of directors who lives in Ṭihrán and has a favourable view of you because you have worked with him previously. If he makes a recommendation to the board, it will be heeded.'[90]

Father and mother returned home unperturbed by the prospect that father was going to be unemployed at a time when the size of their estate in Nayríz had diminished considerably, all their belongings plundered and father's eyesight was deteriorating rapidly. They prayed fervently and consulted regarding what to do next. Finally, they were both inspired to write in detail to Mr Khaḍrá'í and describe the situation to him. Since father was unable to write because of his failing eyesight, he dictated what he wanted to say to one of the older children. He sent the letter in a state of complete resignation, with his hopes set on the bountiful confirmations of Bahá'u'lláh who had provided for him and his family thus far. Three days before the deadline fixed by the board of directors for the termination of father's employment, a letter arrived addressed to the board by Mr Khaḍrá'í. In the letter he emphatically expressed the view that father's leave of absence had to be extended until the completion of his eye treatment. He added that the decision of the board regarding someone who had lost everything he had owned because he was an employee of the company was most unjust. The emphatic tone of Mr Khaḍrá'í's letter, which indicated that father was entitled to unlimited sick leave, left no room for anyone else to express an opinion. The board had no choice but to reconsider its decision. When the new decision was conveyed to father, he and mother gave a sigh of relief and made plans for father's further eye treatment.

As the eye with cataract could not be operated on until the cataract had completely blinded the eye and this process was taking too long, my parents consulted skilful doctors about operating on the eye which had been impaired from childhood owing to chickenpox. The doctors agreed that the eye could be operated on. If successful, father would at least be able to move around without help. The doctors' expert opinion encouraged father to consider going to Ṭihrán, where better medical expertise was available. Thus my parents and Mawhibatu'lláh went to Ṭihrán for the operation. Unfortunately, the operation produced the opposite result. The eye haemorrhaged and became inflamed and very painful. They returned to Shíráz utterly disappointed.

Their eagerness to expedite the process of regaining father's eyesight resulted in his becoming completely blind in the eye which from childhood had only had 10 per cent of its sight. In addition to that, the inflammation resulting from the haemorrhage caused him unbearable pain, which took some time to alleviate. The condition of the other eye with cataract remained unchanged for a considerable time. Finally, father decided that the result of impatience could be the loss of sight in the other eye as well. So he resigned himself to God's will and let things run their course. He recited more and more often the Tablet of Aḥmad, the Long Healing Prayer and other prayers that he knew by heart. Since he could not be active in the teaching field, something he loved dearly and lived for, and as he had to rely completely on mother to hold his hand when he went out, he turned more and more to meditation and prayer, creating for himself a world of ecstasy in which he forgot his ordeal. The older children, Rawḥanieh, Nayyirih and Pouran, took turns chanting prayers, Bahá'u'lláh's poems and Bahá'í songs to him. To calm himself, several times a day he recited the following verse from one of the prayers for the fast:

> Wilt thou cast away this poor one after he hath taken no one but Thee as his succourer . . .[91]

During the long years that father was confined to the house, life was most difficult for mother, who had to manage a large family on father's monthly salary. The salary, which remained static during father's special leave of absence, had to pay for the rental of modest accommodation, the educational fees of several schoolchildren, food and living expenses of a large family and all incidental expenses as well as father's medical bills. Having lived through so many upheavals in the past and having had the pleasure of socializing with people of all backgrounds had taught mother many useful lessons and earned her valuable experiences but during those difficult times her biggest challenge was to make ends meet without the privileges she had enjoyed in the past. Previously, she had always relied upon her husband's hard work to improve the temporary adverse conditions they suffered. During this period she could not do so. Not only was father unable to work, his failing eyesight placed an additional burden on her. She had to be his eyes and help him to move around. For a man as active as father, being confined to the house and unable to read and write was most difficult. Although he was magnanimous about it, people did not know how to relate to his condition, for all his life he had been the helper of the needy and provider of the family. Suddenly he had needs to be met and could not provide as well as he wished. Mother did her best to make everything look as normal as possible. It was her job to make sure that with father's monthly salary the family could live with the barest necessities and survive. The income-generating properties that my parents owned in Nayríz had been drastically reduced in size, for every time adversity visited them they had sold more property and used the money to start again. Thus just when the family was in greatest need, that option did not exist. Father had previously been engaged in business and agricultural pursuits in addition to his office work but at this time that, too, was not possible.

When mother finished her day's chores and had time to spare, she would hold father's hand and go for a walk, take him to a Bahá'í meeting or visit a close relative's home. Those who serve as other people's eyes know that unless you are trained and do this correctly, you are constantly worried that the person in your care may trip over something and fall. This was an added stress to mother's already stressful life but she undertook it without complaint.

As father's eyesight grew worse and it became impossible for mother to be with him all the time, she enlisted the assistance of the children to take him out for short walks every afternoon. I was eight years old when father was going through the most difficult period. I remember taking his hand and going for walks around our neighbourhood. Mother emphasized every time that we should not go to places where we had to cross streets. She knew the hazards of her visually impaired husband and her little girl venturing out, even though the traffic in those days was nothing like it is now and we lived in a quiet part of the city, where uncle 'Abdu'l-Ḥusayn had rented a big house in which also lived Masiḥu'lláh, his wife and son. It was a great improvement on what we initially had when we returned from Kázirún.

It was during those difficult times that father started composing poetry, a hobby he continued to the last years of his earthly life. As he immersed himself in the ocean of the writings and expressed his feelings in the form of poetry, he found relief from the ordeal he was suffering. Gradually the pain subsided and uncertainty and anxiety gave way to happiness, reliance on God and assurance. Father was fortunate to experience the true meaning of the passages of the Hidden Words, such as 'My calamity is My providence, outwardly it is fire and vengeance, but inwardly it is light and mercy.'[92] And 'Close one eye and open the other. Close one to the world and all that is therein, and open the other to the hallowed beauty of the Beloved.'[93]

When he passed beyond the cares and limitations of the world and found himself in the joyous expanse of spirituality, he often dreamed of the Báb, of Bahá'u'lláh and 'Abdu'l-Bahá. And in his wakeful hours he imagined that he was associating with the heroes of the Apostolic Age. He also remembered the joy of being in 'Abdu'l-Bahá's presence. Several months elapsed. One day Mr Ṭarázu'lláh Samandarí, who was later designated by the beloved Guardian a Hand of the Cause of God, invited father and mother to his chamber.[94] After greetings, he invited them to sit down, then turned to father and said that the beloved Guardian's favours had been showered upon him and that he had conveyed the glad-tidings that his eye would be healed. Since father had not written a petition to the Guardian, this news came to him as a real surprise. Mr Samandarí explained:

> Some time ago you and your wife entered my room. Since you did not recognize those present, I felt very sad. In a missive that I sent to the beloved Guardian, I beseeched, on your behalf, that

> your eye be healed. He has honoured you with a response and his loving-kindness has embraced you.[95]

Mr Samandarí then read the passage from the beloved Guardian's message which was about father and, in his own beautiful handwriting, transcribed and gave it to him. It read:

> Jináb-i Áqá Mírzá Muḥammad-Shafí' Nayrízí Rouhani was also the recipient of his [Shoghi Effendi's] loving-kindness and favours. He supplicates for him, from the Court of the Beauty of Oneness, success and the healing of his eye.[96]

The message completely reassured father of the success of the forthcoming operation on his eye, notwithstanding the doubts expressed by the eye specialists. He spent the remaining time before the operation in joy and confidence, relying on divine assistance. Finally, the time arrived for the operation. On 9 Mihr 1948 father entered the private hospital of Dr Mushírí, the eye specialist who had expressed doubts about the outcome of the operation. However, father was not worried, for he had sought healing from Bahá'u'lláh and had been assured of the favours of Shoghi Effendi. When he lay down on the hospital bed, he had before his eyes the beloved Guardian, who had interceded on his behalf.

When the operation was over, the surgeon showed mother what he had removed from father's eye and remarked: 'The rate of success for curing eyes with this condition is not even ten per cent.'[97] For nine days father's eye was bandaged. When the bandage was removed, he opened his eye and to his delight he could see! He received a prescription for glasses. When he put them on, he was overjoyed to see everything around him looking bright and beautiful. He rendered praise to the court of his Best Beloved for the miracle of being able to see again and rededicated himself to His service. After one month's recuperation, father went back to Shirkat-i Jean and resumed his duties, to the utter astonishment of all, friend and foe alike.

## The Eldest Son Pioneers Abroad

After father regained his eyesight and resumed work, the family moved to another rented house. Masíḥu'lláh and his family moved to the same house, which was close to where uncle 'Abdu'l-Ḥusayn and his family lived. As soon as life began to look normal again, we heard whisperings about Masíḥu'lláh planning to pioneer abroad. We children did not know the meaning of the word and had no idea what it entailed. Father was absolutely ecstatic, for since he and his family had reluctantly left Mázandarán, he felt deprived of serving Bahá'u'lláh's Cause through pioneering services. Therefore, he was most encouraging of the project Masíḥu'lláh had in mind. Uncle 'Abdu'l-Ḥusayn, whose daughter was married to Masíḥ, was, however, against it. He had enough difficulty accepting the fact that his daughter had moved out of his house and was now living in another house in the same city. To him the idea of pioneering abroad was insane and completely out of the question. I never heard his wife's reaction to the pioneering plan. She was a gentle and soft-spoken lady. She seemed rather traditional and did not express an opinion publicly, especially if it was contrary to her husband's stance on a matter. Mother, on the other hand, was quite outspoken. She did not contradict father publicly but when she felt strongly about a matter, she found a way to make her views known to those who needed to hear them. When she was informed of Masíḥ's pioneering project, she faced a dilemma. She loved to have all her children by her side or at least nearby. However, Masíḥ was undertaking a project in compliance with the beloved Guardian's call for pioneers to settle abroad. Although she had no objection in principle, she thought the timing was not right. After all, she said, father had just recovered from years of confinement and the family was just beginning to feel a respite from long years of hardship. She also felt that it was too early after their marriage for Masíḥ and Parvín to entertain any idea that involved living apart, albeit temporarily. At night, after the children had gone to sleep, or my parents thought that was the case, I could hear father trying to convince mother in a whisper of the spiritual merits of Masíḥ's pioneering project. Mother, being pragmatic, realized early on that she could not stand between her son and his conscience, especially if it had to do with obligations of a spiritual nature. She also knew that all Masíḥ needed was the consent of his wife to undertake the journey. So she gave her blessing wholeheartedly. Uncle, on the other hand, had always got what he wanted and tried to have it his way in this case as well. When everything else failed, he threatened Masíḥ that he would have to divorce his wife if he insisted on his pioneering plan. Knowing how much Masíḥ and Parvín loved one another, he was sure that his threat would work.

Masíḥ calmly pursued his plans and was not the least intimidated by the threat. To me, as the child I was then, the whole thing looked very serious and worrisome. Later I heard that Masíḥ and Parvín had agreed on a certain course of action and were not going to let anything get in their way, not even the intimidating threats of her father. At uncle's demand, Parvín moved back to her father's house and stayed there for a while. In the meantime, as Masíḥ was completing the necessary arrangements for his trip, uncle had a dream, which made him realize the folly of his objections. In his dream he saw 'Abdu'l-Bahá standing on a hilltop with Masíḥ and father by His side. Uncle and mother were standing at the foot of the hill, scared of climbing up and joining 'Abdu'l-Bahá and the others. 'Abdu'l-Bahá threw a rope down. Mother grasped it and pulled herself up. He threw the rope again so that uncle could do the same. However, uncle was too scared and adamantly refused. After much encouragement and inducement he decided to let go of his fear and grasped the rope to pull him up. To his astonishment, he found himself on the hilltop with others without much difficulty. When he woke up, he realized the dream had to do with the situation he was facing regarding Masíḥ's pioneering venture. He decided to let go of his obstinance and informed Parvín and Masíḥ that he had no objection to their pioneering plan.

Masíḥ, who all along had been encouraged by and benefited from Mr 'Alí Nakhjavání's guidance and advice, left Shíráz in early summer 1949 for the Gulf area.[98] He was the first youth in the province of Fárs to respond to the call of the beloved Guardian to pioneer abroad. He needed some skills to help him settle in his pioneering post. He had never entered a vocational school but because he loved carpentry, he underwent elementary training with a skilful carpenter in Sẖíráz for a time before packing his bags and leaving Sẖíráz and his beloved family to serve Bahá'u'lláh in a faraway land.

From Sẖíráz, Masíḥ took an old bus for Bandar 'Abbas via Dáráb and Lár. I remember so well the morning of his departure and the sadness I felt in my heart at being separated from so loving a brother. The whole family went to the bus station downtown to see him off. Present also was Mr Naḵẖjaváni, who gave Masíḥ a loving hug, sent him off with his best wishes and assured him of his prayers for his success. From Bandar 'Abbas, Masíḥ had to travel by sail boat part of the way and then travelled with a guide on mule back in the desert until he reached his first stop. At the time Masíḥ arrived in Dubai oil had not yet been discovered there and the place was at a primitive stage of development.

Masíḥ's courageous act in responding to the call of the beloved Guardian for pioneers to settle abroad, notwithstanding all the difficulties in his way, evoked incredibly happy emotions in father, which remained with him to the end of his life. After the devastating experiences of my parents and family in their pioneering venture in Maḥmúdábád, this was the best reward they could have. Masíḥ's laudable decision to leave the comfort of his home in order to render service in the pioneering field set the stage for other siblings to follow in his footsteps. As soon as the circumstances allowed, others left for their pioneering posts in different parts of the world.

When father was in the presence of 'Abdu'l-Bahá in April and May 1921, he had humbly requested Him to reveal a prayer for his daily recital. The opening sentences read: 'O my God, O my God! Verily this plant hath yielded its fruit and standeth upright upon its stalk. Verily it hath astounded the farmers and perturbed the envious. O God, water it with showers from the cloud of thy favours and cause it to yield great harvests heaped up like unto mighty hills in Thy land . . .'[99] This prayer, which father faithfully recited every day, had an incredible effect on him. He firmly believed that 'Abdu'l-Bahá's intention was for his children to scatter far and wide and serve the Cause of God in different foreign lands.

There was one thing about Masíḥ's foreign pioneering venture that puzzled many family members and strangers. Coming as it did so soon after father's eye operation, they could not understand why Masíḥ did not wait a while longer and lend his father a helping hand. The answer to that question came when we gathered for our first family reunion, held in London in July 2004, to honour and celebrate the lives of our parents. In response to my question regarding the timing of his departure from Iran, he said he had had no choice, he had had to do it. I could not understand what he meant, so he explained. The following is the gist of his explanation.

When Masíḥ was gravely ill with typhoid and my parents had taken him to Ámul for medical treatment, the medicine he was first given did not prove effective. His condition worsened. A high temperature caused him to fall in and out of consciousness. The doctor was recalled. He came and as a last resort prescribed a cure or kill medication. When the doctor left, father sat by Masíḥ's bedside and prayed. Masíḥ regained consciousness as father was raising his hands and saying, 'O God, I have lost everything and have nothing to offer as a ransom. My eyesight is my most precious possession. Accept that as my offering and heal my son.' The next thing Masíḥ knew, he was awake and absolutely soaked with sweat. The medication had worked. My parents were ecstatic and most grateful for the miracle cure. After several days, they returned to Maḥmúdábád and continued with their day-to-day survival. When it became clear that father's eyesight was failing and the family had to leave its pioneering post, a feeling of uneasiness came over Masíḥ. He did not discuss it with anyone but felt responsible for father's failing eyesight. He prayed to Bahá'u'lláh to restore it and vowed to pioneer abroad at the first opportunity to compensate for the family's departure from its pioneering post precipitated by his illness and father's failing eyesight. When father's eye operation was successful and he regained his eyesight, Masíḥ could lose no time. He had to fulfil his vow. Therefore, he left when he did, no matter what people said. The father and son were the only ones who understood why.

After Masíḥ left, his siblings followed his example and went pioneering as soon as they could. Poor mother, who was very attached to having her children next to her and objected to them living at a distance farther than a few hours away, witnessed their departure from the country one by one. When Masíḥ left home and entered the field of foreign pioneering, transportation was utterly inadequate and postal services painfully slow. Many months elapsed and no letter arrived from him. He had been unable to settle in a fixed spot in the Gulf and was moving from place to place. One day Mr Nakhjavání, who served with father on the teaching committee, told him that Masíḥ had been unable to stay at his intended post and might have to return. The news made father very sad. He expressed his sorrow to Mr Nakhjavání, saying that he had not received any news from Masíḥ for a long time and did not know where he was. Father beseeched him that if he knew where Masíḥ was, to convey to him the following verse:

> O Zephyr! Tell the sacrificial Ismá'íl on my behalf
> Returning alive from the Beloved's abode
> Is not the way to tread the path of sacrifice.

Father knew Masíḥ well and was certain that he would not return to Iran unless the obstacles proved absolutely insurmountable. Nonetheless, he was concerned about his son's plight as he travelled in out of the way places where no Bahá'í had gone before. Mother was beside herself. It was one thing to reconcile herself to the idea of living far away from her beloved son but an entirely different one to have no news from him for such a long time and not know what was happening to him. Poor mother! We all felt the agony of her heart and joined in prayers that Masíḥ would soon reach his destination and we would receive news of his safe arrival.

During those stressful times mother conceived again. She was then 45 years old. One month before she gave birth to a baby girl, named Firishtih, the first letter from Masíḥ was hand-delivered by a Mr Nadímí, a pioneer in one of the Shaykhdoms of the Persian Gulf. I remember the day as though it were yesterday. The joy of our household was beyond description. Father's supreme happiness found expression in the poetry he composed that day. Masíḥ's second letter arrived on the day Firishtih was born, i.e. 1 Murdád 1329 (23 July 1950). This letter conveyed the glad-tidings that Masíḥ had settled where Mr Abu'l-Qásim Faizi and his family lived as pioneers.[100] The double celebration made everyone ecstatic. Father described the mood of the family in his poetry.

## Other Developments and the First Two Daughters Pioneer Abroad

Firishtih's birth busied mother once again, after a nine-year gap, with raising a child and shifted her focus somewhat from missing her son to looking after a newly born infant. About the same time, father transferred from the privately-owned Shirkat-i Jean to a government-owned company called Shirkat-i Panbih, which operated under Sázman-i Barnámih, part of the Ministry of Economic Planning and Development. His impeccable honesty and integrity attracted the attention of his superiors and afforded him the pleasure of doing his job with enjoyment and confidence. Then came a time when a self-seeking person was installed as the director. Father's responsibility for the company's financial affairs made it very difficult for him to work with the dishonest superior. Fortunately for him, some senior officers in the capital were looking for a man with integrity to receive on-the-job training to become a cotton specialist in the province of Fárs. Father was enlisted for the course, which took two years to complete. That training and the certificate he received gave him the necessary skill to travel to the cotton growing areas of Fárs for the purpose of grading cotton for export, thus relieving him of responsibilities for the inventory and financial matters of the company. His salary and privileges as a cotton specialist were comparable to those offered to engineers who had specialized in this line of work. Father's new job opened doors for him to travel every year to several places in Fárs – Jahrum, Fasá, Dáráb and Kázirún, where Shirkat-i Panbih had branches. Thus father's longing to travel and serve the Faith in as many places as he could was fulfilled, for he had to spend four to five months every year in these towns. Wherever his duties took him, he performed his job to the satisfaction of his superiors in the capital, to whom he was answerable, and spent his free time teaching the Faith of Bahá'u'lláh. It was teaching work that gave him energy and kept him happy, no matter how difficult the circumstances of his life were. He was also delighted that he could earn a decent living and provide for the family.

In 1953 the beloved Guardian announced the Ten Year Plan. His messages encouraging the believers to arise, settle in foreign lands and scatter the fragrances of Bahá'u'lláh's teachings far and wide had a great effect on Rawḥanieh and Nayyirih and their husbands, Manúchihr Rouhani and Náṣir 'Alaví. In consultation with one another, they decided to leave Iran and pioneer abroad. Thus the men resigned from their jobs and, forfeiting the privileges to which they were entitled, left Iran for neighbouring countries. It took some time for them to get established in their pioneering posts. Meanwhile, their families remained in Shíráz and we all lived in the same house. It took some time before the women could join their husbands. When the time came, Rawḥanieh resigned from the Department of Health and, together with Nayyirih and their children, left the country. With their departure, mother relived all the emotions associated with separating from her beloved son several years earlier. She wept bitterly and missed being with her loved ones! By then I was old enough to experience with mother the pangs of separation from our loved ones. Father missed them too but did not show the emotions that mother went through. Moreover, the ecstasy he felt in seeing his children respond to Shoghi Effendi's call amply compensated for the agony of separation he endured. I have heard so often that men are very different from women when it comes to feeling and revealing emotions. If it is true, much of it is due to men having been trained to focus their energy on the priorities at hand. Generally, men in those days were the sole breadwinners in their families and had 'more important' things to do than dwell on emotions which did not produce tangible results. Women, on the other hand, spent a lot of time within the four walls of their homes, so were susceptible to being emotional. They rarely engaged in intellectual pursuits, an excellent way to take one's mind off bothersome issues. Thus they had plenty of time to work with their emotions, with which they were most familiar.

## Nationwide Campaign against the Bahá'ís

Rawḥanieh and Nayyirih had not yet left Iran to join their husbands when disturbances against the Bahá'ís began on a wide scale. With the approach of Ramaḍán 1955, a mullá in Ṭihrán spearheaded an anti-Bahá'í campaign and during the Muslim month of fasting attacked the Bahá'ís and their belief from the pulpit of a mosque. His abusive and highly provocative sermons were broadcast every day on the national radio, which reached every corner of the land. Ironically, the holy months of the Muslim calendar, especially Ramaḍán and Muḥarram, are intended to provide opportunities for the followers of Islam to spiritualize and be at peace with themselves and their neighbours. Yet it is during these months that spiritual leaders arouse their followers' religious fervour and induce them to rise against the innocent members of minorities living amongst them. Since Bahá'ís believe in progressive revelation and regard Bahá'u'lláh as the latest Manifestation of God in the line of divine Educators who come from time to time to revive the spirit of true faith in people, the animosity against them is particularly strong, notwithstanding the fact that they believe in the authors of all previous religions.

The name of the mullá chosen for that year's organized campaign against the Bahá'ís was Muḥammad Falsafí. He enjoyed the cooperation and support of the people and the government, for otherwise it would have been unthinkable for the services of the national radio to be so freely placed at his disposal and used to spread hatred towards the members of the largest religious minority in Iran. On the first day of Ramaḍán, Mr Falsafí began his sermons attacking the Bahá'í Faith and its followers. The sermons were broadcast at noon when people were in their homes and could hear them. They were also reported extensively in national and local newspapers. The insinuation and instigation of the said mullá completely transformed the atmosphere in Iran and resulted in disturbances, which became violent in several provinces. In Hurmuzak, a suburb of Yazd, seven Bahá'ís were martyred in cold blood. In Abádih and Ma<u>sh</u>had the persecution of Bahá'ís reached new heights. The indignities heaped upon the believers were beyond description. Some were made to walk on their hands and feet like four-legged animals. The mob then forced them to run through the streets as they pushed them along with broomsticks. Others looked on, encouraging the mob to intensify its torturous behaviour and to carry on inflicting as much harm on the innocent victims as it possibly could. The purpose was to humiliate a people who stood for unity and peace and behaved towards all with love and kindness. A young Bahá'í girl was raped in Ma<u>sh</u>had. Bahá'í holy places, Ḥaẓíratu'l-Quds and property throughout the land were confiscated. The dome of the national Ḥaẓíratu'l-Quds in Ṭihrán was destroyed under the supervision of General Bátmánqlí<u>ch</u>, an army officer in charge of keeping law and order. Bahá'ís in several places were severely persecuted, lost their belongings and were dismissed from government offices.

In <u>Sh</u>íráz the plan involved the destruction of the House of the Báb, the persecution of Bahá'ís in general, the massacre of four hundred Bahá'í families whose particulars had been compiled in a list and included our family and the confiscation of the Ḥaẓíratu'l-Quds and pilgrim hostel.[101] There was no safety or security for Bahá'ís or their belongings anywhere. It was dangerous for them to be seen on the street. Some wealthy Bahá'í families sent their young daughters abroad to escape kidnapping. Others got married and moved away. The Local Spiritual Assembly of <u>Sh</u>íráz appointed nine individuals to take their place in case they were arrested or killed. Several Bahá'í homes and shops were pillaged.

A mob moved towards the House of the Báb on the very day

that Muḥammad Riḍá Sh͟áh arrived in Sh͟íráz for a visit. I remember that day very vividly. We were all at home listening to the national and local news, wondering what was going to happen to us and other Bahá'ís. When we heard that the mob was moving towards the House of the Báb, mother became outraged. She could not sit still and decided to go and investigate. Unperturbed by the objections we voiced, she put on her *ch͟ádur* and left our home, which was situated in the north of the city, quite a distance from the sacred House. After several hours she returned weeping and sobbing. She confirmed that indeed the mob had attacked the House and was intent on destroying it. The advantage of the *ch͟ádur* is that if it is held tightly over the upper part of the nose, so that only one eye is partially exposed, it is most difficult, if not impossible, to recognize the person who is wearing it. Mother had managed to remain anonymous during her investigative visit to the site. She had even asked some of the onlookers what purpose the destruction of the House was going to serve. When she heard that it was being destroyed because it was a Bábí building, she had voiced her opinion that stones and building blocks had committed no crime. She tarried around the House for some time then came back home.

The next stage in the nationwide campaign against the Bahá'ís was expelling them from government offices. All government employees were given forms to fill in indicating their religion. The day that father filled out the form and wrote in bold letters his religion, he was delighted that he would be expelled because of his allegiance to the Bahá'í Faith. The following poem expresses his emotions:

> I worry not about my government job, for my refuge is God
> And the Guardian of the Faith of Bahá is the one on whom I rely.
> If through wisdom He should close on us one window
> That closed window shall lead to many a high road.
> A thousand doors shall open to the Provider of humankind.
> This I firmly believe although to some it appears unsound.
> Should humanity inflict upon me harm, I lament not
> For I am well aware that such pain is my firm foundation.

> I wonder not when people commit injustice; for it's the norm.
> My gaze is fixed upon the just ones with their mighty backbones.
> Should I lose pleasure, comfort, sleep and good food
> I still rejoice that Bahá's bounty is my glory and joy
> Be silent, O Rouhani, and tell the keeper of secrets
> That the garden expanse and flowerbed is where I stand.

Several months before the start of the Falsafí episode father had two dreams, which indicated to him that some terrible events were in the making. In the first dream he saw himself in Nayríz. He was returning home after visiting his fruit garden outside the town. Before reaching home he had to cross a big river whose water was crystal clear. When he entered the house, he saw mother and his mother in the vestibule. They ran towards him and gave him the glad-tidings that Bahá'u'lláh had honoured the house with His presence and was sitting in the hall together with several people who were with Him. They advised father to change his clothes then seek permission to attain Bahá'u'lláh's presence. Father did as advised. After changing his clothes, he stood by the door and through his son Masíḥu'lláh sought permission to be in His presence. When he entered, he saw that Bahá'u'lláh was engaged in conversation with someone in the southern section of the hall. He said 'Alláh-u-Abhá' and bowed. Bahá'u'lláh bade him to be seated. As soon as he entered Bahá'u'lláh's presence, father realized that the hall was infested with mosquitoes. He was overtaken by embarrassment that the room had not been sprayed beforehand and, in his heart, he blamed his wife, his mother and the mother of Mírzá Ṭarázu'lláh, who were standing ready to serve. As soon as the thought crossed his mind, Bahá'u'lláh said, 'We will walk outside until the room is sprayed.' Then Bahá'u'lláh left the room and returned once it had been sprayed. He sat down and bade father to sit opposite Him. He then gave father a copy of *Iqtidárát*, which He had in His hand, and told him, 'Open the book at random and read the page at which it opens.' Father did as instructed and started reading. The passage, which he remembered and wrote down when he woke up, was the passage that says that God has ever been and will continue through eternity to be sanctified above ascent and descent, limitation, closeness and association.[102] Father was then instructed to recite the Tablet of Aḥmad. As he knew it by heart, he prostrated himself before Bahá'u'lláh and recited the entire Tablet in that position. The intensity of the ecstasy he felt was so strong that he woke up.

Father described the dream in a letter written to Hand of the Cause Mr A. A. Furútan, who was then the secretary of the National Spiritual Assembly of Iran, and asked him to interpret it for him. Mr Furútan wrote back and said that the infested air in the room indicated that some unforeseen events were about to happen. He said that mosquitoes that were sprayed represented the feeble in heart and harmful elements in the community who would be tested by those events and whose belief would be shaken. However, he said, their elimination would purify the Cause of God. Mr Furútan added that father and all those who were in Bahá'u'lláh's presence would be under God's care and protection.

Father's second dream came a short while after the first and just before the disturbances began. Father saw that he was with a few other Bahá'ís in a room which could be entered and exited from both sides. They were attending a meeting when they were informed that there were disturbances in Shíráz. There was an uprising against the Bahá'ís and groups had been formed in the streets and marketplaces. 'Abdu'l-Bahá had been wounded and was being brought to the room where the meeting was taking place. The news so badly affected father in his dream that he instantaneously wished he could be martyred. He also wished that 'Abdu'l-Bahá would accept him as a ransom for Himself and the friends. At that moment, one of the stirrers of mischief entered and beheaded father while he was standing. However, his head did not fall on the ground. While father was eagerly anticipating the flight of his spirit to the world beyond, he heard the sound of the mob and saw a group of evildoers encircling 'Abdu'l-Bahá and pressing so hard that His forehead was covered with sweat and He was not given a chance to look towards father and the other friends who were present. Father, his head hanging from his neck, fixed his gaze on 'Abdu'l-Bahá and was longing for a glance from Him. As He was leaving, 'Abdu'l-Bahá turned and looked at father. After several minutes a doctor, who had been commissioned by 'Abdu'l-Bahá to treat father, arrived. He took a box out of his brief-case and applied an ointment, similar to car oil, to the cut areas of father's head and made him whole again.

These two dreams made father apprehensive and greatly concerned about the events that were about to take place. At the same time, the dreams reassured him that he and his family would be divinely protected.

When the government began its extensive scheme to purge its institutions of Bahá'ís, the beloved Guardian instructed the National Spiritual Assembly of Iran to urge the Bahá'ís to be calm and confident of the outcome. That cable reassured father and mother that all was going to end well. About the same time, at the Guardian's instruction, the Bahá'í representative to the United Nations lodged a complaint and all Bahá'í Assemblies throughout the world sent messages to the Sháh seeking justice and restitution of the rights of the persecuted Bahá'ís in Iran. The telegraph office in Ṭihrán was inundated by thousands of cables received from Bahá'ís in almost every corner of the globe, asking that the cruel treatment of their co-religionists be stopped. Thus gradually the situation improved, the confiscated properties were returned to their rightful owners and those who had been dismissed returned to their jobs in the government.

In Nayríz the situation was particularly grave, for the ground was fertile for anti-Bahá'í activity. From the first day of Ramaḍán when Falsafí broadcast his sermons, groups were mobilized against the Bahá'ís and plans made for persecuting and killing the believers and pillaging their properties. The friends had no choice but to stay indoors, pray and hope for a solution. Some went without food for two days. Those who left home to take care of emergencies and pressing matters were attacked ferociously and tortured. Two of the friends, Mr 'Abdu'ṣ-Ṣamí' Shahídpúr, the son and grandson of two earlier martyrs, and Mr Yazdányár, the technical manager of a small hand-operated textile factory set up by the Bahá'ís, were severely beaten. The wounds they sustained were very deep. Many did not expect them to live. After a lengthy period of treatment, they were restored to health and were able to resume work. The Bahá'ís suffered tremendous financial loss as well. Trees were uprooted from Bahá'í-owned orchards, farm produce was destroyed and the Bahá'í cemetery was attacked, with graves desecrated and the walls of the cemetery half destroyed. Two graves were opened but the perpetrators of this heinous act could not exhume the corpses. Since the wicked doers could not reach father, they inflicted considerable damage on the only fruit garden he still owned in the town. When calm was restored, the Local Spiritual Assembly of Shíráz and the special committee appointed for the consolidation of the affairs of the Faith in Nayríz sent father to extend help and distribute the funds especially collected for the relief of the friends there. When his rented car reached Nayríz, it was stoned and with great difficulty he managed to get to the home of his brother, Mírzá Khalíl. In that house every day he met the Bahá'ís of the town and delivered to the needy the sums he had been entrusted to apportion.

The result of the open onslaught on the Bahá'ís by the people and government of Iran in 1955 was this: The thick veil of obscurity which had enfolded the Bahá'í Faith since its inception over a hundred years earlier was rent asunder. The Bahá'í Faith became known not only in Iran but also abroad. The government of Iran realized that the followers of Bahá'u'lláh lived all over the world, that they were outspoken in the face of atrocities inflicted on their co-religionists in the cradle of their Faith and that the fair-minded people and governments throughout the world were carefully watching what was happening in that country. To control the damage its reputation had already suffered and to forestall further disrepute to its international image, the government issued confidential orders to its departments throughout the country to return the confiscated properties to their rightful owners and to reinstate the dismissed Bahá'ís. It took some time for the order to be completely complied with everywhere. In Shíráz, although the House of the Báb was returned to the Bahá'í community, the repair and restoration work could not be done for a considerable time owing to the volatile situation there. It also took some time before Bahá'í activities could be carried out at the level they had been at before the disturbances began.

As the midway point of the Ten Year Plan of the beloved Guardian, which had begun at Riḍván 1953, drew near, the Bahá'ís of Iran were actively engaged in fulfilling the goals assigned to them. The Falsafí episode galvanized them and spurred them on to intensify their teaching efforts. As a result, the pace of progress accelerated both in Iran and abroad in preparation for the celebration of the centenary of Bahá'u'lláh's declaration in 1963.

Father continued his work as the expert in charge of grading for export the cotton grown in the province of Fárs. He also continued to spend his free time teaching the Cause of Bahá'u'lláh. While in Jahrum, he spent his weekends (Thursday afternoons and Fridays) in Fasá giving firesides. He returned to Jahrum to resume his official duties each Saturday (the beginning of the week in Iran). Meanwhile, the children who had come of age and were at various stages of their studies pressured him and mother to let them stop their education and go pioneering. My parents were eager for us to finish our studies first. Since it was a matter of conscience and spiritual obligation, there was no clear and convincing answer. Therefore the discussion kept surfacing every now and then. As Mr Muḥammad-'Alí Faizi was going on pilgrimage, father asked him to present our situation to the beloved Guardian should he ever ask about Nayríz. Father added that he and mother were completely resigned to his will. The Guardian did ask about Nayríz, which provided Mr Faizi with the opportunity to report on the situation there. He then mentioned my parents' names, briefly reported on the children who had gone pioneering and sought his guidance regarding the dilemma the remaining children faced regarding whether to complete their education or discontinue it to pioneer abroad. The beloved Guardian had responded: 'Study first then hurry.'[103] These two short phrases saved us a lot of unnecessary discussion regarding the wisdom of leaving our studies in favour of pioneering or finishing our education that we might be better prepared and equipped to serve the Faith as effective pioneers.

## The Passing of Shoghi Effendi

Father spent the summer of 1957 in Fasá, Dáráb and Jahrum. This time he made Fasá his base and travelled to the other two places for work. Although he was able to travel and was successful in the teaching field, some disturbing dreams made him restless and unhappy. He felt as though some unfortunate event was about to happen but he did not know what it was. Every day after his daily work he went for long walks in the wilderness and spent hours in meditation and communion with the beloved Guardian, whom he longed to visit. The summer months passed, autumn arrived but for him there was no relief in sight. About mid-Ábán (early November) his inner agitation intensified. One night he was invited to dinner together with delegates from Nayríz, who were attending a district convention in Fasá. It was the eve of a 19 Day Feast. The Bahá'ís of Fasá did not turn up, thinking that because of the convention the Feast was cancelled. Father was most upset. He was so hurt that he could not stay. He excused himself and returned to his rented house. On the way, he bought two candles and a loaf of bread. As soon as he opened the door to his house and entered, he burst into tears and wept for a considerable time. He spent that night in prayer and supplication. After midnight, when the electricity in Fasá went out, he prayed by candlelight. When the second candle burnt out and the remnants melted away, father remembered this verse from Ḥáfiẓ: 'He closed the door and entrusted the key to the Possessor of hearts.' Father's unexplainable grief continued until 18 Ábán (9 November). On that day Mr Reyḥání, a prominent Bahá'í living in Shíráz, arrived in Fasá and conveyed to father and the friends the heartrending news of the passing of the beloved Guardian, which had taken place a few days earlier. The news had to be conveyed to the friends in other areas. It fell to father, accompanied by Mr Rafí'í who had a car, to travel to Dáráb, Jahrum and Quṭbábád-i Lár to inform the friends and to attend the memorial gatherings in those towns.

The untimely passing of Shoghi Effendi came as a tremendous shock to Bahá'ís throughout the world but for those like father, who had permission to visit him and who was longing to attain that inestimable bounty, it came also as a grave disappointment and irreparable loss. He blamed the deprivation on his unworthiness. The only thing that lessened the weight of his grief, as he said himself, was the pioneering abroad of three more children.

## More Children Respond to the Call for Pioneers

Pouran was the first of the next three children to enter the foreign pioneering field. To have a career enabling her to work in almost any corner of the world, she had decided several years earlier to become a state registered nurse.[104] Fortunately for her, about the time she was graduating from high school, the Namází Hospital was built and a modern nursing school run by instructors from the United States had been established in Shíráz. The school offered a degree course equivalent to BSc, the first of its kind in the whole of Iran. To be admitted to the school Pouran needed a high school certificate with good grades. Being a studious pupil with an excellent record meant that she was assured a place. However, when the results were publicly announced, it became clear that she had not passed and was required to re-sit the exams. Oh, how bitterly she wept when she saw the results! And with her we all wept, for the repercussions of the failure were immense. We were at a loss to understand how it could have happened and did not know what to do to find out. The one person who did not give in to negative thoughts and was absolutely sure that something had gone terribly wrong was mother. She was furious that her daughter had been treated with glaring injustice and therefore decided to take it up with the Department of Education. She paid them a visit and demanded that the matter be investigated immediately. She may have even threatened them with legal action. Any delay would have negative consequences for Pouran's admission to the nursing school. So mother demanded action and fast. We were not sure how our being Bahá'ís would play out in establishing the facts. But to everyone's astonishment, mother was proved right. In the process of matching the students' names with the marks they had earned, Pouran's excellent results had been swapped with those of another girl who had done poorly in her exams. After investigation, the error became glaringly evident and the records corrected. Thus Pouran entered the prestigious nursing school that drew students from all over Iran. The degree course lasted three years and Pouran passed the exams with high honours. In fact, she got the highest mark and was acknowledged as the top student in her class.

To pioneer abroad Pouran needed sufficient funds and for that she needed to work in Iran for a while. She applied and was offered a job in the hospital run by the oil company Shirkat-i Naft in Ábádán. In the meantime, she contacted the Foreign Pioneering Committee of the National Spiritual Assembly of Iran and was advised to consider settling in the Netherlands, a part of the Benelux bloc (Belgium, Netherlands, Luxembourg). As soon as she had enough to pay her way, she resigned her job and left for the Netherlands in 1959. She was the first pioneer to settle in Haarlem and work towards the establishment of a Local Spiritual Assembly in that city. After nearly three years in the Netherlands, Pouran pioneered to Nairobi, Kenya in 1962.[105]

The other two who pioneered abroad during the concluding years of the Ten Year Plan were Baharieh (the writer) and Mawhibatu'lláh, the youngest son. My departure from Iran coincided with father's retirement, which presaged changes in the life of my parents and the last two dependent children. I left my university studies six months before graduation and went to Ṭihrán in late November 1960. I stayed in Ṭihrán for about a month to acquire a passport and a visa for Nairobi and to receive the inoculations necessary for going to Africa. The realization of my longing to pioneer to a far-off land in Shoghi Effendi's global Plan, which had seemed so remote, was suddenly to hand. Marriage to a man I had never met was the gateway to that heaven. His name was Manúchihr Ma'ání. At the beginning of the Ten Year Plan he had arisen to open Chagos Archipelago, now Diego Garcia, in the Indian Ocean. He had lived in the Seychelles and Kenya for several years and did not wish to return to Iran before the end of the Plan. I must add here that although Manúchihr and I had not met, the two families knew one another from their pioneering days in Maḥmúdábád and had no objection to our out-of-the-ordinary decision to marry without seeing each other. By the end of 1960 I was in my pioneering post in Nairobi and by 1 January 1961 Manúchihr and I were married in the rented Bahá'í Centre in Nairobi. Our marriage was a happy occasion but lacked the presence of any and all family members. A year and one month elapsed. I was in the last week of pregnancy when Manúchihr died after several days of severe pain in the stomach. He passed away on 3 February 1962. Five days later, our first and only child, Sovaida, was born.[106]

## Father's Retirement and Subsequent Developments

Father reached the age of retirement in 1960. He was then 65 years old. The retirement scheme applicable in his case entitled him only to the payment of a gratuity, which he received in a lump sum. To earn a living and provide for the family, which included a teenage son in college and a daughter about to enter secondary school, he decided to reenter the business world. He became an agent in Shíráz for the Firooz Company.[107] For about two years he was engaged in this line of work. However, the restrictions introduced by the government on imported luxury goods, such as radios and refrigerators, the two items most in demand, adversely affected his fortunes and forced him into bankruptcy. For the last time in his life he sold what he had of worldly possessions, which included the remaining piece of property in Nayríz and a parcel of land he had purchased in Shíráz, paid his debtors and freed himself completely from the cares of this world, devoting his life entirely to the service of the Cause of Bahá'u'lláh. After that, he travelled extensively in Iran for the Bahá'í Faith. He also became more fully active in the teaching field in Shíráz. By that time six of the eight children were independent, two of them in a position to provide financial assistance. As the remaining two children became financially independent, a tremendous pressure on my parents was eased and they managed, with help from their sons, to live reasonably comfortably to the end of their life.

## The Passing of Grandmothers

Several months after my departure for Kenya grandmother Núríján passed away in Shíráz at the age of 85. Her death evoked fond memories of the long years she had spent raising her children and grandchildren in the bosom of the Faith. Wherever her grandchildren lived, which included many parts of the world, memorial gatherings in her honour were held. We had one in Nairobi and told our Kenyan friends about her exemplary life. She was indeed a great source of inspiration and courage, an example of fortitude, high-mindedness and detachment, and had a pivotal role in the Bahá'í education of her children and grandchildren. Her death had a great effect on father, her eldest son, who had assumed at a young age responsibility for the family after the untimely death of his own father.

Grandmother Núríján, also referred to as Núríyyih, had been honoured with a Tablet from 'Abdu'l-Bahá which she had memorized and recited often with feelings of joy and spiritual ecstasy. This is a provisional translation of the Tablet:

> Nayríz
> Núríyyih, daughter of Jináb-i Mullá Muḥammad-Shafí'
> He is God! O Amat'alláh! Light is the revealer of created things, for without it all things would be concealed behind a cover of darkness. Since thy name is Núríyyih [light], beseech God that thou mayest uncover the inner realities of human beings and see them in their true reality. Upon thee be Glory.
> 'Ayn 'Ayn

Grandmother Farrukh died in Nayríz several years after grandmother Núríján. Unlike grandmother Núríján, who lived every season of the year with one of her four sons until she died in Shíráz and was given a befitting Bahá'í burial, no specific arrangements were made for grandmother Farrukh who would not submit to a particular schedule. Her natural disinclination to allow others to dictate what was best for her combined with the fact that her children, except for one, were Bahá'ís while the rest of her family were Muslims, made it very difficult for her to firmly adhere to the laws of either religion. She was a kind and pure-hearted woman who wanted to be at peace with everyone. She travelled, while she could, to the different places in Iran where her children lived and spent some time with each. When old and frail, she remained in Nayríz, where one of her daughters lived, and passed away there. Her Muslim relatives did not allow her a Bahá'í burial. She was buried in the Muslim cemetery, which deprived her Bahá'í children and grandchildren from saying prayers at her funeral or later at her graveside.

## The Youngest Son Pioneers Abroad

The youngest son's pioneering aspirations were fulfilled some 18 months after I left Iran. Manúchihr's death served as the catalyst that changed the course of my younger brother's life. He gave up his studies in the middle of 1962 and joined the rank of pioneers. Life was unpredictable and its length no one could foresee, he argued. He wanted to enter the field of foreign pioneering and could no longer delay. He consulted with my parents and Masíḥu'lláh, who facilitated the realization of his dream.

With the departure of their youngest son from Iran, my parents were separated from the male offspring they had longed to have after their firstborn had tragically died. My younger brother was God's bounty to the family and was treated as such. A good part of his childhood years and mine coincided with the most difficult financial times the family experienced. Mother was very concerned about his needs and willing to do whatever she could to ease the pressure on him. If he wanted something within reason that the resources of the family were inadequate to provide, mother would find a way to meet the need even if it meant reducing the family's expenditure on other things. As a sibling immediately preceding him, I often marvelled at the way mother treated him. I was positioned in the family between a sister, tall and strong, whom I could not challenge physically, and a brother I could not rival because he was treated as 'special'. As a child I was curious to find out what made him so. It took me a while to fathom the dynamics at work. Once my little mind had developed enough to understand the intricacies involved, I embraced the reasons and accepted the way that things were. Not only did I learn to exercise detachment early in my life, I also discovered the value of excelling in virtues, which is the domain of every willing soul. Doing well in school, immersing oneself in the ocean of the writings, being kind and generous, courteous and so on, I was told, would really make a person special, not the circumstances of one's birth. The loving family environment we enjoyed helped us to deal sensibly with minor issues when they arose. We learned at an early age to make the most of what our circumstances were. As a result, the love we cherish for one another knows no bounds. Here is the point I am trying to emphasize by taking this brief diversion: the degree of sacrifice that mother made by agreeing without any fuss to let her youngest son leave the country to pioneer. I was not in Iran when it happened but can well imagine how she must have felt.

It was not long after he settled in his pioneer post that my precious younger brother got married. My parents and Firishtih were able to attend the wedding. Soon after the marriage, the newlyweds moved to a country beyond the reach of my parents, thus they never had the opportunity to see their son and daughter-in-law's newly-established home. To compensate, my brother and his family visited my parents annually in Shíráz and later in India, where my parents lived for five years after the Islamic revolution in Iran.

## The First Bahá'í World Congress

With the approach of 1963, the Ten Year Plan of the beloved Guardian was coming to a successful end. At the close of the Plan, on 21 April 1963, the Bahá'í world witnessed the establishment of the Universal House of Justice, the supreme administrative institution of the Bahá'í Faith, coinciding with the centenary celebration of Bahá'u'lláh's declaration, which had taken place in Baghdád in

April 1863. The celebrations were held in London from 29 April to 2 May. Thousands of Bahá'ís from all over the world travelled to the city. A large number came from Iran using different means of transportation. Some came by land. For example, 40 hired a bus from the T.B.T. Bus Company in Ṭihrán and made a trip lasting 40 days, which included spending one or two nights in each of the following countries: Turkey, Bulgaria, Yugoslavia, Austria, Germany, France, Italy and Switzerland. My parents were with this group of travellers, which also included Rawḥanieh and her husband, Manúchihr, as well as uncle Jalál and uncle 'Alí Akbar and their wives. The group celebrated the first day of Riḍván in Frankfurt and visited the Mas͟hriqu'l-Ad͟hkár on that day. They stayed in London for eleven days, five of which were the days of the Congress. They had a fabulous time.

Although father had travelled abroad in 1921 and had visited India on his way to the Holy Land where he met 'Abdu'l-Bahá, for mother, and indeed for many Persian Bahá'ís who attended the Congress, it was the first time they had stepped outside the borders of Iran and into the western world. For those who had lived their lives in areas steeped in tradition and been persecuted for their belief, the Congress was a wonderful opportunity to see the greatness of their glorious Faith which had brought together many thousands of its adherents from all over the world in a spirit of love and unity. They assembled in the heart of the free world to celebrate the hundredth anniversary of Bahá'u'lláh's declaration and to meet for the first time the members of the international institution He had ordained in His Most Holy Book. To be able to greet their fellow Bahá'ís openly and to speak publicly of the tenets of the Bahá'í Faith was to many a true novelty. Yet for others whose children or relatives had responded to the call for pioneers and settled in foreign countries, the Congress also provided an opportunity to be reunited with them for a few days and together enjoy the Congress programme.

## The Youngest Child Pioneers Abroad

My youngest sister, Firishtih, was too young to pioneer during the Ten Year Plan. For many years she was the only child living with my parents after the rest of us had left Shíráz – a true blessing, especially for mother who terribly missed having her other children around. When Firishtih graduated as a chemical engineer from Pahlaví University, the Five Year Plan of the Universal House of Justice (1973–8) was at its midway point. She longed to go to Africa as a pioneer. In 1975 she married Massoud Samadi, a pioneer living in Nigeria, who was visiting Iran that summer. After their wedding they left together for West Africa. With Firishtih gone, my parents had none of their eight children with them in Shíráz. Mahín, who lived with her family in Iran, did not reside in Shíráz, as we shall see. However, my parents had the opportunity to visit Firishtih and her family in Enugu, Nigeria, during an international Bahá'í conference that took place there from 12 to 14 August 1977. That was the only visit my parents made to Africa. My eldest brother, his wife and daughter also attended that conference and enjoyed a wonderful reunion.

Firishtih and Massoud were married for about four years when the Islamic revolution took place in Iran and brought to power fanatical Muslims. The new regime put into action an extensive programme aimed at exterminating the Bahá'ís of Iran and their administrative institutions. The regime executed and imprisoned the leading figures of the Faith and those active in the teaching field. They severely persecuted other Bahá'ís. Their programme was gradually extended to include Iranian Bahá'ís who had pioneered abroad. Embassies were instructed not to renew the passports of active Iranian Bahá'ís living in foreign countries. The aim was to force them to return to Iran and face the consequences of their activities for the Faith they believed in and served with heart and soul. Firishtih and Massoud were among such Bahá'ís. To obtain legal status in another country willing to help the stranded Bahá'ís, they emigrated to Canada. They stayed in that country long enough to obtain Canadian passports. While there, they continued their fields of study in chemical engineering and soil analysis. As soon as they had their new passports and Master's degrees, they and their two children reentered the pioneering field. This time they settled in Ciskei, a homeland in South Africa, which needed pioneers. They later moved to Pretoria, where they still live.

## My Parents' Remaining Years in Iran

My parents continued to live in Shíráz after father's retirement. As one by one their children left, they had more and more time to devote to carrying out manifold Bahá'í services. They were particularly active in the teaching field and both served on the Bahá'í teaching committee of Shíráz for many years. Father also travelled throughout Iran and offered assistance with teaching and deepening projects wherever help was needed. During the same period he organized his notes, interviewed many people of Nayríz, both Bahá'ís and non-Bahá'ís, who had valuable recollections to share, and wrote the history of Nayríz in two volumes, entitled *Lama-'átu'l-Anvár*. When he travelled to Ardistán for Bahá'í work, he also interviewed the Bahá'ís there and gathered material for the history of the Faith in that town. The manuscript he prepared was in the hands of the publishing committee of Iran when the revolution took place. The fate of that manuscript will, we hope, become clear as the situation in Iran improves. Father also wrote his memoirs, which he entitled *Kháṭirát-i Talkh va Shírín*. Efforts to have them published during the last years of his life were unsuccessful. The process of review, preparation of the manuscript for publication and other formalities took longer than expected. Finally, they were published in 1993, nearly a decade after he had passed away.

One of the services father rendered to the Cause of Bahá'u'lláh in Iran before the Islamic revolution was visiting Bahá'í communities on behalf of the regional pioneering and consolidation committee based in Shíráz, of which he was a member. He and a member of the Local Spiritual Assembly of Shíráz, Dr Iraj Poostchi, visited Sarvistán and Haftú regularly in 1344 (1975–6). Once a month they participated in the joint meeting of those two Assemblies;

every other month they attended a consultative session of all the Assemblies in the area, held alternately in Sarvistán and Haftú.

During a trip that took place on 19 Shahru's-Sulṭán 122 (11 February 1966), father and Dr Poostchi were informed by the secretary of the Local Spiritual Assembly of Sarvistán that owing to unfavourable circumstances it was inadvisable for them to meet in that town. They therefore proceeded to Haftú where they intended to meet with the Bahá'ís individually and encourage them to go home front pioneering. As they were meeting with the chairman of the Local Assembly and another believer, a messenger arrived from Sarvistán conveying a message that at the instigation of Mr Kashfí, the preacher and religious leader of Sarvistán, the inhabitants of the town had come together, secured the support of the influential people of the area and enlisted the cooperation of the head of the military police against the Bahá'ís. The message added that a document had been drawn up regarding the visit of the Bahá'ís from Shíráz. It further explained that four military police had been dispatched to Haftú to arrest the two visitors and those they were meeting. The police were instructed to take the visitors in disgrace to Sarvistán. Father and Dr Poostchi thought the message was designed to create fear in their hearts. As they were talking to the chairman of the Assembly, and another Bahá'í, four armed police arrived on the scene and detained father and Dr Poostchi. When they enquired the reason for their arrest, they were verbally abused and treated rudely, which made them realize the situation was grave indeed.

The appearance of the police in the village and the foul language they used attracted the attention of the local inhabitants, who gathered around and joined the police in heaping humiliation and abuse on the defenceless visitors. The distance between Haftú and Sarvistán, about four kilometres, was traversed on foot by an unfrequented route. The situation was truly precarious and the visitors were unsure of reaching their destination safely. By the time they arrived at the police station in Sarvistán, the numbers in the mob that followed them had reached three hundred. Father and Dr Poostchi thought it best not to utter a word, for the mob could have used anything said as a pretext to do as they pleased.

In Sarvistán the detainees were kept in the police compound from 10:00 a.m. to 3:00 p.m. without food and water while surrounded by vicious people who never stopped using foul language. The police enjoyed watching the Bahá'ís being humiliated. They even encouraged the mob to intensify the abuses. However, they did not allow anyone to inflict bodily harm on the detainees, for they were fearful of unforeseen consequences for which they would have been responsible. At 3:00 p.m. the chief of the police arrived and began his interrogation with foul words and threats. When he was asked the reason for the arrest, he took out his pistol and threatened to kill both men. He then said that because they had come into his area of jurisdiction without his permission, he was going to cut their legs into pieces. He then searched the detainees' bags. He started with Dr Poostchi's bag, reading the Bahá'í literature and papers it contained. With every page that he read he offered several obscene phrases and words. He then searched father's bag and saw the pamphlet entitled 'The Bahá'í World Faith' and a piece of poetry father had composed in praise of Bahá'u'lláh and the Universal House of Justice. He concluded that father was a Bahá'í teacher and was in the area to teach the Bahá'í Faith and his activities were thus considered to be subversive. Father said that in the Bahá'í Faith the priesthood did not exist and no individual believer enjoyed the position of a mullá, leader or teacher. He added that all Bahá'ís had the duty to respond to questions about the Faith but they did not proselytize. The chief of the police asked, 'Tell me, what has brought you here?' Father answered that he had friends in the area and he had come to visit them. Moreover, he said that he was a businessman, as evidenced by some of the contents of his bag. It took a while for the prosecutor to calm down, complete the file and prepare a statement which was to be signed by the detainees and witnessed by the town's notables, such as the mayor. The detainees did not agree with a phrase charging them with forming groups. The prosecutor refused to correct the statement. The accused stated their objection in writing at the foot of the statement before signing it. The completed file was sealed and entrusted to three military policemen, who took the file and the detainees to Shíráz, where the case was to be adjudicated.

In Shíráz, after the intervention of the Local Spiritual Assembly and Colonel Vaḥdat,[108] the accused were released on bail. After release, guided by directives from the Local Spiritual Assembly, father and Dr Poostchi lodged a complaint with the provincial government, the national security apparatus and the regional office of the military police. Investigations were in process when disturbances began which led to the Islamic revolution.

The turmoil Iran witnessed during the last year of Muḥammad-Riḍá Sháh's reign turned the country into a place where lawlessness was the order of the day. As the political situation deteriorated, life for the Bahá'ís of Iran became more hazardous. Their rights had never been fully respected under the Sháh's rule. In fact, whenever his authority was challenged, to divert people's attention from what was at stake, he let them loose to do to the Bahá'ís what they could not ordinarily do under the law. Bahá'ís had always been turned into legitimate scapegoats and over the years nothing in this respect changed. The situation repeated itself during the last years of his rule when, with the full knowledge of the government, Bahá'ís again became targets for religious persecution. Being a prominent Bahá'í teacher in Shíráz, father's life was in real danger, as evidenced by the Sarvistán episode.

## The Islamic Revolution

Father was about 85 and mother 77 when Iran's government underwent a total change, culminating in the establishment of the Islamic Republic in 1979, which made opposition to the Bahá'í Faith and extermination of the Bahá'ís a top item on its list of priorities. As a first step in the process, the revolutionary guards targeted members of Bahá'í institutions and prominent teachers of the Cause of God. They imagined that once the people they considered Bahá'í leaders were removed, other believers would give up their belief. They ignored the fact that since the inception of the Faith many such schemes had been tried and failed.

Knowing how the radical Muslims in S͟híráz despised father for his Baháʼí activities, my siblings who lived abroad were worried for his safety. They consulted together and convinced my parents to leave Iran for India. My parents complied in the hope that after six months the situation would improve and they would be able to return. They therefore left whatever they possessed in their house, locked the doors and gave the key to their granddaughter and her husband, who then lived in S͟híráz. They left Iran for India with two suitcases containing items most essential for their daily living. Among the things father left in the house were his research papers, notes, drafts of articles he had written, manuscripts, poems and other items of sentimental value.

For mother that house held many fond memories. Every summer she received some of her children there who came to pay her and father a visit. She lived all year long waiting for the summer to arrive to see her children around. The ecstasy she felt when re-united with them was beyond description; it was reflected in her countenance and demeanour. It was a wonderful scene to behold. When she got news that one of her children was going to visit, she started making preparations well in advance and asked everyone she knew, 'Do you know who is coming?' She would then give them all the information she had regarding the forthcoming visit. This enabled the visiting children to see the many Baháʼís who wished to see them during their stay in S͟híráz. When the guests came, mother and father received them with much love and warmth and made them feel at home. I vividly and fondly remember the taste of the tea and cookies that mother served to the friends who came to see Sovaida and me when we visited my parents in early 1971. For mother that house and the memories it evoked meant a lot.

The house was in the vicinity of the Baháʼí Centre in Kúy-i Yag͟hmá. It was a big house with subsidiary buildings and belonged to Masíḥuʼlláh. After my parents left Iran for India the house was confiscated, its contents pillaged and it was razed to the ground. The land was then incorporated into a Ḥusayníyyih situated on its eastern side. The expansion that that Islamic institution enjoyed as a result of incorporating usurped Baháʼí properties gave it a tremendous boost; indeed it benefited from the cruelties meted out to the innocent Bahá'í owners and occupants.

## The Fate of the Daughter Who Remained in Iran

My sister Mahín was the only sibling who remained in Iran after the revolution. She and her husband, Na'ím Vaḥídí, were employees of the Ministry of Education and served the people of Iran for many years with honesty, sincerity and perseverance. When the Islamic revolution occurred, their services were rewarded by orders of dismissal from their jobs, humiliation for being members of the Bahá'í community and persecution for not recanting their belief in Bahá'u'lláh.

Mahín and Na'ím had got married in the summer of 1960. Unlike my other siblings who could not wait to go pioneering for the Faith, Mahín and Na'ím decided to remain in Iran and serve the country and its people to the best of their ability. Among the services they rendered was working in Bandar-i Lingih, a place with an inhospitable climate in the south of Iran, which was also a home front pioneering goal. When their term of service in Bandar-i Lingih ended, they returned to Ṭihrán. They were living there when the Islamic revolution took place. As the new regime began its elaborate scheme of cleansing government departments and offices of Bahá'ís, those employed by the Ministry of Education were the first ones to be dismissed, hence both Mahín and Na'ím lost their jobs. In a cynical ploy to make their jobs so attractive that they would be persuaded to hang onto them, they were first given impressive salary rises then summoned for interrogation and threatened with dismissal unless they recanted their Faith. The documents representing Mahín's promotion three months prior to her dismissal and the decree notifying her of the termination of her services owing to her allegiance to the Bahá'í Faith are available for those who want to see hard evidence.

Several years elapsed. The situation in Iran deteriorated rapidly, adversely affecting the situation of the Bahá'ís, particularly those who had been government employees and had no other source of income. Mahín and Na'ím considered leaving Iran for the United States where their sons lived. Unfortunately, several days before their departure, Na'ím, whose love for the land of Iran and its rich heritage had been tested and proved genuine many times before, had a massive heart attack. He passed away in December 1984. He was buried unceremoniously in the land of His Beloved for which he had a tender love and attachment. The regime had confiscated not only the Bahá'í holy places and historical sites but also Bahá'í cemeteries and did not allow the Bahá'ís to bury their dead with due honour and respect. Na'ím was buried in a plot of land far away from the city in an unmarked grave, as the government required the Bahá'ís to do.

With Na'ím gone, life was even more difficult for Mahín, a single woman in the Islamic Republic of Iran. Heartbroken and grief-stricken, Mahín left Iran for Pakistan accompanied by uncle 'Abdu'l-Ḥusayn. She spent several months in that country and in Austria waiting for her refugee visa for the United States to arrive. She then moved to Maryland where she still lives with her sons. Her many years of service in the Ministry of Education in Iran entitled Mahín to no retirement or other benefits. Being a Bahá'í was sufficient reason to deny her any and all rights. In fact, the government required the Bahá'ís dismissed from government service to return to it all the salary and benefits that they had received from the beginning of their employment until the dismissal date.

## My Parents' Life in India

The elderly Bahá'ís displaced by the Islamic Revolution suffered the most. I know it from the experiences my own parents went through. Although they were happy to live in a country that enjoyed religious freedom, learning another language at their old age proved impossible. They had left behind familiar surroundings and the people they had known all their lives. They had left everything and come out with the barest necessities of life in the hope that they would return after, at the most, six months. How they struggled, especially mother, to live in a hotel room in Panchgani for a considerable time, then move to Poona and settle in a rented apartment, which never looked like a home! Father busied himself with giving Bahá'í classes to those who spoke Persian and he and mother spent their days in anticipation of the time when they would find themselves back in Iran.

Five years thus elapsed. During their stay in India their children living abroad paid them visits. This made them really happy. They also visited the Holy Land, the highlight of that part of their life. Then father fell ill and his condition went from bad to worse until he was bedridden and moved to a private hospital. I visited my parents during that time and saw how they missed being in their hometown with the people they knew. Father's memory had started fading before he fell ill. His illness made the situation even worse. In fact, he was in a coma for some time as a result of the medication his doctor had administered in preparation for an operation, which never took place. He was too weak to undergo the operation. By then he was 90 years old and his brain cells were vulnerable to the effects of the anaesthetic. Thus he never recovered from his illness. But there were times when he was more alert and could engage in a short conversation. During those wakeful times he warned about the dangers surrounding his house in Shíráz. He said that the enemies were after his papers, which were his most precious belongings in that house. He had not been told that his house had been confiscated, his possessions including his papers plundered, and the house razed to the ground.

The friends in India, particularly those in Panchgani and Poona, were very kind and loving. They made my parents feel at home. Life in India was similar in some ways to life in Iran. Besides, many Bahá'ís of Persian extraction lived in various parts of the country, especially in Panchgani, Poona and Bombay (Mumbai), with whom my parents could communicate without difficulty. But mother missed having her children around, particularly when father was very ill. Although we took turns visiting them during that period, there were times when mother was the only caregiver. She was then over 80 years old and herself in need of care. After ten months in the hospital, father passed away on 25 November 1984, coinciding with the eve of the Day of the Covenant. Several of his children attended his funeral held in Poona. The Universal House of Justice sent the following cable to the National Spiritual Assembly of India:

> SADDENED NEWS PASSING FAITHFUL STEADFAST SERVANT THRESHOLD MUHAMMAD SHAFI RAWHANI. HIS LIFELONG SERVICES PROMOTION FAITH CRADLE FAITH UNFORGETTABLE. ASSURE HIS RELATIVES FRIENDS LOVING PRAYERS HOLY SHRINES PROGRESS HIS SOUL. TRANSMIT THIS MESSAGE LOCAL ASSEMBLY POONA.
> UNIVERSAL HOUSE OF JUSTICE

## Mother's Life after Father's Death

When father passed away mother was devastated. She felt lonely and disconsolate. I have never witnessed a life go through such drastic change in such a short time. She became very restless after his death. She struggled hard to retain her independence but soon realized that the new conditions of her life made remaining independent most difficult. She lived for 17 years after father's death and spent most of that time in the United States with my sister Mahín. Not knowing English made communication with other people impossible, unless someone translated everything for her. She also had to depend on my nephews to drive her wherever she wanted to go. She was not used to being dependent on others for everything she wanted to do. She thought going back to India would help. She made two trips back there, the first time for the dedication of the Mother Temple of the sub-continent, the second time with the intention of living there indefinitely. However, after six months she had to return to the United States. She also went to Canada where Firishtih and her family lived. She did not like it there either, especially the cold winter weather in Saskatoon. She visited the Holy Land three times and each time stayed for a month. She attended the Second World Congress in New York in 1992 and saw many of her children and grandchildren there. Before she passed away, she moved from place to place, crossed continents and oceans and lived in several countries.

Each time she made a trip she felt better for several months then became restless again. Finally she decided to return to her hometown in Iran where she could talk with people in her mother tongue and had no problem moving around. Thus 19 years after her departure from Iran, she returned to the country full of hope and anticipation that she would be able to sell the property she had inherited from her father many years earlier. My sister Nayyirih went with her, to help her settle down. At her advanced age living on her own was out of the question. She needed to be with a Bahá'í family who would care for her. Such a family was found and arrangements were made for them to be amply compensated for their service. My brothers made the finances available, even a house was acquired for mother and the care-giving family to live in. Thus mother lived in her home country but away from all her children.

## The Ultimate Sacrifice

The decision to return to Iran seemed unwise but mother was determined to visit her home country before her death. In spite of her advanced age – she was 94 years old – she seemed fit. What bothered her the most were her knees for which she took Advil regularly to relieve the pain. Other than that she had no major complaints. She knew the risks associated with her going to Iran and was aware that her children, except for one, would be unable to visit her there. But mother had an inner urge to see the land of her birth. The thought of living in Shíráz again, seeing familiar faces, speaking the language and breathing the fragrant air of her hometown overshadowed all other considerations. Besides, she thought she could visit Iran for some time, sell the property she had inherited from her father, then return to the United States where she was a permanent resident. However, mother's health began to deteriorate sometime after her return to Shíráz. The pain in her knee worsened. Her movements became more circumscribed. She needed help to move in and out of the house. The Bahá'í family with whom mother lived did what they could to attend to her needs but mother wanted so badly one of her children to be by her side. Her health worsened gradually as the pangs of separation from her children sharpened. Her children could not visit her in Iran because of their active Bahá'í lives abroad. They had left the country to pioneer and all their lives were involved with Bahá'í activities, which made them targets for persecution. Mother was well aware of this when she decided to resettle in Shíráz but she hoped that things would change rapidly, making it possible for her to see them again.

One of my sisters who accompanied mother to Iran paid her a visit every year but could not stay with her for long owing to her own family situation. Mother bemoaned her plight. She had reached the point of no return. Her condition made it impossible for her to undertake another long trip abroad. She felt trapped. How often she was heard to say, 'No one would believe that a mother with eight children would have none around at the very time when her needs were so pronounced!'

Alas, many factors worked together to make the last three years of mother's life so difficult. The only way she could express her feelings of nostalgia was through letters and phone calls. She made good use of these means until about two months before her death. As she was hard of hearing, she would come to the phone and explain her feelings, she would then give the receiver to her caregiver who would relay to her what we said. Mother was an excellent lip reader. She developed this expertise when her hearing began to deteriorate at the age of 80. Being expressive and a good communicator made it possible for her to pour her heart out in her letters and phone calls, so it was easy to know what she was going through and how loneliness had taken its toll. We were happy that at least we could write and make phone calls, keeping the lines of communication open.

Three weeks before she breathed the last breath, the pleasure she had coming to the phone stand, which must have been outside her room, was taken away. She suffered a stroke affecting the movements of the right side of her body. When that happened, no contact by telephone was possible and she was unable to write. I was then in the United States and wrote to her all the more often, knowing how much she needed to feel she was in contact. Then something happened that miraculously made a last contact between us possible. During those gloomy days my closest friend, Ḥabíbih Sabet, who lives in Canada, decided to make a trip to Iran to visit her family in Shíráz after many years living abroad. She informed me of her plans in a phone call. It was the best piece of news I could expect amidst the agonizing feelings I had for my mother's plight. I told her about mother and asked if she would go and see her with messages of abiding love from her children. She was happy to render this service. She left Canada on 10 March and reached Shíráz in time to visit mother in the last days of her life. Ḥabíbih was the only connection I had with my beloved mother during those woeful days. I am grateful to her beyond what words can convey, for what she did meant to me more than the world itself. When she entered mother's room, the first thing she noticed was the spark in her eyes. Although her body was melting away like a candle and she was almost at the verge of collapse, Ḥabíbih emphasized that her eyes retained their brilliance. When Ḥabíbih told mother that she was there on my behalf, mother asked her with a movement of her hand to sit on the bed by her side. She then held Ḥabíbih's hands in hers, put them on her eyes, kept them there for a while and kissed her forehead. Without the power of speech, she could not communicate what she felt. However, her gestures were so genuine, so profound, so pure that words were redundant. Two days later her precious and long-suffering spirit winged its flight to the world beyond. She passed away on 16 March 2001. May she rest in peace, be immersed in the ocean of God's mercy, enjoy the heavenly blessings promised to sacrificial parents who offer their all, as did my parents, to raise their children in the bosom of Bahá'u'lláh's love then let them scatter throughout the world to serve His glorious Cause!

The friends in Iran conveyed to the Bahá'í World Centre the news of mother's passing. Upon receiving the news the Universal House of Justice instructed its secretariat to send through an intermediary a letter in Persian dated 26 March 2001. Here is the English translation of that letter:

> The news of the passing in Shíráz of the beloved handmaid of God, Khánum Ṭúbá Rouhani, saddened the supreme Body. Kindly assure her survivors through the friends in Iran that the Universal House of Justice will offer supplications in the Holy Shrines for the progress of her enlightened soul. Undoubtedly the undertakings of her children in the fields of service and their servitude to the Abhá Beauty will be the cause of her rejoicing in the Abhá Kingdom.

During the three weeks between mother's stroke and her death, we did everything we could to find a way to enable at least one of us to visit Iran and be with her. My youngest sister, Firishtih, started making preparations in earnest, notwithstanding the hazards awaiting her. She had originally pioneered to Nigeria but had to emigrate to Canada with her family to obtain valid passports enabling them to return to Africa as pioneers. For her return to Iran she needed a valid Persian passport. She went to the Iranian consulate in Johannesburg, explained the situation and appealed to them to facilitate her visit to Iran. She told the person in charge that she had not seen her elderly mother for several years, that her mother was living the last days of her life and that they both longed to see one another one more time. The man in the consulate showed sympathy for her plight and was kind enough to promise her that a Persian passport would be issued. However, he said, the place of residence to be noted in the new passport would be Iran. Although Firishtih had lived outside Iran for more than 25 years, her foreign residence had never been acknowledged or recorded accurately by the Iranian authorities. Her place of residence needed to be stated factually in the passport to enable her to leave Iran without problem. Persian passport holders who are not foreign residents cannot leave Iran without an exit visa. Acquiring an exit visa was most difficult for Bahá'ís, especially if the Bahá'í in question was as active in Iran and abroad as Firishtih was. In effect, she could go to Iran but there was no guarantee that she could leave the country again. The authorities in Iran could hold her in the country indefinitely, they could also detain and try her for being an active Bahá'í. Any number of things could have happened had she gone without sorting out the question of her foreign residency. As Firishtih was frequenting the premises of the Iranian consulate in Johannesburg, mother's vitality was fast diminishing. She spent her waking hours sitting in her bed gazing at the door of her room hoping that Firishtih or another one of her children would walk in. Firishtih's efforts to convince the relevant authority to give her the passport she needed for a short trip to her home country were unsuccessful. As she was considering the option of returning to Iran without sorting out the question of her foreign residency, mother passed away deprived of seeing her youngest child once more on this earthly plane, the child she had raised with tender love and care after all her other children had left home and to whom she was most attached.

Another sibling also tried to reach mother during the last days of her life. Nayyirih had accompanied mother to Iran three years earlier, had stayed with her for a while and arranged for her accommodation in Shíráz. She had also visited her twice. But now that mother needed her the most, for reasons beyond her control, she could not reach her in time to render meaningful assistance. When she successfully dealt with the obstacles in her way, she could not book a seat on a plane. In that particular year, pre-Naw-Rúz celebrations coincided with Ramaḍán, the Islamic month of the fast, and the Feast of Sacrifice. As a result, planes going to Iran from abroad were fully booked well in advance. Nayyirih finally managed to secure a seat but arrived in Shíráz several hours late. She arrived in the afternoon of 16 March 2001; mother had passed away that morning at 9:00. Mother's plight during the last years of her life reminds me of the story of Job. The suffering he endured as a consequence of his love for God visited mother in a different form. His suffering was so horrendous that he complained. He was then restored to health and regained what he had lost. Mother endured patiently right to the end. Her radiant soul winged its flight to the world beyond in a state of absolute detachment to shed splendour upon the path of the lonely and deprived.

Nayyirih arrived in Shíráz in time for mother's funeral. She and her eldest daughter were the only ones among mother's several children and many grandchildren who saw her off to her permanent resting place.

The loving and faithful friends of Shíráz, among whom mother had lived for so long, gave her a befitting funeral. With their flowers, prayers and tears they said goodbye to mother on behalf of the rest of us who longed but could not be there. Top of the list of people who spent considerable time with mother during the last weeks of her life are uncle 'Ali Akbar and his wife 'Ishrat Khánum. They and the friends looking after the affairs of the community in Shíráz, as well as numerous other relatives and friends, made mother's last days as happy as it could be under the circumstances. They did for mother what her children could not do owing to circumstances beyond their control.

'Ishrat Khánum told me on the phone that an angel was holding my mother's hand when her precious spirit was released from the cage of this world. That angel was Mr Qudratu'lláh Rouhani (no relation). That piece of information comforted my bereaved heart more than words can describe. I do not know Mr Qudratu'lláh Rouhani and may not have the pleasure of getting to know him in the future but want him to know how grateful my siblings and I are for the angelic deed he performed on our behalf.

## Reflections

Father and mother were two very different individuals yet similar in some respects. Their traditional backgrounds, the era and the place in which they were raised, the difference in age and the disparity in their educational achievements did not conduce to an equal partnership. Nonetheless, they were each other's complement. With their marriage they formed a stronghold which withstood numerous tempests. Both made superhuman efforts to raise their offspring in the bosom of the Bahá'í Faith. Their common goal was to get the children to the point of being self-sufficient then send them off to serve the Faith as best as they could.

The dynamics working in my parents' lives, especially the way they died, have occupied my thoughts since the day my mother died. Father always enjoyed an enviable state of resignation and detachment that seemed inborn. To him, whatever happened in life, if one had done one's best within one's circumstances, was for the best and represented God's will. He always did his best and was content with the outcome. Many were the times in his eventful life that he faced catastrophic storms capable of blowing him away completely but which he miraculously survived, albeit at very high financial cost.

In mother spirituality and practicality lived side by side. Struggling to make things happen the way that she wanted was a part of her personality. She could be resigned and detached but only after she had tried and failed to make something work differently. Even then she would have a hard time giving up. She had a good mind, which remained sharp to the end. She used it to get what she thought was best. Lack of proper education, I firmly believe, prevented her from attaining her preordained measure, as was the case with many talented women of her age. Father, on the other hand, enjoyed a trained mind, which was put into excellent use professionally and for carrying out Bahá'í activities until it started fading when he was in his late eighties.

Father enjoyed certain advantages over mother. He was a man in a society that accorded the masculine half of humanity extraordinary rights, opportunities and privileges. He was well-educated, something the society acknowledged and respected. He was the breadwinner. Providing for the family accorded him and men of his generation the privilege of being considered the family's head. That was the way society defined 'headship'. He was about a decade older than mother, which was the norm for marriages among people of my parents' age. The disparity in age worked to the men's advantage, for older people traditionally commanded and received more respect. This applied within the family as well.

When it came to Bahá'í activities, especially pioneering, father prevailed. Mother deferred to father not only because it was the traditionally accepted thing to do but also because she truly believed that he knew best. However, nothing seemed to come to mother effortlessly. For instance, father could not be happier than seeing his children pioneer to different parts of the world. He firmly believed that was what 'Abdu'l-Bahá wanted for them. Mother had no argument with that but every time one of the children left home, she struggled with pangs of separation, overcome with motherly emotions. At times the struggle seemed overwhelming but she invariably emerged unscathed.

As the end of father's earthly life drew near, he was in a coma and rarely knew what was going on around him. Though my parents lived in Poona, their children living abroad visited them from time to time. When father was hospitalized, mother was by his side all day long. The children also took turns visiting them. During the last days of his life my sister Nayyirih was with my parents and lent them a helping hand. When he died most of the children attended his funeral.

In contrast, mother was alert to the end of her life. Although physically frail, she knew what was going on around her. Bereft of her spouse who had died nearly two decades earlier, she had high hopes of seeing at least one of her children by her side before leaving this world of dust. But it did not happen. That last attachment, my daughter says, her grandmother overcame just before her death. Sovaida believes that mother left this world and whatever pertains to it completely detached and that included the attachment of seeing her children one more time in her earthly life. She let go of the only worldly attachment onto which she had tenaciously held until almost the end. When she achieved that state of detachment, the cage of her body broke open and the bird of her spirit soared to the summit of ultimate sacrifice.

The mother and grandmother who had given so much of herself to help her children and grandchildren to attain their highest aspirations in every field of endeavour had none of them to hold her hand in the end. Wishing to have at least one of her eight children with her before she died would not, under normal circumstances, have been too much to ask but, unfortunately, in her case it was. I recall a time when I asked whether she wanted me to leave my services at the Bahá'í World Centre and go to live with her. Her response was: 'You mean leaving God's work and doing mine! How can I in good conscience consent to that?' What a splendid mother she was!

May her radiant soul and that of my father be immersed in the ocean of God's mercy and forgiveness, may the heavenly recompense for their sacrificial efforts be beyond measure!

## The Fulfilment of a Lifelong Dream: The Story of My Pioneering

If I, like Abraham, through flames must go,
Or yet like John a bloodstained road must run;
If, Joseph-like, Thou'd cast me in a well,
Or shut me up within a prison cell –
Or make me e'en as poor as Mary's Son –
I will not go from Thee,
But ever stand
My soul and body bowed to Thy command.[109]

I was raised in a family consumed with the love of Bahá'u'lláh. My ancestors on my father's side became Bábís when Jináb-i Vaḥíd taught the Bábí Faith in Nayríz. They fought with him in the fort of Kh̲ájih, later in the Battle of the Mountain. Some were killed and became martyrs. Some were sent to Sh̲íráz as captives. Those who survived the ordeals became Bahá'ís and were persecuted for their belief in the new Faith. On many occasions my parents lost their worldly belongings and had to start all over again. Yet suffering persecution for adhering to the principles of the Bahá'í Faith not only failed to daunt us, it actually gave us the courage to stand out and glory in being the lovers of humankind. To love human beings of all backgrounds required scattering throughout the globe and sharing with them the tenets of a new world order brought by Bahá'u'lláh.

When I was growing up as a child I often heard people in family circles and community meetings of all kinds talk about pioneering. By the time I was old enough to understand what it meant to yearn for something, I wanted with my whole being to go pioneering. The fire of yearning was so intense that no sacrifice necessary for its realization seemed too great. I assessed the prospects for my pioneering abroad regularly after I came of age. Unfortunately they looked very bleak until suddenly a whirlwind of events changed everything.

I had always wanted to study philosophy or law. I was naturally drawn to these fields of study but the means to achieve them were not in place. The then fledgling University of Shíráz had no programme leading to a degree in either discipline. I graduated from high school in the academic year 1957–8. Going to Ṭihrán to study at the university was the only solution but that was out of the question for two important reasons: 1) Since many Bahá'ís had congregated in Ṭihrán, Shoghi Effendi strongly discouraged the Bahá'ís from sending their children for further studies there. My parents would not go against the wishes of the Guardian of the Faith. 2) The financial resources of the family would have been stretched to the limit had I gone there to study. I had two younger siblings still in school, who were completely dependent on father's salary for their education. My going to Ṭihrán would have placed a real strain on the family's budget. So I did the only thing I could under the circumstances, which was to enter the University of Shíráz and study Persian literary works. My only consolation was that in doing this I was enhancing my knowledge of the Persian and Arabic languages – the study of Arabic grammar and literature was a part of the curriculum – enabling me to understand the writings better. Moreover, Islamic philosophy ranked high on the list of compulsory courses that I had to take to fulfil the requirements for a bachelor's degree in Persian literature. I diligently studied at the university, knowing that what I was studying was unlikely to help me find a job when I went pioneering. I finished the first two years of a three-year degree course with high honours. I sat and passed exams for three-quarters of the total credits required for graduation. I was in the third year of my studies when the prospect of pioneering abroad pulled me away from my beloved family, hometown, studies, friends and everything that I held dear.

My longing to pioneer which I had held ever since I was ten years old was put to the test when doors miraculously opened for me to leave Iran and settle in East Africa, then ruled by the British. Going through the open door had one condition attached to it: marrying someone who had lived in the area since 1954, someone I did not know at all. This condition I would have probably dismissed as totally unreasonable had I not been so enthralled by the prospect of fulfilling a lifelong dream.

For an unknown and unexplainable reason, I wished to marry someone I did not know. This was something I openly talked about with my friends. They were concerned that no one would consent to marry me without knowing who I was and how I looked. If such a person did not exist, I would stay unmarried, was my response. However, I did not have to wait long for the opportunity to come my way.

In the summer of 1960 I was informed by a visitor to Shíráz that Manúchihr Ma'ání, a pioneer living in Seychelles and Kenya since 1954, did not want to return to Iran but wished to get married if the right candidate were found and consented to marry him. The visitor was Fírúz Ma'ání, Manúchihr's brother. Fírúz mentioned this after he learned of my longing to go pioneering, which overshadowed all other considerations in my life at that time. Fírúz and his wife, Faraḥ Khánum, had come to Shíráz from their pioneer post that summer to visit the House of the Báb. While in Shíráz they came to see my family, whom Fírúz remembered from 1943–4 when the two families had pioneered to Maḥmúdábád in Mázandarán. At that time I was about four years old and Manúchihr about 16. As he was in high school and Maḥmúdábád lacked facilities for higher education, he was left in Ámul to finish school. Thus he was the only member of his family who did not get to know mine.

During his visit to Shíráz, Fírúz praised Manúchihr's pioneering services and teaching successes in Africa. During that visit I learned that Manúchihr was one of eight brothers in his family – all of them Bahá'ís in good standing and well-educated – that he was an ardent lover of Bahá'u'lláh, that he had given up everything in life in order to become a pioneer in Shoghi Effendi's World Spiritual Crusade, that he had behind him years of sacrificial service and that he was the embodiment of Bahá'í virtues. What Fírúz had to say about his brother evoked our praise and admiration for his pioneering services but did not seem at the time to have any relevance to my life.

After that visit, unbeknown to me and my family, Fírúz wrote to Manúchihr describing his visit and saying that since I had an intense yearning to go pioneering, if he were to make a marriage proposal, I would most probably respond positively. Manúchihr was tempted but proceeded with caution. He asked that his father, Kalímu'lláh Ma'ání, and brother, Fayḍu'lláh, who lived in Ṭihrán, make a trip to Shíráz, meet with me and submit a report. If they confirmed Fírúz's assessment, he would take it from there. They came and did as asked. Before departure, they discussed with my parents the subject of my marriage to Manúchihr. They wanted to be sure that my parents would not have any objection to their daughter marrying a person they knew only in absentia. I was then attending a summer school in a suburb of Shíráz, unaware of what was going on. My parents' love for Bahá'u'lláh's Cause had been repeatedly tested and they invariably proved that they put the Faith before all other considerations. They did not object to my marrying, pending, of course, my consent. Father's only concern was the continuation of my education after marriage. Manúchihr's father had promised that it would pose no problem. Mother's apprehension revolved most of all around the geography of the place and its distance. Africa was too far away and she did not know when she would see her daughter again, that is, if I said yes to the proposal. None of her children had pioneered to such a distant place. Moreover, no family member could be present at my wedding. The anomalies of the situation were too many, which made her feel rather uncomfortable. When I was informed at the summer school of the prospect of combining marriage and pioneering, I declared my acceptance but refused to leave the summer school before it was over.

I must emphasize here that ours was not an 'arranged' marriage in the way it is traditionally defined. My parents knew and appreciated the fact that without my consent and that of Manúchihr the marriage could not take place, regardless of how eager and enthusiastic they and other family members were. The arrangement was between Manúchihr and myself and involved making a commitment to get married prior to seeing one another. Is this the ideal or right thing to do? I don't think it is, under normal circumstances. But in our case it proved right. In fact, it was much more ideal than many marriages based on romance which turn sour and fall apart because of the two parties' lack of commitment and high expectations that cannot be met.

Another point worth mentioning here is that although my family, my friends and members of the community respected me for who I was and the way I did things, I don't believe they fully understood my personality. The one who understood me better than anyone was father. Let me explain. As soon as the news of my 'engagement' broke, there were whispers. How could a woman of her age and prospects, at the threshold of graduating from university, agree to leave everything behind and hasten towards an unknown future and destiny, some people asked. The idle talk bothered my mother and others but I was unperturbed, as was my father. Those who liked to speculate about my reason for taking such a drastic step were unaware that I was bored with the routine and 'normal' way everyone behaved. I craved for things out of the ordinary. I wanted to serve the Faith in places few had dared to tread. I wanted to see how people of other races and cultures lived. I had lived 20 years of my life in Iran. The time had come for me to go and explore other parts of the world. If I could obtain what my heart desired in addition to getting married to someone who had proved his love for Bahá'u'lláh, it was more than what I had bargained and hoped for. When mother saw how confident I was in pursuing a course of action that sounded 'crazy', she gave her consent.

To obtain a passport, I needed a letter of invitation from someone living abroad. Manúchihr's brother Daryúsh, who lived in Austria, provided the letter. It took several months for the formalities to be completed. In the meantime, the summer was over. I registered as a final year student in the Faculty of Letters, finishing the remaining credits towards a bachelor's degree. Five months before graduation I received approval for the passport to be issued. I was informed that I needed to go to Ṭihrán to attend to the formalities, such as receiving inoculations for travelling to Africa and making travel arrangements. Thus in early December 1960 I left Shíráz for an unknown destiny towards which a mysterious force had for some time beckoned me. My parents accompanied me on the journey from Shíráz to Ṭihrán, where we stayed with my parents-in-law to be until I left for Nairobi via Baghdád, Beirut, Cairo and Khartoum on 26 December 1960. My parents had no hope of seeing me again. As I was going toward the departure gate at the airport, father called my name. When I turned, he said, 'I just wanted to see your face once again. May God be with you every step of the way!'

The trip was long, arduous and not hazard free. I had never travelled alone to any place. There were times during the trip when I was not sure I would make it to my destination. Although I had studied English in school and attended a few courses offered by the Iran–American Society, my spoken English was very poor. Worse than that was my understanding when people with different accents spoke it. I had four stops on the way and twice I had to change planes. I did not understand a word of the announcements made regarding planes taking off and landing. Fortunately, airports were not as huge as they are today and there were not many departure gates. To overcome the anxiety of missing my plane, I presented myself at any departure gate that I saw passengers going through to board an aircraft. After I did this several times in Cairo, one officer got fed up with me, held me by the hand, took me to a seat in the departure lounge, made me sit and angrily said something which I did not understand. I was happy when he went off duty. It gave me the opportunity to repeat my appearances at the departure gate. Fortunately I was allowed to board a plane not long after the rude officer disappeared from the scene.

The next stop was Khartoum. The plane arrived in the evening. I had to spend a night there and catch an early plane for Nairobi the next morning. I had a voucher to stay at an airport hotel but could not do so because I had not been inoculated against yellow fever, an absolute requirement for those who travelled to that part of the world. I could not get it in Ṭihrán, for the Ministry of Health did not have it. Few Iranians travelled to Africa south of the Sahara in those days. Most of those who did were probably Bahá'ís going pioneering. Thus the demand for the inoculation was very low. I had no choice but to leave Iran without it. As a result I spent my first night in sub-Saharan Africa pacing up and down the airport ground. It may have been for a good reason. Had I gone to a hotel, I am not sure I would have been able to sleep for fear that I might miss my plane. Fortunately for me, while I was pacing the airport in Khartoum, a kind stewardess on duty that night saw my plight, befriended me and made my stay in Khartoum less daunting than it might have been. After 45 years I still remember her kindly face. Her name was Stella.

The last leg of my trip from Khartoum to Nairobi was by BOAC at 5:00 a.m. on 27 December 1960. The plane was delayed for several hours. Finally, at 9:00 a.m. it took off. Several hours later I landed in the city I knew nothing about but had made a conscious decision to make my home. Manúchihr and a few Bahá'í pioneers were at the airport to welcome me. There I saw for the first time what my life partner-to-be looked like in the flesh.

The first thing I learned upon arrival in Nairobi was that my fiancé could not book me a hotel room because he did not know the colour of my skin! It sounded weird to me and I thought it was a joke. Unfortunately, the statement was as factual as a factual statement can be. It was during the colonial times when I set foot in Kenya, a British colony. Segregation of the races was the order of the day. Although Iranians were classified as 'honorary whites' by the immigration authorities, hotels reserved for the 'whites' made reservations on the basis of the colour of the guest's skin. The rules governing racial segregation were rigid and remained in place until Kenya gained independence in 1963. I arrived in Kenya more than two years before its independence. It was in the midst of the Mau Mau movement, which brought about the end of colonialism, the establishment of self-rule and independence for Kenya.

No hotel booking meant that I had to stay with one of the pioneer families for a few days until Manúchihr and I got married. I stayed at the home of Mr 'Aynu'd-Dín and Mrs Ṭáhirih 'Alá'i, an elderly and kind Bahá'í couple. Our marriage took place on 31 December 1960 in the presence of the members of the Local Spiritual Assembly of that city and several Bahá'í and non-Bahá'í friends. I believe ours was the first Bahá'í marriage to take place in Nairobi.

## Manúchihr's Pioneering Venture

It would be unfair to continue this account without explaining who Manúchihr was and the circumstances leading him to that part of the world.

Manúchihr was the fourth of the eight sons of Mr Kalímu'lláh and Humáyún Khánum Ma'ání. Although he was born in 'Ishqábád where his parents lived for some time, his birth certificate specified Mashhad, where it was issued, as his birthplace. He was born in September 1927 and grew up in Ṭihrán. After finishing high school he entered university and studied law. He was also an active member of the Youth Committee in Ṭihrán. His graduation from law school coincided with the beginning of the foreign pioneering campaign set in motion by the beloved Guardian in 1951. When Shoghi Effendi announced the Ten Year Plan and called for volunteers to arise and open the territories where the light of the Faith had not yet penetrated, Manúchihr contacted the Foreign Pioneering Committee of the National Spiritual Assembly of Iran and declared his readiness to open one of the virgin territories of the Plan. He set his heart on Chagos Archipelago, presently called Diego Garcia, one of the most difficult goals of the Plan, and started in earnest making preparations for the journey. The place was so obscure that when he applied for a visa at the British consulate in Ṭihrán, those dealing with his application did not know exactly where Chagos was. After several months' waiting, he received a visa for the Seychelles Islands in the heart of the

Indian Ocean. To the objections he raised that his application was for a visa for the Chagos Archipelago, he was told that only in Seychelles could he apply for a visa for Chagos. With the visa in hand, he left Ṭihrán for <u>Kh</u>urram<u>sh</u>ahr, the point of embarkation for a sea voyage that took him to Bombay (now Mumbai) in India and Mombasa in Kenya, before reaching Seychelles, termed by Shoghi Effendi in his message of April 1954 to the Bahá'ís of the world a 'penal colony'.[110] Manú<u>ch</u>ihr's sea voyage, which started at Riḍván 1954, took two months to complete. He arrived in Mahe, the principal island of Seychelles, in June that year.

When Manú<u>ch</u>ihr arrived in Mahe, the Knight of Bahá'u'lláh for that country, Mr Kámil 'Abbás from Iraq, who had reached there a few months earlier, had left and Mr 'Abdu'r-Raḥmán Zarqání from India, a second Knight for that country, had just arrived.

Upon his arrival in Seychelles, Manú<u>ch</u>ihr investigated the prospects of going to Chagos and found out that the Archipelago was privately owned by a British firm which had the exclusive right to cultivate coconut and export it abroad. He also discovered that the only possible way for him to get a visa for Chagos was to get a job on the coconut plantation. So he began the lengthy process of applying for a job as the prerequisite for procuring a visa. Shoghi Effendi mentions the Chagos Archipelago in his message to the Bahá'í world of 20 March 1955 as one of the eight islands 'as yet unopened by the heroic band battling for the Faith of Bahá'u'lláh' and one of the four 'either privately owned or controlled by private companies'.[111]

Manú<u>ch</u>ihr was determined to fulfil his pledge. He did all in his power to get to Chagos. Shoghi Effendi was apprised of the efforts he made to open Chagos and his encouraging responses through his secretary strengthened Manú<u>ch</u>ihr's resolve to pursue the matter until the goal was won. He even applied to work as a labourer on the coconut plantation. A letter written on behalf of Shoghi Effendi by his secretary to Mr Ma'ání Entessari, dated 16 July 1954, reads in part:[112]

> ... The Guardian greatly values and appreciates your services and devotion.

> He assures you of his prayers in your behalf; that every obstacle may be removed from your path, and ultimately you will win the victory, both in the Seychelles, and in the Chagos Archipelago.
>
> He is aware of the difficulties which you experience, and the deprivations you undergo; but these are the marks of your strength, and the development of your character, and the quickening of your spirit.

In another letter written by Shoghi Effendi's secretary, dated 4 September 1954, we read:

> We will continue to pray that the doors may be opened for Mr Ma'ani to enter Chagos Archipelago.

By late September Mr Raḥmán had also entered the race for opening the Chagos Archipelago, as evidenced by the letter written by the Guardian's secretary dated 20 September 1954:

> The Guardian is of course anxious that Chagos Archipelago be settled, and therefore feels that you and Mr Ma'ani should continue your efforts to reach there, particularly Mr Ma'ani.

Manúchihr's efforts to enter Chagos proved futile. He was refused entry ostensibly because there was no vacancy. The real reason was apparently the authorities' suspicion of his intentions. They could not understand why a lawyer educated in Iran would want to work as a labourer on a coconut plantation in Chagos. No amount of sincere explanation convinced them of his true intention. Manúchihr's qualifications thus worked against him attaining his heart's desire.

When it became evident that it was absolutely impossible for Manúchihr to go to Chagos, he sought the advice of the beloved Guardian, who had originally confirmed his plans to open that group of islands. The telegram sent to Mr Ioas in Haifa on 22 January 1955 reads in part: 'Ma'ani's latest reply no vacancy employment Chagos presently solicits instructions prayers.' The

Guardian's cable response of 24 January 1955 reads: 'Assure prayers advise Maʻani consult NSA. Shoghi'

As instructed by Shoghi Effendi, Manú<u>ch</u>ihr consulted the National Spiritual Assembly of Iran and was advised to remain in Seychelles. Therefore he continued to stay at his pioneer post and struggled to earn a living. Those who lived during the colonial period and tried to find employment in a British colony know that Persian qualifications meant nothing. During the hard times ahead, Manú<u>ch</u>ihr's brother Daryú<u>sh</u>, who was then pioneering in the Gulf, helped him financially. In the meantime, Manú<u>ch</u>ihr spent his days crossing the island on foot to spread the fragrances of Bahá'u'lláh's teachings. He also studied bookkeeping by correspondence.

Finally he found a job in a shop as a salesman and accountant. His income was slim and barely provided for a modest living but he was happy and grateful to have become self-supporting.

As for Chagos, by April 1956 it was still unopened, as evidenced by the beloved Guardian's message of that date:

> Of the hundred and thirty-one territories listed in the Ten-Year Plan, only Spitsbergen, Nicobar Islands and the Chagos Archipelago, as well as eleven territories, which are either incorporated in the Soviet Union or are included within its orbit, remain to be opened by the band of intrepid warriors intent upon enlarging the limits, and spreading far and wide the fame, of the Faith of Bahá'u'lláh.[113]

The one who finally succeeded in entering the Chagos Archipelago as a labourer working on the coconut plantation was Mr Pouva Murday, a newly enrolled Bahá'í from Mauritius. When Manú<u>ch</u>ihr learned of Mr Murday's achievement, he rejoiced and wrote in his diary: 'He is the newly born babe who has traversed overnight the path that others tread in a hundred years.'

The intensive teaching activities undertaken by the early pioneers to Seychelles yielded wonderful results. The first Local Spiritual Assembly of the island was formed at Riḍván 1955 and, together with 23 other places which held 'annual elections of the second year, second decade, of the second Bahá'í century', was listed among the achievements reported in the Guardian's cablegram of 30 April 1955.[114]

While waiting for his visa to Chagos, Manúchihr took the light of Bahá'u'lláh's Cause to Praslin, the second largest island in Seychelles. For a brief account of the opening of Praslin see appendix 3. His arrival and teaching efforts in the island resulted in one of the inhabitants embracing the Faith. When the report of the opening of Praslin reached Shoghi Effendi, his secretary wrote on 10 March 1956:

> He was greatly delighted to learn of the establishment of the Faith in the island of Praslin, which is a supplementary victory of the Ten Year Crusade.
>
> The Guardian feels that you and the other pioneers of Mahe have done outstanding work, which is reaping its fruit at an early date. He feels sure the Master is carefully watching over each and every one of you, and your spiritual reward will be very great.

This achievement was announced by the Guardian to the Bahá'í world in his cablegram of April 1956, which refers to:

> . . . the initiation of auxiliary plans for the promotion of the Faith in the Seychelles Islands and in the Sudan; and of the arrival of a pioneer in Praslin Island forming a part of the Seychelles group.[115]

The establishment of the Faith on Praslin Island was an additional achievement to the goals of the Ten Year Plan. This was confirmed in the Guardian's message of April 1957:

> The number of islands now within the pale of the Faith, situated in the Atlantic, the Pacific, and the Indian Oceans as well as in the Mediterranean and the North Sea, is now over a hundred, seventy-four of which have been opened since the inauguration of the World Spiritual Crusade, including five islands, situated in

The picture of Manúchihr was taken in Nairobi less than two years before his passing

First Bahá'í group formed in Seychelles, 4 February 1955. *Left to right, seated*: Samuel Rioux, Marshall Delcy; *standing*: Manúchihr, Munir Vakil, 'Abdu'r Raḥmán Zarqání

The Greatest Name was made with grass on the shore of the Indian Ocean at Beau Vallon, Seychelles, 10 October 1954

Bahá'í group, Seychelles, 29 March 1955. Manú<u>ch</u>ihr is seated at the far left.

A group of the Seychelles Bahá'ís, 4 November 1956. Manúchihr is standing second from the left.

Local Spiritual Assembly of Seychelles, 30 December 1957. Manúchihr is standing at the far right.

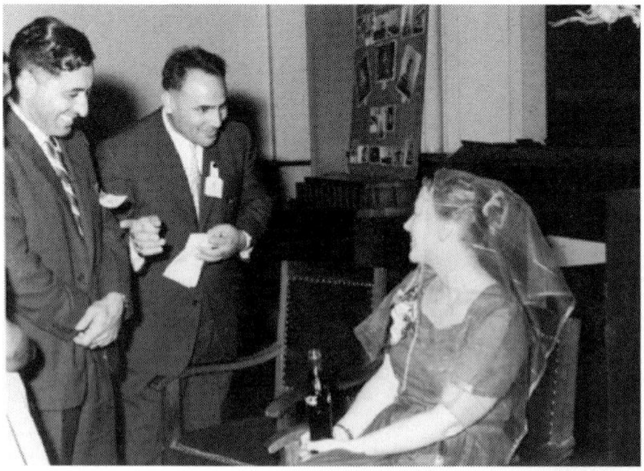

Hand of the Cause Dr Raḥmatu'lláh Muhájir introduces Manúchihr to Hand of the Cause Amatu'l Bahá Rúḥíyyih Khánum during a break in the programme.

Manúchihr and I meet Amatu'l Bahá Rúḥíyyih Khánum. Manúchihr is telling her about Seychelles. Dr Muhájir is in the background.

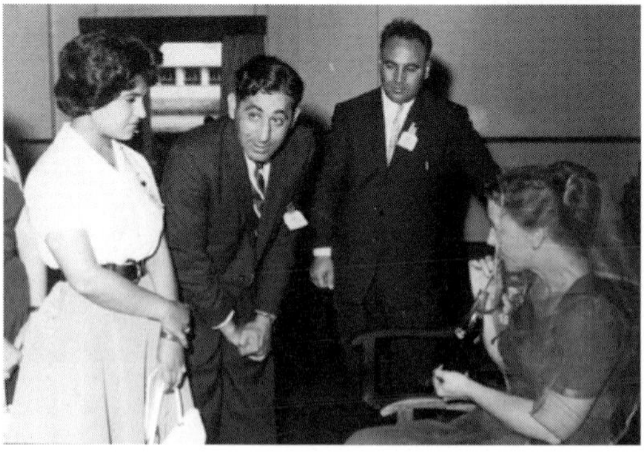

Manúchihr responds to Khánum's questions regarding Seychelles. I am standing on his left and Dr Muhájir on his right.

At the dedication of the Bahá'í Temple, Kampala, Uganda, January 1961

Sovaida and me, taken about 1965

A group of the Nairobi Bahá'ís in the presence of Hands of the Cause of God Amatu'l Bahá Rúḥíyyih Khánum and William Sears, August 1967. Marguerite Sears is seated on the extreme left and Elsie Austin on the extreme right.

Our pilgrimage group, early April 1971.
Sovaida is seated third from the right; I am sitting to her left.

Mother with five of her daughters. *Left to right, seated*: Nayyirih, mother, Rawḥanieh. *Standing*: Firishtih, Mahín, Baharieh. The photo was taken about 1998 in Gaithersburg, Maryland.

Mother and Father in their later years

Ken, Sovaida and Giselle, for whom this book is written, in the gardens at Bahjí, April 2006

the Atlantic and Indian Oceans and not listed as objectives of the Ten-Year Plan.[116]

Manúchihr's efforts in spreading the redeeming message of Bahá'u'lláh among the people of Seychelles were tireless and constant. On 18 February 1957, Mr Harold Bibi, an inhabitant of La Digue, declared his belief in Bahá'u'lláh. With his declaration of faith, the third largest island of the Seychelles, situated about 25 nautical miles to the northeast of Mahe, was opened to His Cause.[117] The receptivity of the inhabitants of those islands to Bahá'u'lláh's message, as attested by the meticulous and detailed diary Manúchihr kept, urged him on to continue living sacrificially and devoting the prime of his life to the task at hand. In the process, not only did his youthful years roll away but with them also went his health, as will be seen later in this account. His labours of love and the deprivations that he and other early pioneers suffered during the initial years of the Ten Year Spiritual Crusade were tenderly acknowledged and lovingly referred to in the beloved Guardian's message of April 1956:

> A spirit of abnegation and self-sacrifice, so rare that only the spirit of the Dawn-breakers of a former age can be said to have surpassed it, has consistently animated, singly as well as collectively, its participants in every clime, of all classes, of either sex, and of every age . . . Already a few heroic souls have either quaffed the cup of martyrdom, or laid down their lives, or been subjected to divers ordeals while combatting for its Cause . . . The heights its champions must scale are indeed formidable. The pitfalls that bestrew their path are still numerous. The road leading to ultimate and total victory is tortuous, stony and narrow.[118]

The most grievous calamity afflicting the friends in general and Bahá'í pioneers in particular in the Formative Age of the Faith was the passing of Shoghi Effendi on 4 November 1957. Those who had arisen since the inception of the Ten Year Plan and were sustained by his constant encouragement and messages of love and support especially felt the effect of his absence. Manúchihr was one of them. The devastation he felt was indescribable. In the privacy of his lonely chamber he wept to soothe his bereaved heart and prayed for the consolation and protection of the young Bahá'í community of Seychelles. Soon after Shoghi Effendi's passing, the Custodians of the Faith, Hands of the Cause of God residing in the Holy Land, held the reign of the worldwide affairs of the Faith in their hands and ensured the successful completion of the Plan whose crowning achievement was the establishment of the Universal House of Justice at Riḍván 1963, coinciding with the end of the Ten Year Plan.

Manúchihr continued his pioneering services in Seychelles until about mid-1959.

One of the outstanding successes of the Bahá'í community of Seychelles during Manúchihr's pioneering years there was the incorporation of the Local Spiritual Assembly of Victoria. A committee had been appointed by the Assembly to accomplish the task. The members were Manúchihr, Mr Raḥmán and Mr Vakil. They worked assiduously with a lawyer over a lengthy period. Despite strong opposition from some corners, the incorporation of the Assembly was achieved in an extraordinary manner. Not only did it pass the parliament of Seychelles but it also received the royal assent of Queen Elizabeth II. Only two countries in the world have extended such recognition to the Faith, Seychelles being one of them.[119]

When the Faith in Seychelles was firmly established, Manúchihr, with the approval of the Regional Spiritual Assembly of Central and East Africa,[120] pioneered to Kenya. The change of pioneer post was to provide him with opportunities to continue his teaching and pioneering work in a more fertile country with a wider scope for service. Manúchihr's favourable response stemmed from his cherished hope to be able to serve the Faith where he was most needed. Manúchihr was a yearning lover who was ready to offer up his life for the love of his Best Beloved. He was a moth that whirled in constant adoration round the light of the object of his creation. No matter where he was and what he did, his main purpose in living was to serve with heart and soul the Bahá'í Faith, which meant everything to him. He was the embodiment of faithfulness and had a self-sacrificing nature, so that living a martyr's life was an inherent part of his own life.

As stated earlier, it was towards the end of 1960 that Manúchihr, so as not to return from the field of service to his native land and at the suggestion of members of his family, who were eager for him to get married, agreed to put his trust in Bahá'u'lláh and accept the testimony of his loved ones concerning the person who was willing to share with him the rest of his pioneering life. That person was the writer of this account. I was then 21 years old.

## Manúchihr's Illness and Death

Manúchihr's job required him to travel frequently. He was out of Nairobi several days every month. He had to travel very often by country buses in order to keep the expenses of the journey low for the company he worked for and almost invariably fell ill during or immediately after each journey. He had contracted malaria in Seychelles which recurred every time he returned from a trip around the country. Nevertheless he undertook the trips with radiance, carried out his duties conscientiously and with exemplary devotion. He spoke about the Faith with the people he met on the bus and taught the Faith to his business contacts.

The highlight of the first year of our marriage was meeting with Amatu'l-Bahá Rúḥíyyih Khánum during the dedication of the House of Worship in Kampala, Uganda.

The Hand of the Cause of God Dr Muhájir, who knew Manúchihr and his family, introduced us to her. Her words of praise for Manúchihr's past services in Seychelles and the hopes she expressed for our future undertakings on behalf of the Cause strengthened our resolve to rededicate ourselves to the high spiritual ideals of the Faith of Bahá'u'lláh and strive harder for their fulfilment.

After the Kampala conference Amatu'l-Bahá Rúḥíyyih Khánum visited Kenya. She stayed in Nairobi for several days and had meetings with the friends. There again we received her gracious and loving counsels for rendering effective service to the Cause. During that same trip, which was about a month after our marriage, she gave us a wedding gift, something useful, which would help us in our teaching efforts and would be pleasing to Shoghi Effendi, she said. She left a sum of money (one hundred shillings) to be used as initial payment to a local teacher to teach me Kiswahili, enabling me to teach the Faith in Kenya and beyond. We hired a teacher immediately. Her name was Charity Moses. She came to our home three times a week. The lessons continued until the first month of my pregnancy. To learn Kiswahili, I had to improve my English in order to communicate with my teacher. Thus Amatu'l-Bahá's gift enabled me to become conversant in both languages.

Life was not easy for me, especially with Manúchihr being away so frequently. He worked for a pharmaceutical company as a salesman travelling all over Kenya and parts of Tanganyika to promote products. Manúchihr returned from what turned out to be his last trip, in late January 1962, with a mild stomachache. That trip was to the Mount Kenya region. The pain grew steadily worse in the next several days. I was then in the last week of my pregnancy. He visited a doctor who prescribed some pills, which proved useless. In fact they worsened his condition. He was then referred to another doctor specializing in internal medicine. The new doctor hospitalized him. Manúchihr was kept under observation in the Parkland Hospital for three days while his pain got steadily worse. He was in the hospital just at the time when he was so eager to be home for the arrival of our first child. His doctor said that he needed to stay in the hospital for only two to three days for different tests. Manúchihr agreed to be hospitalized in the hope that he would be out in time to take me to the hospital for the delivery of our baby. Alas, that was not to be. On the third day of his hospitalization he was extremely weak. He was in pain and had a high temperature. After several days of excruciating pain and fever, he was sent for an x-ray. The x-ray centre was in downtown Nairobi. I went with him. The x-rays showed that he had pancreatitis. It was only then that the doctor decided to operate. However, it was too late. Before going to the operating room, Manúchihr received an injection, probably to sedate him. After that he went into a coma and remained unconscious until the early hours of the next morning. His doctor then admitted that he was unable to do anything to save Manúchihr's life. When all hope was lost, one of the friends sent a cable to the Bahá'í World Centre asking for prayers for his recovery. Immediately after the first cable, a second one was sent announcing that Manúchihr had passed away.

Manúchihr seemed to know that he was not going to make it through the illness. When he was beset by severe and intolerable pain, which changed his serene and cheerful face and made him restless, he turned to Bahá'u'lláh with absolute meekness, imploring Him with tearful eyes to end his life and spare him the agonizing pain. When the pain, which came at irregular intervals, subsided, he expressed longing for the arrival of our baby, due the same week. As he was being prepared for the operation, he said goodbye and emphatically exhorted me not to worry or grieve if he died, lest my sorrow and grief affect our child's happiness and well-being.

The first inkling I received about the gravity of Manúchihr's condition was when the specialist, who was keeping him under observation for so long, turned to me outside his hospital room and said rudely, 'What do you think you can achieve by hanging around here? Why don't you go home and take care of your own needs?' Granted that I was in the last week of pregnancy and likely to go into labour any time but, I thought, what right did he have to question me in such a rude manner and ask why I was there? After all, he was the overconfident doctor responsible for not doing anything to alleviate Manúchihr's pain in a timely manner. Was this his admission of failure? I could not determine. I had been terribly lonely in the hospital during the three days Manúchihr was under observation and was hanging on to the hope that he would get better in time to take me to the hospital. Instead of receiving words of kindness and support, I was being questioned for doing the only thing I could under the circumstances: standing by my husband's bed when no other family member or friend was there. His words, like a sharp sword, lacerated my heart and soul. I was so hurt that I could not utter a word and this is one of my peculiarities: When I am deeply hurt, I do not speak. So I stood there and stared at him. When he left, I reentered Manúchihr's room. He looked frightfully weak. I stood by his bed, feeling for the first time scared and uncertain about the unknown future that awaited me. Those who have pioneered to remote areas of the globe know that the most difficult aspect of pioneering, especially in those days, was the heart-wrenching loneliness one felt.

The haughty doctor ordered that anaesthesia be administered. He was probably trying to prove that he was doing everything he possibly could to save Manúchihr's life. But it was too late. Manúchihr was far too weak to undergo an operation. He remained unconscious under its effect through the afternoon and evening. When the word spread that Manúchihr was not going to make it, many friends, Bahá'í and non-Bahá'í alike, came to see him as he was lying in bed unconscious.

Manúchihr was never operated on owing to his critical condition. Some of the Bahá'í friends who had come to visit him that afternoon and found him so ill arranged for another specialist to examine him and express a second opinion. By the time the second specialist was located and brought to his bedside, it was 11:00 p.m. on Friday, 2 February. The second specialist confirmed that his illness was fatal, saying that it was too late for the operation to yield the hoped-for result. Manúchihr gained consciousness in the early hours of the following morning. He did not talk and looked extremely weak. I called his name. He responded graciously. I adjured him to rest peacefully. He answered affirmatively in a meek and submissive way. My heart was torn because it suddenly struck me like a thunderbolt that he was actually dying.

After half an hour he rolled to his side and blood poured from his mouth. This confirmed my terrifying realization. How could he die so young and at a time when I needed him the most? How could he leave me on my own in a strange country and at the mercy of so cruel a world? These were the questions I kept asking myself. After a while, when all was quiet around him and as I and a few friends at his bedside were silently praying, he suddenly and unasked uttered his name thus: Manúch Ma'ani.[121] We could not understand the purpose and significance of his saying his name at that time and in that manner. Those were the last words Manúchihr uttered during what appeared to be the last conscious moments of his earthly life. The hospital authorities kept him alive by putting him on some elementary type of life support until 11:00 p.m. on Saturday, 3 February. His precious soul, eager to join his Best Beloved, left the cage of his body at that time. The news of his passing was communicated to the Custodians of the Faith in the Holy Land. The cable read:

> HANDSFAITH, BOX 155, HAIFA
> HEARTBROKEN GRIEF SORROW ANNOUNCE PASSING ABHÁ KINGDOM DEVOTED PIONEER DEDICATED KNIGHT BAHÁ'U'LLÁH[122] MANOUTCHEHR MAANI ENTESSARI STOP HIS FIRST CHILD EXPECTED NEXT WEEK SUPPLICATE PRAYERS. YAZDI

In response, the following cables were received on 6 February 1962:

> YAZDI, CARE FIROOZ, NAIROBI
> DEEPLY REGRET SUDDEN PASSING DEVOTED STEADFAST KNIGHT BAHÁ'U'LLÁH MANOUTCHEHR MAANI SERVICES CRUSADE UNFORGETTABLE CONVEY LOVING SYMPATHY WIFE. HANDSFAITH

> BAHARIYYIH MAANI, CARE FIROOZ, NAIROBI, KENYA
> PROFOUND SYMPATHY SUDDEN PASSING MANOUTCHEHR DEVOTED SERVANT FAITH KNIGHT BAHÁ'U'LLÁH LOVING PRAYERS SHRINES YOUR HEALTH PROTECTION DIFFICULT PERIOD. HANDSFAITH

Amatu'l-Bahá Rúḥíyyih Khánum sent the following cable on 8 February:

WHATEVER GOD DECREES WE ACCEPT BE BRAVE PRAYERS LOVE WITH YOU GREAT ORDEAL. RUHIYYIH

Manúchihr was buried on 5 February 1962 at 4:00 p.m. in the Bahá'í section of the Langatha Cemetery in Nairobi. His funeral was attended by a number of Bahá'ís and friends from the Christian, Hindu and Zoroastrian faiths. When the news of his death spread, loving letters of sympathy poured in. Appendix 4 contains an anthology of them.

After Manúchihr passed away, unbeknown to me a friend consulted a lawyer who had offered to sue Manúchihr's doctor on my behalf. The lawyer believed that he could sue the doctor for negligence. Had the doctor administered strong antibiotics in a timely manner or had he operated in good time, he said, Manúchihr's life would have been spared. He offered to file a malpractice suit against the specialist who treated Manúchihr, and suggested that after the case was settled, which he was sure to win, he would receive ten per cent of the money he could make the doctor pay. The information was passed on to me. The thought that Manúchihr's life had ended prematurely because of the doctor's negligence agitated me terribly. For 24 hours I toyed with the idea of making him pay for failing to take the steps that would have saved his life. The more I thought about it, the more agitated I became. I prayed hard to be led to the right course of action. I realized that money was not going to make me happy. What had happened to Manúchihr I considered God's will. Besides, I did not think that the doctor's action or inaction was deliberate, although emotionally I never stopped blaming him for having acted irresponsibly. I let him go free lest greed on my part or the lawyer's would ruin his reputation and prospects. I did not sue the man for his failure to take timely action to save Manúchihr's life but ended up paying his exorbitant bills, which I paid to the last penny from my meagre resources. The grief that doctor caused me was so immense that I did not want to see his face again. Fortunately, I never did, either during the decade I lived in Nairobi after Manúchihr's death or ever since my departure from that city.

## The Fate of Manúchihr's 'In Memoriam' Article

It has been a practice since the time of Shoghi Effendi that when a pioneer dies in his/her pioneer post, an 'In Memoriam' article covering her/his services to the Faith appears in the volume of *The Bahá'í World* covering the period in which the death takes place. This practice continues to date and is a public acknowledgement and appreciation of those who responded to the call for pioneers, who persevered in their posts under difficult conditions and offered up their souls away from home and loved ones.

During the days of my intense grief, I was asked through a friend in Nairobi to prepare an account of Manúchihr's life and pioneering services in the Ten Year Plan. The account had been requested for inclusion in volume 13 of *The Bahá'í World*. The person who conveyed the message asked that I submit the account through him. To do that, I carefully read, as painful as it was in those days, Manúchihr's diary covering the six years that he had spent in Seychelles. Since my English was poor, I wrote the account in Persian and gave it to the friend who acted as an intermediary. He promised either to translate it himself or have it translated by a competent person before forwarding it to the Bahá'í World Centre. Volume 13 of *The Bahá'í World*, covering the period 1954 to 1963, almost all of the Ten Year Crusade, took many years of preparation. The volume includes the final years of Shoghi Effendi's ministry and the intervening years between his passing in 1957 and the establishment of the Universal House of Justice in 1963. When it finally came out in 1970 I noticed, to my utter dismay, that the 'In Memoriam' section made no mention of Manúchihr, whose pioneering services embraced all but one year of the period covered by that volume. It hurt me to the core. I felt obliged to bring the omission to the attention of a person involved with the preparation of the volume. When I gathered sufficient courage to raise the issue, the answer I received did nothing to alleviate my sorrow. It was too late to do anything about it, I was told.

## The Birth of Our Child

After Manúchihr's death I could not step into the home in which we had lived, every corner of which evoked in me the loving memories we shared in the short span of time we had spent together. Moreover, the rent was beyond my means to pay. From the hospital where Manúchihr died, I was taken to the home of Mr and Mrs 'Alá'í, the elderly pioneer family from Iran with whom I had stayed for three days before our wedding. I stayed there again for three days before I was taken to the hospital for the delivery of my baby.

I was afraid I would not be able to make it to Manúchihr's funeral, for I was due any day. I was the only family member present and could not fail to accompany him to his permanent resting place. Since he had died on a Saturday night, we had to wait until the following Monday for the funeral. The burial took place in the afternoon of Monday, 5 February. Twenty-four hours later I started having contractions. They increased overnight. At 5:00 a.m. on 7 February I was taken to the hospital.[123] After 19 hours of labour our precious daughter was born at 15 minutes past midnight. I called her Sovaida, the name Manúchihr and I had jointly chosen for her during the early months of my pregnancy.

The death of my husband followed almost immediately by the birth of our daughter reminded me of a dream I had had many years earlier. Several years before I left Iran for Africa I dreamed that I was in a very big hall. 'Abdu'l-Bahá was seated on a high bench at the head of the hall. He had a book in His hand. It looked like *Some Answered Questions*. I was kneeling before Him on the floor. He opened the book to a page and gave it to me to read. As I was reading it, to my utter astonishment and surprise and for no reason at all, it closed in my hand. I was completely bewildered. Lifting my eyes, I turned to 'Abdu'l-Bahá in a state of imploration and supplication, but did not utter a word. He took the book, opened it to a page again and gave it back to me. I received the book gratefully. As I was trying to find out whether it was the same page, I woke up. I knew the dream was significant but had no idea what it meant. When the book of Manúchihr's life closed and almost immediately thereafter the book of my daughter's life opened, I realized what the dream was about.

So much had happened in such a short time: Manúchihr returned from a trip, fell ill, was hospitalized, passed away, I went to the hospital, our first and only child was born, yet our parents and siblings were uninformed of what was happening. A cable had been sent to the National Spiritual Assembly of Iran informing them of Manúchihr's death and asking them to inform the families concerned. My family received the news after ten days. The National Spiritual Assembly of Iran asked the Local Spiritual Assembly of Shíráz to inform my parents. The Local Assembly met and decided to send one of its members, Colonel Vaḥdat, together with uncle 'Abdu'l-Ḥusayn, to apprise them of what had transpired. All this took several days. In the meantime, I was in the hospital wondering how I could continue living in Kenya with my newly-born baby, with no job, no pension, no hope, no interest, no experience and a broken heart heavily weighed down with grief and unbearable pain. I was then 22 years old. I did not know how to bring up my daughter the way that Manúchihr and I had hoped. I had no means of livelihood; Manúchihr's salary stopped in the month he passed away, his hospital and doctor's bills had to be paid, my qualifications in the field of Persian literature did not presage engaging in gainful occupation. I did not know how I could stay in the country and provide for our barest daily necessities. My prospects were bleak. However, one thing was certain: I was determined to remain in my pioneer post. In fact, the thought of having to leave my place of service terrified me. I recall distinctly my consternation and disbelief when a friend suggested, before I went to the hospital, that I could stay in Nairobi until my baby was born, then arrangements would be made for me and the baby to return to Iran. My categoric answer was, 'I have come here as a pioneer; no matter what happens, I will stay.'

## My Life after Manúchihr's Death

The new situation presented the friends in Nairobi with a dilemma. They did not think that it was a good idea for me to stay yet they wished not to be unkind to someone whose world had been abruptly turned upside down. What they hoped for was that I would come to my senses and decide to return to the place whence I had come from. They perceived me as a liability. I was an inexperienced mother with no particular skill, I could not go to work, my English was poor and I had no one to lean on in times of need. In brief, I had nothing going for me and the friends feared that I would have no choice but to depend on them for my survival and the survival of my baby. They had enough on their hands. Having to help with the day-to-day life of a naive mother and her infant child was too burdensome, something they could do without. So they looked for subtle and not so subtle ways to get the point across to me. The subject of my departure from Nairobi was not directly discussed, yet I was told that the Regional Spiritual Assembly of the Bahá'ís of Central and East Africa had made available a ticket for my return to Iran. I thanked the messenger and through him the Assembly but stated that I preferred to stay at my pioneer post. Others offered to pay my way back to Iran, I was told. They thought the only thing that kept me from returning home was the absence of a ticket or lack of finances. When the friends lost hope that I would ever realize the impracticability of my plan to remain in Kenya, they employed different tactics. They told me nicely that everyone was busy and no one had the time to take care of someone else's needs. Although somewhat subtle, the statement was unambiguous. And although uttered lovingly, it was nonetheless hurtful. The next remark was as loving as the previous ones but candid. Should I wish to stay in Nairobi, I was told, I needed to know at the outset that I could not expect help from others. The purpose was, of course, to discourage me from making a decision that I would live to regret, so to speak. But it was to no avail. If there was one thing I knew for certain at the time, it was my inner desire to stay, no matter what sacrifices it entailed.

I must say here that I could well understand the friends' uneasiness and deep concern regarding my decision to remain in Nairobi. If I were fluent in English, if I had a good source of income, if I had useful skills to earn a living, if I were older than 22 and more mature or if I had family on the spot to lend me assistance when needed, the friends would not have been so eager for me to leave. Unfortunately, my circumstances were what they were but going back to Iran I considered out of the question. Thus I had no choice but to accept the conditions of my stay and work assiduously towards overcoming the obstacles in my way. I was under no illusion that on my own I could not succeed but I had absolutely no doubt that Bahá'u'lláh's confirmations would be with me. Notwithstanding this knowledge, the discovery, so soon after Manúchihr's death, that I was on my own was as painful as it was difficult. I had had many trials before but this was by fire. Fortunately, I never doubted the correctness of my decision to stay regardless of the seemingly insurmountable difficulties ahead.

Divine assistance during my grief-stricken days and months ahead was truly tangible, especially when my sister Pouran arrived. With her arrival everything changed for the better. By the time she came, six months had elapsed and I had considerable practice in living on my own. The longer I lived in Nairobi, the more independent I became. The irony is that the degree of independence I gained was not in the end to the liking of those who advocated it at first! Unwarranted expectation, unreasonable assumption and miscommunication made a bad situation worse. A harsh remark was expected to make me aware of the consequences of my decision and lead me to pack my belongings and leave. When that failed, it was assumed that I would fulfil what antiquated tradition required of women in my situation. Since I was a young widow raising a child on my own, away from family and in a foreign land, it was considered proper for me to seek and follow advice. I appreciated the necessity of consultation, which applies across the gender line, but warded off interference in my personal affairs, so did not give it much thought. Moreover, I had become accustomed to my newly-found independence. I had found it at a high cost and was unwilling to let go of it for the sake of appeasing some friends. When people expressed unsolicited views about matters, such as whether or not I should send my daughter for music and ballet lessons, I weighed them in the balance of the writings of the Faith and did what my conscience dictated. This 'attitude' of mine was displeasing to those steeped in tradition. Had there been a man in my situation living in the same place and doing the very same things, I wonder how he would have been treated?

I well remember those sorrow-laden days and how my back bent under the weight of manifold challenges while trying to stand upright to avoid imposing on the kindness of the friends or giving the impression that the weight was too great to bear. What enabled me to cope were the outpourings of divine grace, for which I render God praise. I was provided with the opportunity to rely on God's assistance alone and given the means to experience it. Although the remark was terribly painful and harsh when it was uttered, later I realized it was a blessing in disguise. It taught me to be detached and free from expectations, no matter what my circumstances were. It taught me early on to stand on my own feet, no matter how wobbly they seemed. It also taught me to trust the mystic voice, which amidst my agonizing and hurt feelings, cried out from within and urged me constantly to persevere and hope for brighter and more joyous days ahead.

## Doors of Hope Fling Wide Open

I stayed in the hospital for ten days after Sovaida's birth. The normal length of time spent in the hospital after delivery in those days was a week. I stayed longer because of a temperature I developed about the time I was to be discharged. During my stay in the hospital I was completely bewildered, for I had no idea where I was going to stay afterwards, how I could earn a living, how I was going to raise my child and how to deal with the weight of my grief under which I was being crushed. The only tangible thing at that time was my overwhelming sorrow. I was sorry not only for my plight but also for my little girl who had entered this world in the midst of my miseries. I tried so hard to withhold my tears when she was being breastfed. She was the only bright spot in the darkness of my gloomy days. Her bright, radiant and innocent face rekindled in the depth of my heart the lamp of hope, which had been extinguished with the tempest of Manúchihr's passing and the succeeding tests and difficulties. When the sea of anguish surged in my heart while carrying her in my arms and the tears poured down my face, she opened up like a tender bud and brought glad-tidings of future happiness and better days ahead. Soon she learned to move her delicate fingers on my cheeks and look deeply into my eyes with a smile as though wanting to dry my tears and say that she knew what I was going through, that it was okay to weep, that I was no longer alone. She gradually filled the vacuum that Manúchihr's sudden departure from the world had created in me.

With Sovaida's arrival the blessings of God rained down upon me with such force that everyone was amazed. The visible signs of Bahá'u'lláh's power and might encompassed us in such ways that surprised those who thought I was about to sink into a bottomless well of misfortune and misery.

The news of the tragic death of Manúchihr, whom my family had not met, reached them at a time they expected to hear the news of Sovaida's birth. I can well imagine the shock they received. Once informed, they gathered together in Shíráz, prayed fervently and decided that they would extend financial assistance to enable me to stay in my pioneer post, if that was my wish. The decision was conveyed in a cable, which assured me of arrangements being made for my stay. I received the cable the day before I was discharged from the hospital. A detailed letter followed and relieved me of my deep concern about the continuation of my pioneering service. The arrangements made it possible for me, at least for the time being, to live in Nairobi without financial difficulty. Moreover, my brother Masíḥ offered to come to Nairobi and help me to resettle. Knowing the important work that he was doing at his pioneer post, also being aware that seeing a family member at a time when I was emotionally vulnerable would intensify my separation anxiety, I thanked him for his loving consideration but suggested that the cost of the trip be paid to the fund in Manúchihr's name.

In the meantime, the car and furniture we owned were auctioned and the proceeds went towards Manúchihr's doctor and hospital bills. My own doctor, a real angel – his surname was Adamson – who had seen me through pregnancy and continued to see me until six weeks after delivery, submitted no bill for his service. When I enquired, he responded that he was in no hurry to get paid. When I insisted, he sent a token bill. What a difference between two men practising medicine! One so careless with my husband's life but brisk in submitting exorbitant bills; another tenderly looking after my baby's life until delivery and weeks thereafter, yet hesitant to bill me under the conditions I was in. God be praised for the second type of doctor. They instil hope in the hearts of the hopeless and prove that humanity is not dead.

After I left the hospital it took me five weeks to find affordable accommodation. Meanwhile, I lived with the Rupp family, Italian Bahá'ís from Ethiopia, for one week and with the Yazdi family for four weeks. The accommodation I acquired was a room in the home of an Asian family. They were Ismá'ílís. It was the same room that Manúchihr had rented when he had first moved to Nairobi. It was very basic and had one condition attached to it – that I did not wash my baby's nappies in the bathroom basin.[124] There was a tap in the garden, which I used for the purpose. During the time I was out in the garden washing Sovaida's nappies and clothes, she was in the room either playing by herself or asleep. She was a wonderful child, quiet, well-behaved and good-natured.

The Bahá'í friends visited me when they could. Manúchihr and I had a non-Bahá'í friend, Mrs D'sa, who was originally from Goa, India. Manúchihr had met her and her family aboard the ship which had brought him from Seychelles to Mombasa. Mrs D'sa and her daughter, Cynthia, visited me every afternoon on their way home from work. Mrs D'sa treated me like her own daughter and gave me motherly advice regarding how to raise my child. It was as though God had placed her there to be my guardian angel.

Something else helped me considerably during the days and

months immediately after Manúchihr's passing. The loving sentiments expressed in the letters and cables of condolence that kept pouring in calmed the ocean of sorrow surging within my inner being and bound together the pieces of my broken heart. Although none could change the reality of the situation I faced, nonetheless the spiritual and moral support they lent was incredible. Words of encouragement and sympathy warmed my chilled heart and lifted my drooping soul. Some of these letters, either in the original language or in translated form, are included in appendix 4.

There are times when I traverse the expanse of my distant memory and reach the threshold of the intense grief occasioned by Manúchihr's death. When I enter that sanctuary, everything is fresh and clear as though it happened yesterday. The lapse of over four decades has done little to mitigate the intensity of the feelings and emotions that surged within me. The bundle carefully deposited in the recesses of my memory remains untouched and is accessible at all times. The agonizing pain and misery that separation from a loved one brings is so real that it can be touched. What has changed is the world in which I live, which has changed the nature and quality of the life I lead.

## Watching the Plight of the Less Fortunate

The house in which I had rented a room was adjacent to another a few metres away. From the only window in my room I could clearly see the back of that house, which was occupied by an Asian family.[125] They had a deformed daughter about eight or nine years old. She was disabled and had no control over when and where she responded to the call of nature. At the back of their house there was a cement platform. The only fixture on that cold bleak platform was a water tap. The platform was used for washing clothes, utensils and the disabled girl. Every morning a woman, probably the mother, held the tiny deformed child by her hands and feet, took her out of the house and placed her on the cement platform to clean. As the child screamed – she knew what was coming to her the moment she was taken out of the house – the woman opened the tap in full and let the pressure of the water wash away the waste discharged from the girl's body overnight.

Every day when I woke up in the morning I dreaded looking out of the window lest I see that heartbreaking scene. I could avoid seeing it by not looking but as soon as I heard the child's scream I knew what was happening. The child's suffering, the anger and pain in the face of the mother, as well as the daily repetition of the scene made me forget my ordeal and realize how gracious was God to me. As I prayed for the mother and the child, I praised God for the evidence of His bounties and blessings which my child and I enjoyed. It is an established fact that when we see people who are worse off than we, we feel grateful for what we have.

## Pouran's Arrival Makes a World of Difference

After Sovaida's birth I occupied myself with my daily chores, with my thoughts and with reading Manúchihr's diaries of the six years he had spent in the Seychelles. When I felt gloomy and sad, I was happy that Manúchihr was not alive to share with me my sorrowful life. Ironically I felt worse when I was with people and things seemed to be going well, for at those times I missed Manúchihr all the more and wished he were with me to share the joy. Thus in a strange way I learned to like being alone and occupied with my thoughts.

Six months thus elapsed before Pouran's efforts to move to Nairobi bore result. She was then pioneering in the Netherlands where she worked as a state registered nurse in Haarlem. Her American training at the Namází Nursing School in Shíráz, augmented by several years of experience and the midwifery courses she had taken in the Netherlands, proved to be great assets and were useful in earning her a visa to work in an English hospital in Nairobi. Her arrival in August 1962 was the greatest gift Sovaida and I could have had. She was truly God sent. Had she not arrived when she did, I don't know how we would have survived our ordeal. When she saw our modest accommodation and unsatisfactory living conditions, the first thing she said was: 'This is not the way to live with an infant. We have to get you better accommodation, somewhere we can live together.' That was, naturally, music to my ears.

Being a nurse working in an English hospital entitled Pouran to free accommodation in what was called 'Sisters' Mess' (a place adjacent to the hospital where resident nurses lived). But that was not what Pouran wanted. Living outside the hospital environment meant renting accommodation which was much more expensive but she had come to be with us and, true to her intention, that is what she did. We searched and found decent, modest accommodation in a guesthouse close to the hospital.

With Pouran's arrival our life brightened up and became much more meaningful. There was someone I could talk with, confide in, get advice from and learn childcare from. Gradually I became alive again and learned to do things other than those that pushed me more and more into isolation. We enjoyed doing things together, such as participating in Bahá'í activities, going on teaching trips, attending conferences and so on.

One of the major projects we undertook soon after Pouran arrived in Nairobi was attending the first Bahá'í World Congress in London in April–May 1963. While we were preparing for the trip, I learned that I had a huge problem to deal with.

At the time of the first World Congress Sovaida was about a year old. To be able to travel abroad, she needed to be in my passport or have her own. Until then she only had a birth certificate issued in Nairobi. I thought it was a simple thing to have her name entered in my passport and initiated correspondence about this.

In the 1960s there was no Iranian embassy in Kenya, Tanganyika (present-day Tanzania) or Uganda, which formed British East Africa. Few Iranians lived in the three countries under the colonial rule and those who did were all Bahá'í pioneers. The closest embassy was the one in Addis Ababa, Ethiopia. We could also refer matters to the embassy in London. I sent to the Persian embassy in Addis Ababa my passport together with Sovaida's birth certificate and a letter explaining that we were taking a trip to London and needed Sovaida's name to be written in my passport. The embassy asked for a marriage certificate. I sent them a copy of our Bahá'í marriage certificate. The certificate was rejected and the entry of

Sovaida's name in my passport refused. I wrote to the embassy in London and explained the situation. The same argument was put forward. A civil marriage certificate was what they needed. Manúchihr and I did not have a civil marriage because the Local Spiritual Assembly of Nairobi was trying to get Bahá'í marriage recognized in Kenya at the time and we had been advised that since Bahá'í marriage was soon to be recognized, we did not need to have a civil marriage, which meant not having a civil marriage certificate. I informed the embassy of the non-existence of the civil marriage certificate and explained that since my husband was dead, there was no way I could procure one at that late date. They offered to enter Sovaida's name in my passport but would have to specify that her father was unknown. I could not accept that. The communication continued for some time. They were adamant in their refusal and I was persistent in my request. Finally I was told that whenever I went to London, I should visit the embassy and present the case in person. I seized the opportunity and informed them immediately that I would be happy to oblige but without Sovaida's name in my passport I could not go to London or anywhere else. The consul was then on vacation. His deputy saw nothing wrong with writing Sovaida's name in my passport to enable us to take the trip. The name was thus written without mentioning anything about the father. The passport was returned to me with a short letter saying that while in London I should go to the embassy and present the case for further consideration.

Faithful to the promise I had made, I visited the embassy in London after the World Congress and talked with the Iranian consul there. He read the file and informed me that his deputy had made a mistake by entering Sovaida's name in my passport. I was bewildered and could not understand why. I told him that since the Kenyan birth certificate clearly stated Sovaida's particulars, including her parents' names, and since Manúchihr's death certificate stated that he was deceased, there should not be any problem establishing the facts. He explained that a birth certificate issued by a foreign country was insufficient for the purpose of obtaining legal status in the country of origin. He added that his deputy should have insisted on a civil marriage certificate. To emphasize the point he was trying to make, he said that even a Muslim marriage certificate would not suffice in that kind of situation. However, he said that it was too late to rectify the mistake, so he would just let it ride. We will see later in this account how that providential mistake helped to solve a more serious problem when Sovaida and I made a trip to Iran in early 1971.

In London we saw, in addition to my parents, two of my siblings and their spouses, as well as many family members and friends who had come to attend the Congress. It was an emotional reunion, which made it hard for us to separate from our loved ones again. However, we drew much strength and courage from seeing one another. After the Congress we returned to our respective areas of service with stronger resolve to do our utmost to serve our glorious Faith. We did not see our parents and siblings again for eight years. Foreign pioneering in the mid-20th century for many middle class Iranian Bahá'ís who responded to the call and left for the far corners of the globe had many rewards and opened before them horizons undreamed of. It provided the pioneers and their children with excellent opportunities for learning foreign languages, receiving a good education and acquiring wonderful skills. However, for those who only had meagre resources and did not do very well financially, pioneering entailed many sacrifices. One such sacrifice was going for a long time without seeing one's family. Pouran and I earned enough to live and serve the Faith in our pioneer post but could not afford to take long trips, the cost of which were prohibitive.

## Achieving Financial Self-Sufficiency

To be truly independent I needed to earn a living and become financially self-sufficient. By the time assistance from the family stopped, Pouran had a secure job and we could live on her salary and my small savings. However, I needed to stand on my own two feet and do something useful with my life, in addition to being a full time mother to my child. To earn a living I had to acquire certain skills beyond what I had learned about Persian literary works in school and at university. When Sovaida was about two years old, I seriously looked into courses that I could take. As I could not attend college full time and did not have the money for private tuition, I had to settle for skills achievable through teach-yourself books. My options were naturally limited. Out of necessity I started teaching myself Pitman's shorthand, typing and bookkeeping. My poor English was, of course, a big stumbling block, which I had to overcome fast. Typing and bookkeeping were not as problematic as shorthand was. Although I learned the outlines and gained sufficient speed to take down what was dictated, transcribing the outlines into proper English was a daunting task. Fortunately, my memory was good and it came to my aid when I was confused regarding certain outlines that could be transcribed in more ways than one. When unsure, I looked up the meaning of all the words and phrases represented by the confusing outline and chose the one that made most sense in the context of the sentence or passage I was working on. At times this kind of exercise kept me busy for many hours. However, the tedious work I had to do in transcribing shorthand outlines helped to improve my English. My perseverance enabled me to gain confidence and with confidence I managed to obtain the certificates necessary to apply for a job. That felt really good. The next hurdle to overcome was finding a job.

When Sovaida was about two and a half years old I put her in a nursery school run by a very kind and good-hearted Catholic woman, Mrs Gladys D'Souza. She was at that time being temporarily assisted by her wonderful sister, Mrs Kathleen Andris, herself a teacher. They became very good personal friends of ours. Although the older sister has since passed away, I am still in touch with Kathleen, who lives in Australia. With Sovaida in school, I was ready to go to work, but finding employment when the market was flooded with prospective candidates was not easy.

Kenya gained independence in 1963. The Mau Mau movement prior to independence struck terror in the hearts and caused the security situation to deteriorate. Fortunately, my English was not good enough to know what was going on in the country. My ignorance served as a blessing. However, living conditions became more difficult. Many foreigners left the country fearing unforeseen complications, one of which was new legislation by the government to make it difficult for foreigners to obtain jobs that Africans could do. Secretarial positions fell into that category.

Independence eased the plight of the Africans and pushed blatant racial prejudices into the background but it did not change the situation of foreigners like Iranians who were neither white nor black. Before independence we were not white enough to enjoy the privileges they had, afterwards we were not black enough to be entitled to the privileges that independence brought. Jobs were reserved for Africans; foreigners could find employment if they were specialized in something Africans could not do or had a lot of money to invest. I belonged to neither category. After a while my efforts to secure a job yielded the hoped-for result. I first got a job with the Industrial and Commercial Development Corporation. When my prospects improved, I left that job and got one with the Fiat Company. I was happy that I had a good job until one gloomy day I was called to the Immigration Office. I was told to go there with my passport. I did as I was told. Upon arrival, the officer took my passport, cancelled my temporary resident's visa and said something in the form of a reprimand. He then stamped a two-month visitor's visa in my passport and handed it back to me. I protested vehemently. He said that I had a dependant visa, which was rendered invalid when my husband died. 'If you want to work in Kenya,' he said, 'you need a work permit.' He further explained that a work permit acquired for me by one firm was not valid for working with another.[126] He said that I had broken the law and for that reason he cancelled my visa. I took issue with his statement and said that I expected to live and die in Nairobi just as did my husband, and that my dependant visa gave me the right to do that. The officer looked at me as if I were completely out of my mind. When he realized that I was naive but serious, he showed compassion and explained to me why things did not work that way. He added that he had studied my file, knew about my unfortunate circumstances and therefore did not want to make my situation worse than it was. He then told me all the things that I needed to do during the two months my visitor's visa was valid. He said that I could keep my job, although it was illegal to work with a visitor's visa. What I needed to do was to get Fiat to complete certain documents and send them to the Ministry of Work. The procedure, he explained, was for the Ministry of Work to send the file to the Immigration Office for its review and recommendation. When the file got to him, he would recommend that I be granted a work permit. With that recommendation on my file, I was sure to get the necessary permit to work, he said. I thanked him profusely for his advice and got up to leave. As I was shaking his hand, he looked into my eyes intently and said, 'If you divulge to anyone what I just said, I will deny it outright and make sure that you are on the next plane to where you have come from.' He then asked if I understood what he was trying to say. When I promised that I did, he let go of my hand.

For the next two months my prayers were focused. I prayed for divine assistance and confirmations to enable me to stay in Kenya but I knew that I had to be detached in case that course of action did not work out. The immigration officer, an English gentleman, kept his word and made sure that everything worked out the way that he predicted. I did not see him again and may not do so in the future but am most grateful for his having been so compassionate when I needed it desperately. I was on the verge of having to leave the country, for I had no work permit. Without a work permit, I could not work and without work I could not stay in the country. Again, Bahá'u'lláh sent an angel to guide me through the darkness of that gloomy situation and help me to emerge.

In 1966, after five years' stay in Kenya, I became a permanent resident. Permanent residency made it possible for me to change my job without legal constraints. I immediately applied to the Rockefeller Foundation for a job opening at the University of Nairobi. The Foundation's University Development Programme needed an executive secretary. I was offered the job, which required me to work 30 hours a week and paid me a good salary with generous benefits. This new development was made possible only through the outpourings of Bahá'u'lláh's favours and opened the door to further attractive prospects. Working at the university provided me with the opportunity to take academic courses free of charge. I enrolled as a student and took courses in Islamic history, African traditional religion and religion in general. One of the purposes of my enrolment was to satisfy the requirement of the newly established Department of Religious Studies to include the Bahá'í Faith in its syllabus. In response to an application that the department consider including lectures and seminars on the Bahá'í Faith, we were advised that it would be done if at least three Bahá'í students enrolled in the courses offered by the department. Two other Bahá'í students registered for such courses and the Bahá'í Faith was for the first time included in the syllabus of a university department in Kenya. Having a well-paid job made it possible for Sovaida to receive the best education possible in Kenya. She also developed her talents in music, ballet and languages by taking extracurricular courses at school and at the Nairobi Cultural Centre.

In 1967 Pouran left Nairobi for Copenhagen, where she married 'Abdu'lláhí H. 'Abdí, a devoted believer from Somalia. After six months in Denmark, Pouran pioneered to Mogadishu, 'Abdu'lláhí's hometown. They lived in Somalia until the harsh economic conditions and the unstable political situation in the country forced them to leave for the United States in the mid-1980s. They are presently living in California together with their daughter Maryam.

By the time Pouran left I was well established in my new job and had ample opportunity to serve the Faith in a variety of ways. Sovaida and I continued to live in Nairobi for almost ten years after Manúchihr's death. During that decade, especially the first few years when Pouran was with us, we travelled to various parts of Kenya and Uganda. Wherever we went we witnessed the evidences of Bahá'u'lláh's abundant confirmations.

## The Fire

As soon as I had a well-paid job, I planned to go with Sovaida to the Holy Land on pilgrimage. With a secure job and good, regular monthly income, the only impediment to attaining our heart's desire was removed. I sent an application for pilgrimage to the Bahá'í World Centre and after some time received confirmation that we could start our pilgrimage on 29 March 1971. In those days there was a weekly flight from Nairobi to Tel Aviv. To make it on time for pilgrimage on 29 March, we had to leave Nairobi on the 26th and spend the intervening days in Tel Aviv. All arrangements were made for the trip, including obtaining visas and traveller's cheques. As we were taking this long trip, we thought it would be nice also to visit our family in Iran for the first time since I had left the country ten years earlier.

The days of the fast (2–20 March) went by and the eve of Naw-Rúz (21 March) arrived. There were celebrations in the Bahá'í Centre on the evening of 20 March. Before getting dressed for the celebrations, I cleaned the apartment and went out with Sovaida to do some last minute shopping. When we returned after half an hour, we saw smoke pouring out of the square building in the centre of the city, called Regal Mansion, where our apartment was situated. We enquired and were told the building had caught fire because one of our neighbours had lit a match to start a primus without realizing that a gas balloon attached to a gas cooker in the same kitchen was leaking. When she struck the match, the excess gas in her kitchen caught fire and spread through the flimsy roofs to 20 other apartments in the building. I asked Sovaida to stay outside while I went in to rescue my bag containing my passport, our tickets and traveller's cheques. She objected vehemently. Her loud objection attracted the attention of the police and firefighters on the scene. They prevented me from entering the building. So we stood there and watched helplessly as the building burned. The first thing coming to my mind was that our pilgrimage was off, for without passports and money we could not undertake the trip. Heartbroken and despondent we left the scene of the fire and went to inform a dear Bahá'í friend, Shahnaz Meshkin Bleam, of our plight. She and her brother, Shahram, who was visiting her at that time, were attending the Naw-Rúz celebrations at the Bahá'í Centre in Nairobi. They came immediately.

When the fire was brought under control, I asked Shahnaz to look after Sovaida so that I could go inside and see what could be rescued. Police objected on the ground that the building was unsafe. Sovaida tearfully pleaded with me not to risk my life. Shahnaz and her brother got permission to go in at their own risk. They tried to salvage whatever they could. The wardrobe containing my bag in which my passport and the travellers' cheques were kept was untouched by the fire. They grabbed the bag and returned to us with wide smiles. Other items surviving the fire were our books and some documents kept in a closed bookcase which had been thrown into the courtyard by firefighters. The contents, although damaged, were rescued. Almost everything else in the apartment was either burnt or stolen by looters who had gone in as soon as the fire had broken out. The handbag had survived because it was in a closed area. Lack of oxygen and the firefighters' quick response had kept it safe. It was an unbelievable experience. I did not care if everything else had gone up in smoke. What mattered to us most was that handbag containing the items we needed to take our long-awaited trip. I was homeless for a second time in ten years but happy and grateful that Sovaida and I could go on pilgrimage and refresh our souls. For those who may wonder whether we were covered by insurance or received compensation, the answer to both questions is no. We stayed with Shahnaz and her family until 26 March, the date of our departure for the Holy Land.

## Pilgrimage

Sovaida and I left Nairobi for Tel Aviv on Friday, 26 March 1971. Fortunately, the time between the burning down of our apartment and the date of our departure from Nairobi was short and matters arising from the fire that needed immediate attention were many; thus we had no time to dwell on the unpleasantness of the experience we had gone through or to worry about where and how we were going to live upon our return. I was so tired and overwhelmed that I could not think ahead. Racing against time was a blessing, for I just enjoyed what came my way and refused to entertain negative thoughts.

The first time I showed any reaction to the fire was in the Haifa pilgrim house on the second day of our pilgrimage. My emotions took me by surprise. As we were sitting in the room with the *mandar*, the Hand of the Cause of God Mr Furútan, one of the four Hands residing in the Holy Land, asked how we were doing. He knew us from a trip he had made to Nairobi. He also knew our families well. I casually mentioned that we had just survived a fire. In response to his further questions, I explained that the fire had destroyed our apartment and consumed its contents. He was sad to hear of our plight and expressed kind sentiments, which touched my heart. I looked around and saw expressions of sadness on the faces of my fellow pilgrims. It may sound strange but it was everyone's loving reaction to what had happened that made me break into tears. I had seen and heard from the friends in Nairobi, Bahá'í and non-Bahá'í alike, sincere and heartfelt expressions of sympathy after the fire but I had never reacted the way that I did on that day. What caused it was the memory of an incident which had occurred soon after the fire. The memory of that incident came rushing to my mind and made me break down.

On the Monday morning after the fire I took Sovaida to school and explained to the principal and her teachers why she was not wearing the school uniform. They understood and let her go to her class. I then went to the half-ruined apartment to look in the debris for two rings: one was the Greatest Name ring that my mother had given me before I left Iran, the other my wedding band. It was my practice to remove these when I was cleaning. Before the fire broke out on Naw-Rúz eve, as I was cleaning the apartment and washing clothes, I had taken them out and placed them on a table in the living room. On the day after the fire, when I was searching for my rings, someone walked in. I was pleasantly surprised to see a friendly face. He was a dignified elderly gentleman who had recently moved to Nairobi. I did not know him well personally but knew of him and the wonderful services he had rendered to the Faith. I thanked him for taking the trouble to pay me a visit under those conditions. He expressed sadness for what had happened and said that he had come to convey a message on behalf of a couple of friends. I listened attentively. He started with a question: 'Do you not think there is a good reason for whatever happens in life?' I responded positively, not knowing what he was leading to. He continued by saying that the fire happened for a good reason and suggested that I would do well to ponder upon what had happened and try to understand why among all the Bahá'ís in Nairobi this had happened to me. I asked him to elaborate. He refused. I did not know what to make of it. I tried to fathom the intent from his facial expressions. They were eloquent and unmistakable. In his view and the view of those whose message he had come to convey, the fire was in consequence of something I had done wrong and was meant to teach me a lesson. In an instant the record of my deeds during the decade I had lived in Nairobi flashed before my eyes. I had made mistakes and many were my shortcomings but what warranted that particular affliction at that particular juncture, I could not tell. Had I been the only victim, I said to myself, the suggestion would be plausible. However, that was not the case. Many people had lost their possessions in that fire. However, I was singled out for condemnation in the court of the biased opinion of a few who had chosen a kind and willing messenger to convey a crude message in the worst of circumstances. As these thoughts went through my mind, I felt the warmth of another fire raging. It was the fire of anger ignited in my anguished heart by so unkind a remark. Had I let it blaze, it would have consumed my soul, then the anger used as justification by the ones who were ever ready to prove me guilty without just cause. Having recognized the signs, I said calmly: 'I may deserve what has come my way but is it fair that many others affected by the fire should have suffered because of me?'[127] He did not dispute the conclusion I had drawn from his statement, nor did he answer my question. I tried hard to conceal the emotions that stirred within me, while he did his best to avoid looking me in the eye and to say exactly what he had come to achieve.

Over the years I had learned to conceal my feelings and pretend that I was unaffected by the hurtful remarks made every now and then by the same few individuals who were otherwise very loving and kind people, not only to me but to everyone else. However, that day the chalice of my patience was full to the brim and the ceiling of my tolerance quite low. I knew that I had to remove myself from the volatile scene before I said something I would regret. So I thanked the dear man for his advice, abandoned my search for the rings, said goodbye to him and left the place. I had too many things to deal with and could not allow emotions to stand in the way. Three days after that unfortunate encounter, Sovaida and I left on our long-awaited pilgrimage.

Thus when Mr Furútan and my fellow pilgrims showed genuine sympathy and loving-kindness, the whole experience came to me like a torrent. All of a sudden I lost the ability to master my emotions. Tears withheld for so long rained down my face uncontrollably. Being so far away from my familiar surroundings in Nairobi, where I had been turned into what some perceived as a hard human being with a strong and independent personality, helped me to behave normally. The pressure that had built up in my heart for a decade could no longer be contained. The floodgates were forced open and the reservoir of my suppressed feelings gushed out. I wept and wept until I had no more tears to shed. Then I was calm as though nothing had happened. I felt no pressure. I was light like a feather soaring high on the wings of the spirit and consigning the unpleasant incident to the realm of oblivion. The emotions only resurfaced in their intensity when I put pen to paper to write this account.

My weeping caused my fellow pilgrims to think that I was shedding tears for the loss of my worldly possessions. Only I knew why I was weeping but did not want to divulge, nor could I, the reason. I erroneously thought that I had safely buried the unpleasant experience in the tomb of concealment. Little did I know that I had my limits, that a powerful trigger in favourable circumstances would break the seal and that I would be overcome by the emotions I had tried so hard to hide. When the remark was made, I was determined to stand erect under the overwhelming pressure I felt and let not anything mar the experience of our pilgrimage. Now that I am three and a half decades older and, it is hoped, wiser, I know that feelings, good and bad, have a strange way of resurfacing. When I came on pilgrimage, I was young and felt strong. Like all young and strong people, I believed that I could bury all unpleasant experiences in the recesses of my memory, never to deal with them again!

Weeping has always been my solace. It is such a great blessing to be able to cry. When I finished weeping on that second day of pilgrimage, I did not tell anyone why I had been so overcome with emotions. I just let people draw their own conclusions. Some of our fellow pilgrims, who felt for the plight we had suffered, made offers to assist financially. They were surprised when their offers were declined. I assured them that Sovaida and I were fine, that our financial situation was not a cause for concern, but said nothing further.

The pilgrimage was a true blessing, for it helped me to focus on more important things. The nine glorious days we spent at the Bahá'í World Centre were unforgettable. We have many fond memories of that wonderful experience. It was a God-sent opportunity to refresh our souls and turn a new page in the book of our lives. We enjoyed tremendously the great times we spent visiting the sacred Shrines and the holy places. The Bahá'í World Centre community in those days was very small compared with what it is today. We spent quality time with the three Hands of the Cause of God who were then in Haifa – Mr Paul Haney, Mr 'Alí-Akbar Furútan, Mr Abu'l-Qásim Faizi – as well as members of the Universal House of Justice. While on pilgrimage we forgot about the world, its sufferings and cares. We focused on the present and basked in the embracing warmth it so generously proffered.

Being on pilgrimage opened for us portals we did not know existed or could be entered. In a way, that pilgrimage shaped our future. Unbeknown to us, the Universal House of Justice was looking for a bilingual person to carry out certain duties at the Bahá'í World Centre. Spending nine days on pilgrimage provided the opportunity for some members, such as the late Mr Gibson and Mr Nakhjavání, to get to know us better. My qualifications in the secretarial and administrative fields, as well as my Persian literary studies, were needed at the World Centre. So enquiries were discreetly made regarding prospective candidates, without actually telling them the reason. In the early years of the establishment of the Universal House of Justice, serving at the Bahá'í World Centre was not by application. Those who were needed to carry out certain functions there were invited by the Universal House of Justice to join the staff, after ascertaining their qualifications and availability.

## Visit to Iran and the Unforeseen Problem

After that wonderful experience at the Bahá'í World Centre, we proceeded to Iran. This was my first visit there since I had left it over ten years earlier. Our reunion with the family after so many years was exciting and emotional. We spent a few days in Ṭihrán with my sister Mahín and her family. We then proceeded to Shíráz where my parents and youngest sister, Firishtih, lived. The bus trip from Ṭihrán to Shíráz brought back the experiences of more than a decade earlier. Although I was a grown woman and had a nine year old child with me, my mother did not think it was safe for us to travel alone! She came to Ṭihrán to accompany us to Shíráz. At first I thought it was an unnecessary exercise but when we disembarked to eat in roadside cafe restaurants or to use the inadequate facilities along the way, I realized what a blessing it was to have her with us. During the decade I had been away the infrastructure had improved but the mentality of the male passengers and their treatment of women was the same. Having my mother with us provided a measure of security and protection.

During our stay in Shíráz we visited Kázirún where uncle 'Alí-Akbar and his family lived. That visit refreshed for me the childhood memories of the war that had taken place some 25 years earlier between government forces and tribal rebels. The victory of the rebels cost my parents everything they had and endangered our lives. The war changed the course of our lives in ways previously unimagined.

When Sovaida and I returned to Ṭihrán to prepare for our departure from Iran, we learned that we needed an exit visa.[128]

When applying for the required exit visa, I learned with horror and disbelief that I was free to go but could not take Sovaida with me, that it was unlawful for an underage child to live in a foreign country without a legal guardian! How convenient, I thought. For nine years the government had done nothing to provide for the protection and education of that child. It had not even enquired about her well-being during those difficult years. Now it was going to block her return to the place where she was born and raised? The painful truth was that the laws of Iran, even under the Sháh, did not accord the mother guardianship of her underage child or children when her husband died. Those who automatically enjoyed the right of guardianship were, in priority order, the father's father and the father's brother(s); competency and suitability did not matter. The mother could be given the right if the father's father and the father's brothers signed a legal document giving her such right. Well, this was completely out of the question for several reasons: 1) By supporting the groundless claims of one of his sons,[129] Manúchihr's father had lost his membership in the Bahá'í community and therefore could not have acted as Sovaida's legal guardian. By the time we visited Iran, the subject was moot anyway, for he had passed away a year or two earlier. 2) Three of Manúchihr's six brothers, all dedicated and faithful Bahá'ís, had pioneered abroad and lived in various countries. Although they would have readily signed the document, it would have taken several weeks for the formalities to be completed. In the meantime, I would have lost my job in Kenya. 3) The whole thing sounded like a joke. I had raised Sovaida for nine years on my own without the government showing the least interest and concern. Now suddenly the authorities felt that there was a problem about who was the legal guardian!

As my vacation was coming to an end, urgent action was needed to solve the problem. However, the Ministry of Foreign Affairs and the Passport Office, two entities with which I had to deal, were in no hurry. Their response to my application and pleadings was that I could go and leave Sovaida behind. That, too, was out of the question for obvious reasons.

One of my three brothers-in-law who lived in Ṭihrán was

Dr Daryúsh Ma'ání. He took me to see someone he knew in the Ministry of Foreign Affairs and together we went to see the director of the Passport Office. He reviewed my file and carefully examined my passport. When he saw Sovaida's name in my passport, he wanted to know how it had got there. I explained the circumstances. He smiled and said, 'The person who entered your daughter's name in your passport unwittingly accepted your right and role as her legal guardian.' He picked up the telephone and said the same to the person in charge of issuing exit visas. That person asked that the matter be conveyed to him in writing. The director immediately summoned his secretary and dictated a letter to that effect. While we were sitting there, the letter was typed, signed and given to us. We left his office with the letter, fully confident that on that basis we would be given the needed visa. When we presented the letter to the man in charge, he threw it before us and said, 'A typed letter is not accepted. The director must write it in his own hand.' We retraced our steps to the director's office and explained with embarrassment what the problem was. He smiled, took the letter from us and, in his own hand, confirmed at the foot of the letter what the typed version stated. We took the letter back to the exit visa section, not knowing what other obstacles we would face. Fortunately, the man dealing with us earlier was not at his desk. The person working at the desk next to his saw no problem with the letter and issued the visa.

When Sovaida and I occupied our seats on the plane leaving Mihrábád airport, we gave a sigh of relief. While I was dealing with all the complications placed in the way of our return to our pioneer post, I was not sure whether I would succeed in setting foot outside Iran again, at least not until Sovaida had come of age. However, Bahá'u'lláh's bountiful confirmations, which had seen us through so many difficulties before, came to our aid again and made it possible for Sovaida and me to return to our field of service.

## Departure from Kenya

Upon our return to Nairobi we booked accommodation in the family quarters of the YWCA (Young Women's Christian

Association), a Christian-operated hostel where women of all faiths and backgrounds could stay. The representative of the Rockefeller Foundation, Dr James S. Coleman, paid me a visit there to express his sympathy and regret for the loss of our home in the fire. He added that if I decided to rent another apartment, the Foundation would furnish it for me. I thanked him for his generosity but said that I needed time to think about it. The more I thought, the less convinced I was about the advisability of spending time and energy making yet another home from scratch. Besides, we were happy at the YWCA. It provided us with a wonderful opportunity to teach the Faith. We lived there for about six months.

It was about the end of October when a letter arrived from the Bahá'í World Centre. It was from the Universal House of Justice extending to me 'a cordial invitation to come to the World Centre for service on our staff. We are asking the Secretariat to write you in more detail about the conditions of work . . .' The letter, which was dated 21 October 1971, also stated:

> We know that you will be concerned about your daughter's schooling. There is a church operated girls' school (with a few boys attending) near our offices which provides instruction in English up to General Certificate of Education examinations in a number of subjects, and, of course, there are the state operated schools giving instruction in Hebrew. The children of Mr and Mrs Hushmand Fathea'zam attended the English-speaking school, and the Fathea'zams will be able to give you more definite information about curricula and standards of instruction.
>
> If you are able to serve at the World Centre, we would appreciate your letting us know as soon as possible the date of your availability as the member of the staff presently handling this work expects to return to Persia approximately December lst.

When the letter arrived, I talked it over with Sovaida, who was then about nine and a half years old. I wanted her to be a part of the process of making a decision impacting her life more than it did mine. She was delighted at the prospect of having the opportunity to live at the Bahá'í World Centre; so was I. At that time I understood the wisdom of the fire that consumed our worldly belongings, for I did not need to worry about what I was going to do with our possessions. I responded in the affirmative to the invitation and said in my response of 29 October:

> Although I have not yet received the details about the conditions of work at the World Centre from the Secretariat, due to urgency of the matter, I am writing to say that, according to my terms of appointment with the Rockefeller Foundation, I am required to give one month's notice before I terminate my work at the University of Nairobi, i.e. if I am required to be at the World Centre on lst December, I should submit my resignation and give notice on lst November. However, since Sovaida (my daughter) does not finish the third term of her school until 5th December, I wonder if we could leave Nairobi on or about 15th December and be at the World Centre about that time. Should it be necessary for us to come earlier than that, we will, of course, make alternative arrangements to leave Nairobi about the end of November.

I tendered my resignation to the Rockefeller Foundation on 30 October 1971 and gave one month's notice as of that date. Two weeks later Mr Nakhjavání informed me by telephone that the school in Haifa no longer provided instruction in English. He said that the Universal House of Justice wanted me to have this information immediately. He also said that the House of Justice would offer compensation for the losses incurred in case the new situation affected my decision to relocate to Israel. The gist of that telephone conversation was confirmed in a letter from the Universal House of Justice dated 15 November 1971. To emphasize the Supreme Body's concern for the education of children and the welfare of families who are invited to serve at the World Centre, I share the contents of that letter:

> In our letter to you of October 21, 1971 we referred to a church operated girls' school in Haifa which we felt would be suitable

> for dear Sovaida. We have just been informed that the courses for an English-based education are being discontinued at that school, and that there are no other recognized schools in Haifa with English as their language of instruction.
>
> This is a radical change from the conditions under which you accepted our invitation to come to the Holy Land for service at the World Centre. We are, therefore, sharing this information with you at once.

The letter then listed various possibilities that existed in Haifa for Sovaida to continue her education in English, including 'an unofficial branch of an American school in Haifa being operated by one American teacher', 'the same church school in Haifa which offers its courses in Arabic', 'Hebrew schools', 'the possibility of arranging for private tutors to instruct Sovaida in English'. The letter continued:

> From your letter of October 29, 1971 we realize that you must have by now tendered your resignation from your present employment, but in view of the new circumstances we realize you must have an opportunity to reassess the situation. In arriving at a decision you should bear in mind that while we still need your services here, you should in no way feel obligated to disregard what you consider to be in the best interests of your child's future education, in order to respond to the invitation of the House of Justice. Furthermore, if you find that by deciding to remain in Nairobi you would have incurred any material losses in connection with your employment, you should feel free to write to us and we will be glad to offer you whatever may be necessary.
>
> We are praying at the Holy Shrines for your guidance in arriving at the right decision.
>
> With loving Bahá'í greetings,
>
> (Signed) The Universal House of Justice
>
> P.S. As requested by telephone, please cable your decision.

Sovaida and I consulted about the letter and how the information it contained could affect the way she continued her education in Haifa, if we decided to proceed with our original decision to relocate to Israel. We went over the different possibilities and what each entailed. She confirmed that she would like to go to the school in Haifa which offered courses in Arabic. She had always wanted to learn Arabic and this was a God-sent opportunity, she said. Thus I confirmed our original decision by cable, as asked.

Before leaving Kenya, Sovaida and I visited Mogadishu, Somalia, Pouran's new pioneer post, where she lived with her husband, 'Abdu'lláhí, and their daughter, Maryam. Mogadishu was very different from Nairobi in every respect. The airport was small and in the middle of nowhere. When our plane landed, we saw nothing but sand. Camels walked freely a short distance away. The sound of bells attached to their legs attracted our attention. They looked unperturbed by what was going on. The weather was hot and humid. The people were tall and slender. The women went swimming wearing long garments. We arrived during the period when a communist regime was in power. We met with the Bahá'ís during the several days we were there and were highly impressed with the calibre of the believers. We found them well-informed of the tenets of the Faith and very devoted. We returned to Nairobi a few days before our departure for the Holy Land.

On 17 December 1971 we left Nairobi, which holds for me both fond and hurtful memories, and settled at the Bahá'í World Centre, where I have been ever since.[130] After six years of schooling, Sovaida went to the United Kingdom for higher education. After becoming a barrister at law, she did her master's degree (LLM) in International Law at Pembroke College, Cambridge. She presently lives in Washington DC together with her husband Kenneth Patrick Ky Ewing, and their daughter, Giselle Rúḥíyyih Ewing, for whom this book has been written.

# Appendix 1

## Major Events in Nayríz Associated with the Bábí–Bahá'í Faith

Nayríz enjoys a prominent place on the map of events associated with the Bábí and Bahá'í Faiths. The person who introduced the Bábí Faith to Nayríz was Siyyid Yaḥyá. He later became known as Vaḥíd, meaning unique or the sole one,[1] a title bestowed upon him by the Báb after He espoused His claim to be the promised Qá'im. Siyyid Yaḥyá was renowned in Iran for his erudition. Upon becoming a Bábí, he travelled extensively to teach the Báb's message. Nayríz was the last place he visited to spread the Bábí Cause. His heroic efforts to establish the truth of the Báb's assertion in that small town claimed his life. Although he and many early Bábís were killed for their faith, the Cause of the Báb flourished in Nayríz. The Bábís of the town later espoused the Cause of Bahá'u'lláh, whose advent the Báb had heralded, and suffered severe persecution. Before discussing the soul-stirring events that took place in Nayríz over several decades, a brief account of the life and services of Siyyid Yaḥyá Vaḥíd is necessary.

### Family Background

Siyyid Yaḥyá was the son of Siyyid Ja'far Kashfí. We do not know the name of his mother but know that she was from Yazd. It is not known how many wives Siyyid Yaḥyá's father had but it was not uncommon for Muslim men of his time to have a wife in every place they established a residence. Siyyid Ja'far had residences in several locations in Iran and Iraq. He is believed to have had 15 children: eleven sons and four daughters.

Siyyid Yaḥyá's paternal grandfather was Siyyid Isḥáq. He was from Dáráb, a town in the province of Fárs. He later moved to Iṣṭahbánát, another town in the same province, where his son, Siyyid Ja'far, was born. Siyyid Ja'far's vast knowledge and his ability to unravel divine mysteries won him the title Kashfí (the one who unravels mysteries). He enjoyed widespread fame and established residences in Najaf, Iṣfahán, Yazd, Ṭihrán, Brújird and Iṣṭahbánát. He died in Brújird about 1851. He is reported to have met the Báb in Mecca and accepted His mission through his son Siyyid Yaḥyá.

Siyyid Yaḥyá was born in Yazd about 1809. In his childhood and youth he acquired extensive knowledge and became one of the renowned religious leaders of his time. He made Yazd his home and married there; the name of this wife is unknown. Siyyid Yaḥyá had four children from his first marriage: one daughter, Ṭúbá Khánum; and three sons, Siyyid Aḥmad, Siyyid 'Alí-Muḥammad and Siyyid Mihdí. The last two have also been referred to as Siyyid Muḥammad and Siyyid Muḥsin.

Siyyid Yaḥyá's second wife, Ṣughrá Khánum, was from Nayríz. She was daughter of Shaykh 'Abdu'l-'Alí; the name of her mother is unknown. Ṣughrá Khánum lived in Nayríz where Siyyid Yaḥyá had established a second home. They had one child, Siyyid Ismá'íl.

## Siyyid Yaḥyá's Acceptance of the Báb and His Services to the Bábí Cause

In 1844 Siyyid Yaḥyá, at the age of 35, visited Ṭihrán and stayed with his brother, Siyyid Isḥáq. While in Ṭihrán he learned of the Báb's advent and decided to travel to Shíráz to personally investigate the truth of His Cause. Muḥammad Sháh and his prime minister, Ḥájí Mírzá Áqásí, eager to obtain reliable and firsthand information about the Báb and His mission, and confident of Siyyid Yaḥyá's knowledge, integrity and devotion to Islam, asked him to report back to the Sháh the outcome of his investigation. The Sháh is purported to have provided him with a horse for the purpose. Siyyid Yaḥyá accepted the mission and set out for Shíráz.

In Shíráz Siyyid Yaḥyá was the guest of the governor of Fárs,

Ḥusayn Khán, a well-known opponent of the Báb. To make arrangements for meeting the Báb, Siyyid Yaḥyá established contact with his old acquaintances Ḥájí Siyyid Javád-i-Karbilá'í and Mullá Shaykh 'Alí, entitled 'Aẓím, who had become Bábís. They familiarized him with the tenets of the nascent Faith and led him to the Báb's presence in the house of His uncle, Ḥájí Mírzá Siyyid 'Alí. Siyyid Yaḥyá met with the Báb several times. According to his testimony, each meeting witnessed the resolution of some of his questions and made him humbler and more convinced. He was totally persuaded of the truth of the Báb's mission when He revealed, unasked, a commentary on the Súrih of Kawthar. The length of the commentary, its style, the speed with which it was revealed and the manner of its revelation confirmed Siyyid Yaḥyá in the truth of the Báb's claim. The Báb conferred upon Siyyid Yaḥyá the title Vaḥíd and this is the name by which he is generally known by Bahá'ís throughout the world.

The Báb encouraged Siyyid Yaḥyá Vaḥíd to arise and spread far and wide the new message he had espoused. He is also believed to have given the new convert a sword as a gift. At His behest, Vaḥíd first travelled to Burújird and acquainted his father with the Qá'im's claim. He then submitted the report of his investigation and his acceptance of the Báb's Mission to Muḥammad Sháh through Mírzá Luṭf-i 'Alí, a confidant at the Sháh's court. Some sources say Vaḥíd returned to Ṭihrán and tried, without much success, to teach the new Cause to his old acquaintances and friends. Vaḥíd continued his travels and visited Kurdistán, Iṣfahán, Ardistán, Ardikán, Yazd, Ṭihrán, Qazvín, Qum, Káshán, Khurásán and Fárs. In each place he acquainted the members of his family with the tenets of the Bábí Faith. He also announced, often from the pulpits of mosques, the coming of the promised Qá'im.

According to Fáḍil-i Mázandarání in *Ẓuhúru'l-Ḥaq,* Vaḥíd also visited the Báb in Máh-Kú on foot, after his visit to Qazvín. This has not been confirmed by other sources. Vaḥíd returned to Ṭihrán in the winter of 1848 and met Bahá'u'lláh in His house. He also met Ṭáhirih, who was then staying as a guest in Bahá'u'lláh's house.

When the episode at the shrine of Shaykh Ṭabarsí in Mázandarán had reached its climax, Vaḥíd began preparations to join the defenders of that Bábí stronghold. Bahá'u'lláh then returned from Mázandarán and advised him of the futility of such an attempt.

Vaḥíd returned to Yazd on Naw-Rúz (21 March) 1850. As was the custom, the 'ulamá and notables came to his house that day to welcome him back to the city. A provocative remark by Navváb-i Raḍaví, an adversary of the Báb, provided Vaḥíd with a welcome opportunity to proclaim the Báb's mission and His teachings to the assembled guests. That proclamation and the ensuing developments caused uproar in the city and threatened Vaḥíd's life. To avoid further deterioration of the situation, Vaḥíd left for Nayríz, accompanied by two of his sons, Siyyid Aḥmad and Siyyid Mihdí, together with two attendants. His wife and the other two children went to stay with her parents. Vaḥíd's house in Yazd was plundered and demolished in that incident.

With much difficulty Vaḥíd travelled sometimes on foot, at other times on horseback through unsuspected mountain routes to Bavánát in Fárs. He was warmly received by the inhabitants of Bavánát, who knew and admired him. Vaḥíd's proclamation work there yielded great results. Ḥájí Siyyid Ismá'íl, the Shaykhu'l-Islám, and a number of Vaḥíd's acquaintances embraced the Cause of the Báb, and some accompanied him to Fasá, another town in the province of Fárs.

Unlike Bavánát, the people of Fasá showed no interest in the new message. From there Vaḥíd proceeded to the shrine of Pír Murád in the vicinity of Iṣṭahbánát, where one of his sisters lived with her family. A number of the inhabitants of Iṣṭahbánát came out to meet Vaḥíd and 20 of them accompanied him to Nayríz. Vaḥíd had visited Nayríz several times previously and was well known to its inhabitants, who respected him highly. On his way to Nayríz, Vaḥíd tarried for a few days in Runíz (situated between Iṣṭahbánát and Nayríz). A large number of prominent people from Nayríz travelled to Runíz to extend a warm welcome to Vaḥíd and accompanied him back to their town.

## Vaḥíd's Arrival and Teaching Activities in Nayríz

Accompanied by the inhabitants of Nayríz who had gone to Runíz to welcome him, Vaḥíd arrived in Nayríz on 27 May 1850.[2] Vaḥíd's visit to the town to preach the new Faith was at a time when the people there were disenchanted with the despotic rule of the governor, Zaynu'l-'Ábidín Khán.

Upon arrival in Nayríz, Vaḥíd went to Masjid-i-Jámi' in Maḥallih Chinársúkhtih and announced to an eager congregation that he was the bearer of wonderful glad-tidings but postponed disclosure until a larger audience was present. When the mosque and its surrounding areas were packed with people, Vaḥíd explained the circumstances attending his acceptance of the Báb as the promised Qá'im and invited the congregation to pay allegiance to Him. Hundreds from Maḥallih Chinársúkhtih and many from other sections declared their belief upon hearing the news. After Vaḥíd accomplished this, he decided to leave Nayríz. However, the insistence of the new converts induced him to remain.

The enthusiastic response of the inhabitants of Nayríz and their support of Vaḥíd aroused the animosity of the apprehensive governor. Some of his relatives, oppressed and imprisoned by him, had been freed by the Bábís and had joined the ranks of the new converts. Vaḥíd's popularity, as evidenced by the welcome he received in Runíz, his success in securing the allegiance to the Bábí Faith of a large number of the inhabitants of the town and his prolonged stay in Nayríz caused Zayn'ul-'Ábidín Khán to turn against him.

To challenge Vaḥíd's authority and remove him as a threat, the governor addressed a message to the Bábís warning them in the strongest language of the dire consequences of espousing the new Faith. The message went unheeded, as did the appeal to Vaḥíd to leave Nayríz. These developments incensed the governor. He issued orders for the confiscation and use of the residence of Áqá Siyyid Abú Ṭálib, the Kad Khudá of Maḥallih Bázár, a new convert, for attacking Masjid-i Jámi', where Vaḥíd preached daily. He then went to Qaṭrúyih and raised a sizeable army of cavalry and infantry to attack the Bábís. He also apprised the governor of Fárs,

Prince Fírúz Mírzá, the Nuṣratu'd-Dawlih, of the developments and requested assistance.

## The Outbreak of Fighting

When information regarding Zaynu'l-'Ábidín Khan's plan reached Vaḥíd, he responded by despatching 20 of his companions, headed by Shaykh Hádí, to fortify the fort of Khájih in the vicinity of Maḥallih Chinársúkhtih. They hurriedly prepared the place for defence and stockpiled food. The army prepared by Zaynu'l-'Ábidín Khán in Qaṭrúyih arrived in Nayríz overnight and camped near the governor's residence in Maḥallih Bázár. Another group of armed men took position in Shaykh Abú Ṭálib's residence, overlooking Masjid-i Jámi'. In the first assault, one of Vaḥíd's old and venerable friends, Mullá 'Abdu'l-Ḥusayn, was wounded. The unprovoked military action tested the faith of some of the new converts. It also prompted Vaḥíd to ride out, in the company of 72 brave and staunch Bábís, to the fort of Khájih. Others joined him gradually until the number reached six hundred. Included in this number were some prominent people from Maḥallih Bázár. This boosted the morale of the Bábís. Vaḥíd's commitment to the Bábí Cause and his ability as an outstanding teacher and leader stood the test when the governor's army, headed by his eldest brother, 'Alí Aṣghar Khán, surrounded the fort and cut off its water supply. Vaḥíd sent a message to the governor asking that water be returned to the fort. The message was ignored. Vaḥíd sent a small band of his followers in the dead of the night to attack the encamped army. In the ensuing fight 'Alí Aṣghar Khán was killed and his two sons were captured alive. The defeated governor and his army returned to Qaṭrúyih, reported the incident to the governor of Fárs and requested urgent help.

Vaḥíd, well aware of the intention of the relentless enemy, organized the Bábís inside the fort, assigning them specific tasks. They further fortified the strongholds and dug a well to provide water.

The first emissary despatched by Zaynu'l-'Ábidín Khán to the governor of Fárs was captured in Hudashtak by a Bábí and sent to the fort of Kh̲ájih to face charges. Zaynu'l-'Abidín Kh̲án sent more emissaries to the governor of Fárs with valuable gifts and pleas for help. The governor of Fárs acted by despatching the Hamadání and Síláḵh̲urí regiments headed by 'Abdu'lláh Kh̲án (or Mihr 'Alí Kh̲án), the Sh̲ujá'ul-Mulk, and Muṣṭafá Kh̲án Qarágúzlú, fully equipped with heavy artillery. He also authorized them to conscript soldiers from the areas surrounding Nayríz. Consequently, a huge army surrounded the fort of Kh̲ájih, dug trenches, set up barricades and bombarded the Bábís' positions. The defenders of the fort fought heroically and inflicted a humiliating defeat on the combined armies of the enemy. The number of Bábís martyred in this battle was 60 according to a Bábí source and 150 by another account. The victorious defenders were steadily reinforced by fresh recruits from Nayríz. Their number, despite the return to town of some who could not endure a prolonged confrontation, is said to have swelled to over one thousand. Further attacks ordered by Vaḥíd resulted in more striking victories for his followers and completely frustrated the resolve of the army to continue the fight.

## The Martyrdom of Vaḥíd

Realizing that the war could not be won through military confrontation and desiring to end the fighting, the enemy resorted to treachery. The governor of Nayríz, the commanders of the two regiments and the army officers consulted and adopted a scheme. They first suspended their attacks for a few days, then addressed a written appeal to the besieged, accompanied by a copy of the Qur'án, to which they had affixed their seals, asking for a ceasefire to allow both sides to negotiate a peace treaty. Vaḥíd knew intuitively that the invitation to negotiate a peace treaty with the promise that he would not be harmed was nothing but a trick. But to show respect for the Qur'án and to expose the enemy's suspected scheme, he responded positively. He accepted the invitation and set out for the camp of the enemy, accompanied by five attendants. Before leaving the fort, he advised his followers not to abandon their strongholds and to await his specific instructions.

The governor and army commanders received Vaḥíd and his attendants with due respect. They knew that if any harm befell Vaḥíd, his followers inside the fort would retaliate fiercely. They devised a plan to get the Bábís out of the fort before they dealt with Vaḥíd mercilessly. They asked Vaḥíd to address a letter to the occupants, advising them to proceed to their homes since a peaceful solution had been reached. Knowing the intention of the enemy, Vaḥíd wrote two contradictory letters and instructed the bearer, Ḥájí Siyyid 'Ábid, one of his attendants, to destroy the letter he had written at the request of his hosts immediately after he left the camp and to deliver the second letter warning the occupants of the evil designs of the enemy. Ḥájí Siyyid 'Ábid, induced by the enemy, betrayed his master and presented both letters to the governor, who encouraged him to destroy the second letter and deliver the first. The treacherous design of the enemy and the betrayal of a confidant produced devastating effects for Vaḥíd and the Bábís. When presented with the letter, the occupants of the fort were uncertain of the wisdom of abandoning their strongholds but the instructions in Vaḥíd's handwritten message and Siyyid 'Ábid's verbal assurances left no room for doubt, so they complied. No sooner had they evacuated the fort than they were confronted by a column of the enemy forces which opened fire on them. A second column took position near the fort immediately after it had been vacated and opened fire, making it impossible for the Bábís to return. Although trapped, the besieged fought heroically. Many of them perished in this incident; the number is estimated at 350. Some survivors managed to reach Nayríz, intending to seek refuge in Masjid-i Jámi', but one of their bitter enemies had taken position there and shot whoever approached. They dispersed and went into hiding but were sought out and arrested. The wealthy and influential among them were held in Nayríz, others were either killed under torture or sent in captivity to Shíráz accompanied by the heads of their fellow Bábís. This was to signify the triumph of the authorities. In Shíráz the male captives were executed and the women and children, after untold humiliation and ridicule, set free.

When Zaynu'l-'Ábidín Khán and his accomplices were assured

of the dispersal of the Bábís, they consulted on how to circumvent their solemn oath in order to get rid of Vaḥíd. A ruthless officer named 'Abbás-Qulí Khán, undeterred by those who had pledged to protect Vaḥíd's life, stepped forward and offered to carry out their design. He declared that he had not participated in the oath and was not bound by its obligations. His act induced others, who had lost their kinsmen in the war, to follow suit. They wound Vaḥíd's turban, the sign of his lineage, around his neck, tied him to a horse and dragged him through the streets, accompanied by the loud sound of drums and shouting of the populace. They inflicted upon him whatever harm they could. He was beheaded just before he was dead. They stuffed his scalp with straw and sent it as a trophy to Fírúz Mírzá, the governor of Fárs, together with other severed heads of the Bábís. Vaḥíd's martyrdom occurred on 18 Sha'bán 1266 (29 June 1850), ten days before the Báb's martyrdom.[3] He was then 41 years old. His martyrdom ended the first Bábí uprising in Nayríz.

## Continued Persecutions Bring about Second Bábí Uprising

When the episode at the fort of Khájih ended, the Bábí community became a target for severe persecution. The wealthy and renowned were singled out; the purpose was to extort their wealth. To escape such treatment, the surviving men left Nayríz and became fugitives in the surrounding mountains and neighbouring towns. The women and small children were left without protection or support and were ridiculed, ostracized, abused and tortured. During this time a heroic Bábí youth named Mírzá 'Alí, entitled Sardár, remained in the vicinity of the town and provided material and moral support for these valiant souls. He was later joined in his humanitarian efforts by Khájih Quṭbá.

A few of the Bábís left for Ṭihrán to plead for justice. They were spotted near the capital by a caravan from Shíráz, arrested and sent to Shíráz where they faced execution. Another Bábí, a survivor of the fort of Khájih episode, Mullá Muḥammad, whose twelve-year-old blind brother had been tortured to death before the eyes of his mother, went to Ṭihrán to take revenge on the despotic Sháh whom he held responsible. There he joined two other Bábí youth in their attempt on the life of Náṣiri'd-Dín Sháh on 15 August 1852. The effects of the ensuing turmoil exacerbated the already volatile situation in Nayríz.

When the level of persecution reached its zenith, the Bábís decided to take decisive action. The fugitives established contact with each other and with Mírzá 'Alí Sardár and Khájih Quṭbá. Nineteen of them met and planned a strategy to get rid of Zaynu'l-'Ábidín Khán. Five Bábís volunteered to carry out the decision. One morning they attacked the governor as he entered the bath. The five Bábís and the governor died in the incident. The governor of Fárs at this time was Prince Ṭahmásb Mírzá, the Mu'ayyadu'd-Dawlih. He received repeated requests from the family of Zaynu'l-'Ábidín Khán, along with valuable gifts, to deal with the Bábí threat. He appointed Mírzá Na'ím-i Núrí to replace Zaynu'l-'Ábidín Khán and empowered him to take action. Mírzá Na'ím despatched his uncle, Mírzá Bábá, together with manpower and heavy military equipment to Nayríz prior to his arrival. However, knowing that he could not deal effectively with the Bábís through the use of force, he first tried to overpower them by other means. He announced that he wanted to administer justice. A Bábí delegation led by Sardár welcomed him upon arrival. Mírzá Na'ím treated them with kindness and for a while there was calm. He then sent a message to the Bábís asking those who had complaints against the former governor to assemble in the court house on a certain day to present their cases for investigation. On the appointed day, between 130 and 150 Bábís, including Sardár and Khájih Quṭbá, gathered in the court house. Soon they realized it was a trap. The doors of the court house closed, soldiers moved in and they were all arrested. The plan was to send the captives to Ṭihrán to prove the wise and skilful rule of Mírzá Na'ím. However, their deceptive plan was thwarted. The inhabitants of Qaṭrúyih, one of the dependencies of Nayríz, arose in rebellion. In order to subdue the offenders, Mírzá Na'ím decided to make use of the available Bábí force and skill. He apologized to Sardár and the other Bábís for what he called a mere misunderstanding. He then briefed them on the uprising in Qaṭrúyih and requested their support to deal with the situation. If they were successful, he said, they would be rewarded by the government with the restoration of their properties. Sardár accepted the challenge and, with the help of the freed Bábís, quelled the rebellion in Qaṭrúyih. He was thereafter commended by Mírzá Na'ím, who summoned him and his companions to the government house to receive compensation.

Fully aware of Mírzá Na'ím's secret designs, Mírzá 'Alí asked the governor to send a representative with sufficient men to take over affairs in Qaṭrúyih. He also advised the governor that having been away from home for so long, he and his companions preferred to visit their families before attaining the presence of the governor. Thus Sardár and the other Bábís returned to their homes and started making preparations to defend themselves. As they proceeded, the Bábí fugitives and their relatives joined them. When the number of willing warriors reached 361 (19 x 19), they consulted and organized themselves under the leadership of Mírzá 'Alí Sardár, with Kh̲ájih Quṭbá appointed as his deputy. In the last month of 1268 (early 1852) they were fully prepared to defend themselves and their families. Mírzá Na'ím realized the magnitude of the Bábí threat and knowing that he no longer could effect the arrest of the Bábís peacefully, decided to resort to force and arrest enough Bábís to despatch to Ṭihrán in fulfilment of his original plan. However, his forces met with the Bábís' fierce resistance and retreated. A further confrontation took place during which seven Bábís were arrested, imprisoned and subsequently put to death. Following this incident the Bábís collected their wives and children and took to Bídbukh̲úyih in mountains south of Nayríz, where they made extensive plans for their defence. From there they proceeded to a higher and more defensible position called Darb-i S̲h̲igift. They were followed by government forces. Sardár instructed the Bábís to attack. In a series of encounters the forces of the governor suffered heavy casualties and retreated, allowing the Bábís to recover a considerable amount of firearms and heavy artillery.

One night the Bábís besieged the headquarters of the armed

forces in Nayríz and killed many of them. After this episode the Bábís took position in Bálá Ṭárum, the peak of the mountain. They set up 19 strongholds in defensible heights. Each stronghold was entrusted to a responsible person who was assisted by a group of 18 other Bábís. One of the 19 strongholds was assigned to a woman known as the mother of Samí'; the members of her team were all women. As a considerable time was needed for the army to reorganize and receive reinforcement for a fresh attack, the Bábís had a time of respite. During this period it was necessary for some Bábís to go to the town to obtain food, which resulted in occasional clashes with the inhabitants of Nayríz. The reference by one historian to Kh̲ájih Quṭbá, also known as Mírzá Ḥusayn-i Quṭb, intimidating and terrorizing the people of the town must be to such encounters.

### The War of the Mountain (Jang-i Jibal)

The continued persecution of the Bábís, the attempt on the life of the Sh̲áh, the murder of Zaynu'l-'Ábidín Kh̲án, the constant provocation of the 'ulamá and feelings of vengeance entangled both sides in a war much fiercer in intensity and broader in scope than the first one. It is known as Jang-i Jibal (the War of the Mountain) and it took place about the end of 1852 to early 1853.

After the first few encounters, which resulted in the defeat of the government forces, Mírzá Na'ím sent a detailed report of developments to the central government and the governor of Fárs requesting urgent help. He also made extensive preparations to attack the organized Bábí community, whose number had increased considerably since the first upheaval in 1266 (1850). He gathered an imposing force, some say of ten thousand men supported by heavy artillery, and ordered an all-out attack. Their strategy was to surround the mountain and entrap the Bábís, who had to fight their way down daily to obtain water. This continued until Sardár led a well-planned general attack. Concurrent with the assault from the mountaintop, the Bábís set ablaze the storehouses containing wood and thistles and inflicted heavy losses on the retreating army. Mírzá Na'ím and his entourage escaped.

Following Mírzá Na'ím's humiliating defeat, a decree was issued calling upon all tribes, clans, villages and towns in the surrounding area to participate in the war. The army received a tremendous boost. Aḥmad Khán-i Bahárlú with five hundred of his renowned horsemen ascended the mountain from the direction of Íj and Dáráb to the south. The armed forces and their supporters surrounded the mountain from every direction. The Bábís' food supplies and ammunition diminished with every passing day. Sardár advised his companions of the gravity of the situation and asked those who could not bear the consequences to leave; none did. The heroic Bábí leader mounted his horse and, as was his normal practice, set out with 18 other Bábís to quell the attack. Although he succeeded in his attempt, he was fatally wounded. He returned with great difficulty to his stronghold, where he died and was buried. After his death, the Bábís continued the fight. They rationed the available food. Towards the end the warriors' sustenance was a few figs a day, women offering their daily portions of figs to the men to enable them to fight. When the supply of figs came to an end, the remaining warriors tied the hems of their robes and charged down the mountain to launch a last united assault on the enemy. Thus the second Bábí uprising in Nayríz came to an end.

One source[4] suggests that when Sardár was killed a message was sent to the Bábís to surrender. They asked the armed forces to retreat as a sign of goodwill to enable them to bury their dead. The army retreated one kilometre. The Bábís used the opportunity to send their women and children home, it says. Then they advised their adversary of their readiness to fight to the last breath, fulfilling the pledge they had made to fight and die together. The same source gives the number of the captured women at the end of the war as 603.

The Bábí survivors went into hiding. A widespread search ensued and those found were often tortured and killed. Among them were 40 women and children who were burnt to death when the cave in which they had taken refuge was set ablaze.

The heads of those who were killed, numbering two hundred,

were sent to Shíráz together with a similar number of the wounded and several hundred women and children. Many of the Bábís were executed in Shíráz by order of Ṭahmásb Mírzá. A number of the aged had been chained and sent on foot; some died owing to the hardships they endured. The women and children, who were forced to ride on unsaddled mules, were held in Shíráz. After a period of immense humiliation and torment they were freed. Many of them perished on their way to Nayríz. Mullá 'Abdu'l-Ḥusayn, a Bábí survivor of the first and second episodes, who could not keep pace owing to his old age, was beheaded after the caravan left Shíráz for Ṭihrán and his head was carried along on the journey. When the caravan reached Ábádih, according to a royal decree, the heads were buried there. Only a small number of the wounded, 28 in all, survived the journey to Ṭihrán. Fifteen of them were executed upon arrival in the capital, while others were released after two years of imprisonment and torture.

### Later Developments

The War of the Mountain started more than two years after the martyrdom of the Báb and ended about the time Bahá'u'lláh was released from the Síyáh-Chál and banished to Iraq. It signifies the rapid growth of the Bábí community of Nayríz after the first upheaval; it also demonstrates its determination and capacity to withstand brutal and unjust treatment. Despite the abominable atrocities it suffered after the termination of the second war, the community gradually regained its strength and became a focal point of Bábí, and later Bahá'í, activities. Some of the Bábí survivors went to Baghdád and attained Bahá'u'lláh's presence. One of them, Mullá Muḥammad Shafí', returned to Nayríz and played a leading role in effecting a reconciliation between the community and the authorities which lasted until 1909. He was also instrumental in educating the community in the tenets of the Bahá'í Faith. What happened to the Bahá'í community of Nayríz after that date is covered in the main text.

# Appendix 2

## Excerpts from the Memoirs of Mr Muḥammad-Shafí' Rouhani of His 39-Day Pilgrimage in April/May 1921

### I

'Abdu'l-Bahá admitted us to His presence immediately upon our arrival in Haifa. There were seven of us from Nayríz accompanied by Náẓimu'l-Mulk. We were led to a small room to the north of the blessed House. We entered with utter humility and attained the honour of union.

We had been advised beforehand not to kneel before 'Abdu'l-Bahá. We were told to enter, say Alláh-u-Abhá and await His instructions.

We followed this advice and bowed one by one as we entered. With supreme dignity 'Abdu'l-Bahá welcomed us and bade us to be seated. The power of prostration was taken from us. We were like dead bodies in His presence. While He was leaning back, He said in a captivating voice, 'Welcome! You sustained many difficulties during your journey . . .'

As there were seven pilgrims from Nayríz, 'Abdu'l-Bahá turned His loving attention to us, asked after the friends there and said, 'Nayríz is a sacred place. The pure blood of many martyrs was shed on its soil. Among the martyrs is Áqá Siyyid Yaḥyáy-i Vaḥíd, who had committed to memory thirty thousand traditions. He was foremost among the 'ulamá of Iran. Also among them was Ḥáj Muḥammad-Taqí-Ayyúb, who, as the gamblers say, risked his all. He sacrificed whatever he had in the path of God. He was tortured and made to suffer greatly. Finally he went to Baghdád and became the recipient of endless bounties.'

## II

The second day after our arrival was the first day of Riḍván. On that day 'Abdu'l-Bahá and His family went to Bahjí to visit the Shrine of Bahá'u'lláh. At His behest, bus tickets were obtained for all the pilgrims to go to 'Akká and visit the Most Holy Shrine. As we entered the bus and were introduced to the person in charge, he manifested extreme respect for 'Abdu'l-Bahá and expressed delight that we were the followers of 'Abbás Effendi.

We were dropped off at a place about one kilometre from Bahjí. From there all of us walked towards the Shrine while singing a song, the opening verses of which are:

We the followers of Bahá
with dilated hearts
from the beginning of creation
to the end of time
are proclaimers
of the Greatest Name:
Alláh-u-Abhá! Alláh-u-Abhá!

And all of us, with cries of exultation, responded by repeating the last verse. When we reached a curve in the path near the Bahjí tea house and saw before us in the distance the blessed figure of 'Abdu'l-Bahá, we stopped singing and approached Him with absolute courtesy and humility. We bowed and uttered the greeting of Alláh-u-Abhá. With a heavenly smile He said, 'Welcome!' Then with much compassion and in a very humorous way He pretended to scold us, saying, 'You have publicly disgraced us! There was a time when no one dared say "Alláh-u-Abhá". Now you raise the cry of praise and glorification and openly utter the greeting of "Alláh-u-Abhá" as you come to the Blessed Shrine.'

## III

One day the writer and another pilgrim from Nayríz were taken ill and were confined to bed. Dr Luṭfu'lláh Ḥakím was our physician. The illness deprived us of the bounty of attaining the presence of 'Abdu'l-Bahá for a few days. I was able to leave my sick bed on the eighth day of Riḍván. I joined the other pilgrims at the pilgrim house. However, the condition of Ḥáj Amru'lláh, the other pilgrim, worsened. 'Abdu'l-Bahá issued instructions for the German doctor to visit the patient and help Dr Ḥakím in his attempts to cure him.

On the ninth day of Riḍván we again left Haifa, at 'Abdu'l-Bahá's behest, and went to Akká. On that day we visited the Most Holy Shrine, the Garden of Firdaws[1] and the Garden of Riḍván, which was also called by Bahá'u'lláh the verdant island. Dr Ḥakím was directed by 'Abdu'l-Bahá to remain in Haifa and watch Ḥáj Amru'lláh's condition, which had become critical.

Unfortunately, on this trip I developed diarrhoea. In the morning the matter was reported to 'Abdu'l-Bahá. He ordered that one and a half litres of milk be boiled. I was to drink it when it was cold. With this prescription I was completely cured; the immediate cure was obviously effected through His blessed will.

Two days later something happened that astonished us all: 'Abdu'l-Bahá was sitting in the little garden in front of the Shrine of Bahá'u'lláh[2] and a group of us were in His presence. He was talking to us when Dr Ḥakím arrived from Haifa and sought permission to attain 'Abdu'l-Bahá's presence. Permission was granted. He, panic-stricken and perturbed, said, 'One of the patients from Nayríz is in a critical condition.' 'Abdu'l-Bahá said calmly, 'He will be all right.' Dr Ḥakím, who had given up hope and was certain the patient would die by the time he returned said, 'My Master, even the German doctor has no hope for him; he is moribund.' With a special gesture, which is His alone, and with considerable force, 'Abdu'l-Bahá repeated His assurance, saying, 'He will be all right,' and then He dismissed Dr Ḥakím. There were some candies on the table. 'Abdu'l-Bahá took one of the candies known locally as

Turkish delight, gave it to Dr Ḥakím and said, 'You may also give this to the patient.' The doctor took the candy, backed out respectfully and returned to Haifa. On the twelfth day of Riḍván, when we returned to Haifa, Ḥáj Amru'lláh was out of bed, looking well and very much alive. He joined us in the pilgrim house near the Shrine of the Báb.

## IV

One evening 'Abdu'l-Bahá granted audience to a large number of the friends in the hall of His house. With a captivating eloquence and in a state of joy and delight, He said, 'No government was able to seize the fortress and port of 'Akká but when God willed it, it was conquered by two British cavalrymen. ('Abdu'l-Bahá with the use of His two fingers emphasized the figure two). He then said, 'It is the will of God that this Faith should advance; therefore, nothing can hinder its progress or check its growth. All the religions of God have been like this in the beginning. We are holding a pickaxe in our hand ready to build but we see that the building is raised by itself. [At this point 'Abdu'l-Bahá related the story of Abú Muslim-i Khurásání[3] and the seemingly trivial circumstances that contributed to his victory over the forces of Ibn-i Marván and remarked that 'the same force is in operation now'.]

## V

One afternoon 'Abdu'l-Bahá was in the garden of His house pacing the path when He admitted a group of us to His presence. We were completely immersed in the bountiful ocean of His eloquent utterances when someone informed Him of the arrival of Áqá Shaykh Faraju'lláh[4] from Egypt and requested permission for him to attain 'Abdu'l-Bahá's presence. Permission was granted. Shaykh Faraju'lláh came and said one of the well-known scholars of Egypt by the name of Shaykh Muḥammad, with whom he had spoken about the Faith for some time and who had several unresolved questions, had come to Haifa with him to discuss his difficulties and pose his questions in person. 'Abdu'l-Bahá granted permission for them to attain His presence after supper (the pilgrims usually had their supper at the house of the Master and went to the pilgrim house to sleep). After supper we were dismissed and returned to the pilgrim house.

Some time elapsed. I was in a state between sleep and wakefulness when I heard the voices of two Arabs coming up the mountain who were talking together as they were approaching the pilgrim house (the pilgrim house is situated in the heart of Carmel and the voices of those who climbed could be clearly heard in the silent night. Therefore, I could hear their happy conversation. They were so jubilant, methought they had discovered a treasure house). As they drew nigh, they knocked at the door. Áqá Muḥammad Ḥasan, the attendant . . . awoke and opened the door. It became known that the arrivals were Áqá Shaykh Faraju'lláh and his friend Shaykh Muḥammad, the Muftí of Egypt. After arrival they lit the light in the corridor, sat there and started talking together. Sleep was lost to me completely. As I had studied Arabic and could follow their conversation to a measured degree, I understood what they were talking about. In but one meeting 'Abdu'l-Bahá had subdued the heart of the Shaykh in such wise that he had become an ardent lover. Their discussion was so intriguing and the description of their visit with 'Abdu'l-Bahá so exciting that I lost the power to resist. I left my bed and with their permission sat on a chair next to them.

They continued their conversation. Shaykh Muḥammad, addressing Shaykh Faraju'lláh said, 'I worked hard for several years and had selected some very difficult questions which I had noted down to ask. When I decided to accompany you to Haifa, I was thinking that my encounter with 'Abdu'l-Bahá would take a long time before settlement could be reached. However, after discussing one of my problems during the first meeting, the response was so comprehensive and all-embracing that I feel all of my difficulties have been resolved. 'Abdu'l-Bahá has answered all my questions. For example, the problem of fate and free will which seemed to be very complicated and which I thought would have needed a long time to resolve, was disposed of in one meeting. As soon as the first question was discussed, the response was such that my other questions were also answered. It is like a key with which I can open the door to many other questions.'

The Shaykh spent several days in Haifa partaking of the bounty of attaining 'Abdu'l-Bahá's presence. On the night of the Ascension of Bahá'u'lláh I saw him in the Most Holy Shrine and in the presence of 'Abdu'l-Bahá displaying absolute devotion and humility. He was so transformed and appeared so intoxicated with the spirit and filled with enthusiasm that I was envious of him. His tears were unceasing. He evinced such tender emotions at the time of prostrating himself at the Sacred Threshold that everyone present was affected.

This is the story of the meeting with 'Abdu'l-Bahá of one of the Islamic learned men whose transformation I witnessed with my own eyes. I saw how dust was transmuted by alchemy and copper became gold.

## VI

One day as 'Abdu'l-Bahá entered the courtyard and was going up the steps leading to His house, one of the pilgrims approached Him and said, 'My purpose in life is to teach the Cause of God. I beseech confirmations.' 'Abdu'l-Bahá turned back and addressing the petitioner said, 'Every teacher is confirmed and victorious. The Blessed Beauty has said: "Verily, We . . . shall aid whosoever will arise for the triumph of Our Cause with the hosts of the Concourse on high and a company of Our favoured angels."'[5] He then said twice that purity of motive is needed and, alluding to Alma Knobloch, remarked, 'A woman of slight build and of little formal education arose with pure intention and conquered Germany.'[6]

## VII

One day 'Abdu'l-Bahá stepped out into the verdant garden of His house. The pilgrims stood in rows on both sides of the footpath awaiting Him. 'Abdu'l-Bahá called His faithful gardener Ismá'íl Áqá and asked him to bring a basket. 'Abdu'l-Bahá with His own hands picked a considerable number of red roses and placed them in the basket. He then entered the path, followed by Ismá'íl Áqá, who carried the basket. 'Abdu'l-Bahá was extremely happy and, as He walked past us, He gave each a rose and said ['Abdu'l-Bahá's words are paraphrased]:

> Today the news was received that a beauty, divinely blessed, has been martyred in Kirmánsháhán. This youth sought martyrdom from Me. I assured him with this verse, 'O Thou assured soul, return to thy Lord well-pleased and pleasing unto Him.' Now the news of his martyrdom has arrived. I give you these flowers in memory of Áqá Ya'qúb-i Muttaḥidih.[7] He then continued as He walked, saying that when the Blessed Beauty [Bahá'u'lláh] was in Baghdád, there was a flowering tree in the house, which had become weak. Bahá'u'lláh ordered that some blood from a slaughtered lamb be poured around the tree. This was done and the tree became very strong. This is the effect of blood on a tree. Behold the effect that the sacrifice of blood of a youth such as Áqá Ya'qúb-i Muttaḥidih will have on the tree of the Cause.

That day 'Abdu'l-Bahá's words about martyrdom were such that they caused even the most stone-hearted individuals among the audience to desire martyrdom.

In the evening there was a beautiful gathering in the Master's house. 'Abdu'l-Bahá ordered that the letter from Mírzá Yúsif Khán-i Vujdání describing the circumstances attending the martyrdom of Áqá Ya'qúb-i Muttaḥidih be read from beginning to end. The letter closed with the following lines of verse [by Jalálu'd-Dín-i Rúmí]:

Thou hast slain the lovers,
Thy hands are stained with their blood;
Thou hast then performed prayers
Over their bodies, one by one.

'Abdu'l-Bahá again spoke in praise of that beloved youth who had asked Him to be permitted to be the first martyr from among the Bahá'ís of Jewish origin.

## VIII

A meeting was convened one evening in the beautiful garden of the Master's house. At His bidding tea was served. Then two Jews who had returned to Haifa from Jerusalem asked permission to meet with 'Abdu'l-Bahá. Permission was granted. They said, 'We are Jews. We had gone to Jerusalem for pilgrimage. Now that we want to return, it is the time of [heavy rains] and we are fearful that our ship may sink. We have heard that your prayers for people are answered. We have come to you with our need and beseech your guidance and prayers.'

'Abdu'l-Bahá said, 'We will pray, rest assured. From here you should go to Port Said. You will be able to get a ship to take you directly from there to Basra and Bú<u>sh</u>ihr. You will reach home safely.' Then He dismissed them. As they were saying farewell they said, 'We are strangers in this city and have no place to rest tonight.' 'Abdu'l-Bahá said, 'Go to the pilgrim house and spend the night there.' They bowed and left with supreme happiness and humility.

When they left, 'Abdu'l-Bahá said, 'I like them very much. Although they came to us with a need to be fulfilled, they were frank and forthright. The friends should have such an attitude and use this as an example . . .'

## IX

One day a meeting was held in the hall of 'Abdu'l-Bahá's house. A large number of people were present and 'Abdu'l-Bahá, while seated, spoke to the friends. At the end of His talk two small children, four and six years old, whose father was of Armenian background and had embraced the Faith, stood up with their hands over their chests and, with 'Abdu'l-Bahá's permission, recited in very sweet voices a poem which starts with the verse: 'O 'Abdu'l-Bahá, I am helpless, O 'Abdu'l-Bahá, I am homeless, hold Thou my hand, hold Thou my hand.'

It was very interesting to see the extraordinary kindness with which 'Abdu'l-Bahá treated those children. He called them to Him, seated them on His lap and, after showering His special favours upon them, let them go. The two children went to the other side of the meeting hall and sat on the lap of Áqá Ḥusayn-i Kahrubá'í.[8]

## X

One day when we were in the presence of 'Abdu'l-Bahá, He was informed that the British Crown Prince[9] was arriving in Haifa and that the governor [of Palestine] wished to borrow His car, which was the latest model and had been presented to Him by the American friends. ['Abdu'l-Bahá had no objection.]

## XI

One day we were in the presence of the Master in Bahjí. Something came up that prompted 'Abdu'l-Bahá to speak of Nayríz. Áqá Mírzá Aḥmad-i Nayrízí conveyed a request from some of the friends, who had seen us off, that they be blessed and graced by the Master. 'Abdu'l-Bahá said, 'They are all the recipients of favour.' Mírzá Aḥmad said, 'They seek the good pleasure of their Master.' 'Abdu'l-Bahá responded, 'I am well pleased with the friends of Nayríz and the Blessed Beauty is also well pleased with them. How can I be dissatisfied? They have thrice sacrificed their lives in the field of martyrdom.' Mírzá Aḥmad said, 'Our fathers gave up their lives but we are sinners and ashamed of ourselves.' 'Abdu'l-Bahá replied, 'We are all sinners but the bounty of the Blessed Beauty is immense, be assured.'

## XII

On a certain day when a group of pilgrims and resident Bahá'ís were in the presence of 'Abdu'l-Bahá, Áqá Siyyid Muṣṭafá,[10] the renowned Bahá'í teacher from Rangoon, Burma, found an occasion to say that the land of India is like a jungle of different religions and denominations. He said the beliefs, customs and manners are very diverse and superstitions are rampant. 'Abdu'l-Bahá said it was true but He added that the establishment of schools and the promotion of knowledge will eradicate the foundation of superstition.

Áqá Siyyid Muṣṭafá said, 'The friends in India are awaiting the arrival of their Master there.' 'Abdu'l-Bahá said, 'I was inclined to take a trip to Japan, China and India but now there are obstacles in the way. I have accomplished my work. The Mas͟hriqu'l-Ad͟hkár of Turkistán has been built and the foundation of another one in the United States is in place.[11] Today we have received the news that the annual convention has also been convened. The time has come for the friends to take over the work.'

These utterances conveyed the sad news of 'Abdu'l-Bahá's imminent departure from this world but no one dared ask a question except Áqá Mírzá Abu'l-Ḥasan-i Afnán, who was an ardent lover of the Master. Because that venerable man was a trustworthy person, 'Abdu'l-Bahá shared with him the hidden meaning of His utterance. When we returned to Iran we received the news that because Mírzá Abu'l-Ḥasan could not bear the thought of separation from 'Abdu'l-Bahá, he, while the Master was still enjoying good health, wrote his will and drowned himself.

## XIII

I was a youth in my twenties when I came on pilgrimage. As it is a condition peculiar to this age, I had not set a fixed pattern for earning a living and serving the Cause. At times I wanted to leave home and finish my education, then arise and teach the Faith on a full-time basis. At other times, since I was married, I thought of having children and educating them for this work. And yet at other times, I contemplated seeking wealth in order to spend it in the path of service.

As I was sincere in my intention, I knew that once I made up my mind and sought 'Abdu'l-Bahá's assistance, He would grant it. 'But what should I request that would not be harmful?' I asked myself. 'If I request wealth, it may become the cause of negligence; if I seek knowledge for the purpose of teaching the Faith, that knowledge may become a veil.' I was doubtful about what to ask that would be beneficial and in my best interests.

Several nights, before going to bed, I pondered upon the subject and prayed with fervour in order to choose the best option. One night I had a dream which gave me the courage to set aside my own thoughts, leave my affairs in the hand of the divine Physician and implore Him to prescribe for me that which He saw to be in my best interests. However, I knew that in His presence I would not have the power to utter anything, unless He granted me the strength to do so. Therefore I chose a short sentence and practised it well with the intention of reciting it if I ever had the bounty of attaining His presence privately.

Then I mentioned to Áqá Mírzá Dhikru'lláh, 'Abdu'l-Bahá's cousin, that I was longing to attain His presence in private. Because I knew 'Abdu'l-Bahá did not deprive sincere petitioners of reception in His court, I made the necessary preparations for the visit.

I had just received a letter from Nayríz containing the glad-tidings of the arrival there of Mr Náṭiq,[12] a Bahá'í teacher, the establishment of the Míth//áqíyyih School and the news of the inauguration ceremony. Attached to the letter was the text of the speech delivered by my brother. I kept this material with me to present to 'Abdu'l-Bahá because I knew He appreciated receiving such news.

One day when all the pilgrims from Nayríz were in the house of the Master, Mírzá Dhikru'lláh gave me the awaited news. He told me that 'Abdu'l-Bahá was alone in the house of Mírzá Jalál, His son-in-law, and had called me into His presence. I took the items which I wanted 'Abdu'l-Bahá to bless and with exceeding gladness accompanied Áqá Mírzá Dhikru'lláh to the appointed place. With extreme excitement and in a state of utter humility and lowliness I entered the vestibule of the house. Mírzá Dhikru'lláh went in and sought permission for me to enter. Permission was granted. I left the wrapper, which contained several items to be blessed, in the corridor. I then opened the door and saw 'Abdu'l-Bahá seated at a desk. I bowed and said Alláh-u-Abhá. He gave me permission to enter.

I immediately threw myself at His feet, held the hem of His robe and entreated Him tearfully saying: 'O my Beloved! Do not leave me to myself, cause me to move in accordance with Thy will and confirm me in my servitude and obedience to Thee.'

'Abdu'l-Bahá bountifully lifted me up with the hand of His power and with a penetrating voice said: 'God hath confirmed thee in serving His Cause, in elevating His word and in spreading His fragrances.'

This blessed utterance opened before my face the portals of happiness. It imparted hope and assurance to my heart and helped me to know what course of action to follow in my life. I immediately realized that I was not going to become wealthy but knew of a certainty that He would grant me all that was necessary for rendering service.

After I rose to my feet 'Abdu'l-Bahá granted me permission to sit on a chair. He then gave me the courage and the opportunity to give Him the glad-tidings from Nayríz. The news of the arrival there of Mr Náṭiq, of the establishment of the Míth//áqíyyih School, of the inauguration ceremony and of the speeches read by the students of the school was presented to Him. In the end I submitted the handwritten copy of the speech which I had received from my brother Jalál and sought divine confirmations for the teachers and students of the school. 'Abdu'l-Bahá took the copy, read it carefully and added the word '*bárí*' (yea) to a sentence. He then called His amanuensis, who was not there. Therefore, He took the pen and at the foot of the same sheet of paper wrote the following prayer:

> O God, my God! I supplicate confirmation and assistance for those who have arisen to serve Thy Cause and educate the chil-

dren who have been nurtured from the breast of Thy love. O God! Glorify these children in Thy Kingdom and teach them from Thy knowledge. Thou art the Powerful and the Mighty.[13]

Praised be God! 'Abdu'l-Bahá's favours were far beyond anyone's imagination and perception. It was providential that His amanuensis was not there, so that He wrote the prayer in His own handwriting.

It was the custom that unless 'Abdu'l-Bahá clearly dismissed a person by saying: 'May you be in God's trust', the visit continued. Therefore, as He left the room, I followed Him. Outside in the corridor I saw the items I had left there and forgotten about. I presented them to 'Abdu'l-Bahá and just said, 'For blessing.' He took them with the hand of compassion and, while holding them, recited a prayer and returned them to me.

Still he did not dismiss me. As He was leaving the corridor to enter the vestibule, He rubbed His eyes with His Hands and said, 'I am tired. It is the spirit that endures; the body cannot bear it.' Then He recited a verse of poetry, which says: 'Servitude is captivity and lordship a headache'. He then immediately added, 'Servitude is not captivity, although lordship is a headache.'

As 'Abdu'l-Bahá entered the courtyard of the house He ordered that chairs be set up and the pilgrims from Nayríz be called. This was done. As soon as the chairs were in place, 'Abdu'l-Bahá sat down and granted me permission to be seated. The other six pilgrims from Nayríz also arrived and were seated at His behest.

'Abdu'l-Bahá spoke favourably of the friends of Nayríz, of their successes in rendering service, of the arrival of Mr Náṭiq, of the establishment of the Mí<u>th</u>áqíyyih School and He praised Mr Náṭiq. When He was informed that before the arrival of Mr Náṭiq, Mr Muṭlaq and Mr Nabílzádih[14] had visited Nayríz and produced great results, He said, 'Mr Nabílzádih and Mr Muṭlaq are indeed sacrificial.' We were then dismissed.

## XIV

On the first day of Ramaḍán we were in the presence of 'Abdu'l-Bahá together with a group of pilgrims and resident Bahá'ís, such as Ḥájí 'Alíy-i Yazdí, the brother of Ḥájí Muḥammad Ṭáhir-i Málmírí. Because of the difference in the lunar calendar, some of the Muslims had observed the first day of Ramaḍán the previous day. 'Abdu'l-Bahá asked Ḥájí 'Alí whether the people in the market had observed the fast yesterday or today. He replied that some started the fast as from yesterday and some from today.

'Abdu'l-Bahá said, 'Because they have not understood the significance of the fast, they have abandoned the primary purpose and have clung to a secondary matter, thus they have become the cause of division. In the early days of Islam this was not so; it has gradually become like this.' Then He continued, 'Fasting means abstinence from that which increases the appetite for lust and passion. This has been the wisdom of the fast. Just as people abstain from indulging in food, they should likewise abstain from the promptings of the baser self and protect themselves from their evil effects. However, as can be seen,' He said, 'they dispute with each other over the basic principle and instead of spending their extra time in meditating and pondering upon the writings, in performing good and charitable deeds and in suppressing their evil promptings, they are engaged in advancing their personal interests and improving their businesses.'

## XV

As the night of Bahá'u'lláh's ascension drew close, 'Abdu'l-Bahá instructed all the pilgrims and the resident Bahá'ís to go to Bahjí on the eve of the ascension. Therefore, in the company of a group of friends we travelled to Bahjí the day before the ascension and were accommodated in the houses in the vicinity of the Shrine of Bahá'u'lláh. [These houses were destroyed during the ministry of Shoghi Effendi and became a part of the gardens.] At about sunset there was a meeting of the friends. 'Abdu'l-Bahá blessed us with

His presence and spoke about the sufferings of Bahá'u'lláh in a manner which deeply affected everyone.

At the instruction of the Master another gathering of the friends was held at night in the bírúní[15] opposite the mansion of Bahjí. 'Abdu'l-Bahá honoured the meeting with His presence. The Covenant-breakers were watching the meeting from the mansion of Bahá'u'lláh and evinced signs of immense envy and rancour. They tried to attract attention by pretending that since they were the occupants of the mansion, they were Bahá'u'lláh's true heirs. When 'Abdu'l-Bahá was giving a discourse, one of them started chanting one of the prayers of the Blessed Beauty in a very loud voice so that it could be clearly heard. After the prayer, 'Abdu'l-Bahá recited a poem in Persian, the gist of which is this: Once a fox stayed in a paint container for about two hours. When he saw his colourful coat and tail he thought he was a peacock. His claim to be a peacock was nothing but the manifestation of his vain imaginings.

That night the utterances of 'Abdu'l-Bahá revolved around the sufferings of Bahá'u'lláh and immersed us all in an ocean of sorrow. After the talk, when the darkness of the night had enveloped the land, 'Abdu'l-Bahá arose and left the meeting; in a short while He disappeared from our sight. No one knew where He had gone. When the meeting was over, we did not know what to do because He had not indicated how we should proceed.

I took advantage of the opportunity and decided that, since we were deprived of the opportunity of visiting the mansion, I would circumambulate it. As I was walking around the mansion, I recited one of 'Abdu'l-Bahá's prayers. When I finished the prayer, and as I was still circumambulating, 'Abdu'l-Bahá in His white cloak appeared before my eyes. I felt completely lost and did not know what to do. I bowed and said, 'Alláh-u-Abhá.' I had no power to utter anything. I followed Him to the gathering place.

As He stood there, He instructed the friends to form several groups and each group to continue praying and meditating in one of the rooms. 'Abdu'l-Bahá left for the chamber on the second floor of the building in the small garden of Bahjí, which is now called the tea house. It was either through the intervention of providence or the will of 'Abdu'l-Bahá that, when the rooms were being assigned, a room on the first floor of the same building which 'Abdu'l-Bahá was using was allocated to those of us who had come from Nayríz. Hence the appointed night when 'all were sleeping but we were awake engaging in prayer and meditation' was at hand.

'Abdu'l-Bahá was awake in the upper chamber. At about midnight He started revealing a Tablet of visitation in honour of Áqá Ya'qúb-i Muttaḥidih, who was mentioned earlier. We could hear the captivating and melodious voice of 'Abdu'l-Bahá.

Just before the time of the ascension we heard a sound. Thereafter we beheld Khusraw, the faithful attendant of 'Abdu'l-Bahá, descending from the steps of the upper chamber with a lantern in his hand. 'Abdu'l-Bahá followed him down the steps and left the area. Immediately after, we were informed of 'Abdu'l-Bahá's instruction to proceed to the Shrine of Bahá'u'lláh for the recitation of the Tablet of Visitation.[16]

We set off walking behind 'Abdu'l-Bahá until we reached the entrance to the Shrine of Bahá'u'lláh, the Qiblih of the people of Bahá. As I approached the outer threshold, I beheld 'Abdu'l-Bahá standing in the vestibule holding a large bottle of attar, with which He anointed those who entered. We stood in a line and went in one by one. As my turn came to be anointed, I stretched out my hand in such a way that my palm was flat. 'Abdu'l-Bahá lovingly pressed the palm of my hand with His thumb in order to make a hollow. He then poured the perfume generously into it. I was afraid it would spill from the corners of my hand. To avoid losing the precious perfume which 'Abdu'l-Bahá had granted me, I sipped some of it. It burned my throat in such a way that tears started rolling down my face.

After all the friends were anointed, they stood in rows facing the inner Shrine. The Master, who was in front, with a movement of His hand and in a very quiet voice, instructed one of the resident friends to recite the Tablet of Visitation. At that time the learned man from Egypt, who was the travelling companion of Shaykh Faraju'lláh Dhakíy-i Kurdí and who had been completely transformed in one meeting with 'Abdu'l-Bahá, was standing in front of me. He was weeping profusely as 'Abdu'l-Bahá supplicated at the threshold of the Blessed Beauty.

After the recitation of the Tablet of Visitation, 'Abdu'l-Bahá kissed the threshold of the sacred Shrine and backed away. Others did likewise. While the ladies of the Holy Family and other women believers visited the Shrine of Bahá'u'lláh [in those days in the Holy Land the matter of '*ḥijáb*' had not yet been abolished; therefore men and women separately visited the Shrines of Bahá'u'lláh and the Báb], the Master sat on a chair outside facing the sacred spot. For about half an hour He was fully wrapt in meditation in absolute silence and complete lowliness. During that time we were all standing behind Him in utter humility and supplication. When the morning light broke we were dismissed and proceeded to our rooms.

## XVI

On the afternoon of the day of Bahá'u'lláh's ascension, the seventieth day after Naw-Rúz, we had our last meeting with 'Abdu'l-Bahá at Bahjí. Thereafter we had to leave the promised paradise.

'Abdu'l-Bahá called the pilgrims from Nayríz one by one to His presence. He honoured us each with a separate Tablet and, after showering us with His supreme favours and endless blessings, He bade us farewell. When my turn came I prostrated myself as I entered, kissed the threshold and kneeled before 'Abdu'l-Bahá. He pointed to a chair and invited me to sit on it. He quoted a verse of the Kitáb-i Aqdas to the effect that God desires us to sit on thrones. He then graciously gave me a Tablet revealed in my honour, at the foot of which was the following prayer in the handwriting of His amanuensis:

> O my God, O my God! Verily this plant hath yielded its fruit and standeth upright upon its stalk. Verily it hath astounded the farmers and perturbed the envious. O God, water it with showers from the cloud of Thy favours and cause it to yield great harvests

> heaped up like unto mighty hills in Thy land. Enlighten the hearts with a ray shining forth from Thy Kingdom of Oneness, illumine the eyes by beholding the signs of Thy grace, and gratify the ears by hearing the melodies of the birds of Thy confirmations singing in Thy heavenly gardens, so that these souls may become like thirsty fish swimming in the pools of Thy guidance and like tawny lions roaming in the forests of Thy bounty. Verily Thou art the Generous, the Merciful, the Glorious and the Bestower.[17]

The above prayer was revealed at my request for my use on a regular basis. I was then dismissed when 'Abdu'l-Bahá said, 'May you be under God's protection.'

It can be well imagined how we felt: we had been invited to paradise and then dismissed. Methinks life was taken from us and our vitality sapped. The thought of separation from our Beloved reduced us to spiritless bodies.

# Appendix 3

## Taking the Light of Bahá'u'lláh's Revelation to Praslin Island[1]

Four months after his arrival in the Seychelles, Manúchihr was invited by an acquaintance, a Mr Solomon, to visit the island of Praslin situated about 25 nautical miles from Mahe. Mr Solomon was a successful non-Bahá'í businessman living in the Seychelles. The invitation was for the afternoon of 23 October until sunset the next day. Manúchihr accepted the invitation. When he mentioned the trip to Mr Raḥmán, he, too, expressed interest in visiting the island. The two pioneers met at Mr Solomon's shop at 1:00 p.m. on the appointed day and travelled with him in his private car to the seashore. From there they took a 'fast moving' boat to Praslin. Mr Solomon's two young sons and a few others travelled with them on the same boat. The small boat moved at the speed of 15 miles per hour. After an hour and 15 minutes it reached Grand Anse on the western shore of Praslin.[2] To reach land they took another small private boat belonging to Mr Solomon. The party spent from 2.30 to 6:00 p.m. in Grand Anse, had refreshments in a shop belonging to a friend of Mr Solomon, looked around, visited the church and several other places, then proceeded by boat to the other shore. After 30 minutes they reached Baie St Anne where Mr Solomon had a house. They had dinner there and spent the evening.

On 24 October 1954 the two pioneers went for a walk in the small, quiet and sparsely populated town. From the top of an elevation they could see several small islands, such as Petit Soeur, Grande Soeur, Flecite and Curiose (the lepers' island).[3] In Baie St Anne, they got to taste coco-de-mer, the double coconut that produces the largest seed in the world and only grows in that part of the world.

Manúchihr wanted very much to stay longer on the island. Mr Solomon saw his eagerness and responded by extending to him an invitation to stay several more days. Manúchihr accepted with profound pleasure. Others, including Mr Solomon and Mr Raḥmán, returned to Mahe on 24 October in the afternoon.

Manúchihr's sole purpose in remaining longer in Praslin was to spread the fragrance of Bahá'u'lláh's teachings among the inhabitants of the island. He also wanted to visit someone he had met in Mahe on 19 August 1954 who was familiar with the Bahá'í Faith. During his few days' stay in Praslin, Manúchihr travelled extensively on foot to various parts of the island and engaged in conversation with people, intending to introduce them to the redeeming message of Bahá'u'lláh.

On 25 October 1954 Manúchihr visited Providence, situated in the northeastern part of Praslin. The purpose of that visit was to see Mr Tyndale Biscoe, an Englishman familiar with eastern philosophy, religions and poetry. He had read some Bahá'í books while in Madras, India, and was attracted to the Faith. Manúchihr had a standing invitation to visit Mr Biscoe in Praslin. However, they did not meet on 25 October because Mr Biscoe was in Mahe. Later that day Manúchihr went for a walk with a man, a Catholic about 55 years old, whose name was Alzas Babé. After being introduced to the Bahá'í teachings, he expressed interest to know more. He was given the *Bahá'í Teachings* pamphlet and encouraged to read and ask questions.

Manúchihr returned to Providence on 26 October. Fortunately, Mr Biscoe was back and received him warmly. During the next few days that Manúchihr stayed in Providence as Mr Biscoe's houseguest, they talked about Bahá'u'lláh as the second coming of Christ, the history of the Faith and many other subjects. Mr Biscoe was provided with Bahá'í literature, which he read, and received convincing answers to his questions. Manúchihr and Mr Biscoe continued their conversations for several days. Mr Biscoe confessed his belief in Bahá'u'lláh. As a prerequisite for becoming a Bahá'í, he also accepted Muḥammad as a Messenger of God.

After several days' stay in Providence, Manúchihr, accompanied by Mr Biscoe, returned to Baie St Anne on 29 October 1954 and from there went to Grande Anse and then to Mahe.

Another gentleman from Baie St Anne who heard about the Bahá'í Faith during Manúchihr's visit to Praslin and pursued his study of it until he was confirmed in his belief in Bahá'u'lláh was Mr Robert Camille.[4]

## Manúchihr's Description of Praslin

> Praslin is a small island. It is very quiet and has about four thousand inhabitants. Most of them are Catholics. Its important town is Grand Anse; it is the largest and the centre. About two-thirds of the island's population is in this town. Next to Grand Anse is Baie St Anne. The third is Providence. The distance between these towns is from three to four miles. The elevations are not high and electricity exists only in the hospital. There are many Catholic and Protestant churches and the place is very scenic; it is actually known as the Garden of Eden.

In his diary Manúchihr renders praise to Bahá'u'lláh that during his six-day stay in Praslin the word of God reached the inhabitants of that island for the first time. He also expresses the hope that the seeds planted there would soon germinate and yield delectable fruit. About six weeks later, on 5 December 1954, Manúchihr was approached by a visitor from England who was staying in the same hotel, Mr Fluitt. He asked whether Manúchihr was a Bahá'í and knew Mr Biscoe. When Manúchihr responded affirmatively, Mr Fluitt said that he was a friend of Mr Biscoe, had heard from him about the Bahá'í Faith, had read some pamphlets while in England and was now on his way to Praslin to see Mr Biscoe. Manúchihr was delighted to meet Mr Fluitt and hear the news of his interest in the Bahá'í Faith. They talked about Bahá'u'lláh's Revelation. As Mr Fluitt was proceeding to Praslin, he was encouraged to continue the discussion there with Mr Biscoe.

# Appendix 4

## Selected Letters of Condolence in Chronological Order

Translation of a letter from Mr 'Alí Nakhjavání dated 5 February 1962. Mr Nakhjavání was then a member of the International Bahá'í Council:

> Dear spiritual sister, Baharieh Ma'ani, upon her be glory of the All-Glorious
>
> The sad news of the passing of your peerless husband, the true and sincere servant of the Cause of Almighty God, Manúchihr Ma'ání, upon him be God's glory, has affected the hearts in a manner that I am indeed unable to describe.
>
> This frightful news reached us today and made us very sad.
>
> You have, no doubt, received the cable of the Hands of the Cause of God and perused it. Be assured, we have all prayed and will continue to pray in the Holy Shrines with absolute humility and lowliness, for the progress of his precious and sanctified soul, and for the endurance and fortitude of that spiritual sister. That radiant soul truly had no desire except to serve at the sacred Threshold. He was a devoted pioneer in the path of the Cause of God and had been honoured with the title of Knight of Bahá'u'lláh. Be assured that his soul is most joyous in the midmost part of the Kingdom, resting in the Riḍván of His mercy, enjoying reunion with the Lord of bounty, for he spent the days of his life in the path of recognition and faith, living the Bahá'í life, serving and teaching with sacrifice.
>
> When faced with divine decrees which are predestined, we

must be submissive and resigned, we must leave the affairs to the Causer of all causes.

I am sending three packets containing flowers from the holy Shrine of Bahá'u'lláh. Kindly lay them on his fragrant and blessed resting place and say a prayer there on my behalf.

Amatu'l-Bahá Rúḥíyyih Khánum, the dear Hands of the Cause of God and members of the International Bahá'í Council all send you their loving greetings and heartfelt sympathy.

Your brother,
'Alí Nakhjavání

Translation of a letter written on behalf of Hand of the Cause of God Amatu'l-Bahá Rúḥíyyih Khánum by Hand of the Cause Mr Abu'l-Qásim Faizi, dated 6 February 1962:

Dear spiritual sister, Baharieh Ma'ani

. . . Yesterday, as soon as the cable of that dear one was received, Amatu'l-Bahá Rúḥíyyih Khánum, who had met you in Africa and liked you very much, was overtaken by such grief at the disclosure of this distressing news that I cannot recount. Immediately after the meeting of the Hands of the Cause, she stated emphatically that this letter be written and sent to you, so that your radiant and sorrowful heart may be assured of her heartfelt sympathy. She beseeches consolation for you from the divine Threshold and will especially pray that you and your newly born baby may be protected under God's bounty and mercy, and that you may be assisted to continue dear Manúchihr's services with full force, absolute resignation and fortitude . . .

Signed: Faizi

Translation of a letter from Hand of the Cause of God Mr Abu'l-Qásim Faizi, dated 6 February 1962:

Dear Bahá'í sister, Baharieh Ma'ani, upon her be the favours of the Lord, the Most Sublime

. . . Yesterday, in the meeting of the Hands, three cables from you, from Yazdi, and from the Assembly were read. God knows how we felt. I have no word or expression to describe my feelings and the feelings of the friends. It was a mixed feeling of intense sorrow and spiritual joy. We were sorry for you and happy for dear Manúchihr, who was a Knight of Bahá'u'lláh and, as he responded to the call of God in his pioneering place and passed away in a foreign land, he is considered a martyr. Well is it with him and his sublime and sanctified station. There is nothing to be said. I am writing these few words to assure you that I will remember you in the holy Shrines and will humbly and constantly beseech from His holy court everlasting happiness and comfort for you and for your baby.

Amatu'l-Bahá Rúḥíyyih Khánum felt immensely sorry and especially asked me to write the enclosed letter on her behalf.

Convey my sorrow to all members of your family . . .

Signed: Faizi

Translation of a letter from Hand of the Cause of God Ṭarázu'lláh Samandarí, dated 18 February 1962:

Mr Samandarí starts his letter with two excerpts from the writings of Bahá'u'lláh. The first excerpt is from a Tablet revealed in honour of the wife of the Báb. In it Khadíjih Bagum is advised not to grieve over tragic events that occur, for, He says, ordeals have always been and will continue to be the special lot of God's chosen ones. He praises the soul that is well pleased and grateful for what it receives, for God does not give to anyone except that which is better for that person than whatever is created between the heavens and earth. He adds that because people are not aware of this hidden secret, they feel sad when they are visited by calamities . . .

The second excerpt is from a Tablet in which Bahá'u'lláh quotes a verse from the Qur'án about those who leave their homes to pioneer in the path of God and His Messenger. Should such souls be overtaken by death while away from home, Muḥammad says they will be rewarded by God. Then Bahá'u'lláh describes the station of such souls in this Revelation and says:

> They that have forsaken their country in the path of God and subsequently ascended unto His presence, such souls shall be blessed by the Concourse on High and their names recorded by the Pen of Glory among such as have laid down their lives as martyrs in the path of God, the Help in Peril, the Self-Subsistent.[1]

After the above two excerpts, Mr. Samandarí says:

> To a bereaved pioneer, the wife of a martyr in the path of God, Mr Ma'ani, upon him be God's mercy and His glory.
>
> Praised be God, the Glory of the All-Glorious! Your peerless husband, after many years of pioneering service and true endeavours, and after marriage with that spiritual, illumined, forbearing, thankful, submissive and resigned handmaid, winged his flight, at the behest of the Almighty and in response to His pervasive decree, to the Kingdom of God. He discarded this temporary garment, entered the kingdom of sanctity, took shelter under the shadow of the Sidratu'l-Muntahá, the holy Tree of Life, under the tabernacle of glory, and became, according to the explicit text from the Abhá Beauty, a martyr in the path of God and reckoned as such from the Exalted Pen . . .
>
> Those lands are in need of sacrifice that the seeds already sown may be watered and the saplings already planted may be nurtured. May the new-comers in the Faith increase in their steadfastness, certitude and assurance, and each one of them – even as a straw today may become a mountain tomorrow, a drop now may become a lake in the future, an insignificant speck of dust in this day – be transmuted into a brilliant star shedding its light all over that region.
>
> As you know, Cyrus Samandarí was only 21 years old when he, after the passing of the beloved of the world, the peerless pearl

of the luminary of the Covenant, may my life and the lives of all His lovers be sacrificed for his sanctified and illumined remains, hastened impatiently like an eager lover to join his Beloved, and chose that land as his eternal abode.[2] Then a second precious soul joined that symbol of detachment,[3] and now Mr Ma'ani is the third one. 'We have glorified the two with a third' was realized in the world beyond. It is now realized in the world of dust as well.

Soon the blaze of the Cause of God in those regions will reach the heavens and will illumine that horizon in such a manner that it will shed light upon neighbouring lands.

Therefore, you should be happy for having offered such a ransom, do not express sorrow; immerse yourself in the ocean of happiness and gladden the hearts of the friends of God. Try to become an example to others, cling to the cord of patience, and hold fast to the hem of forbearance. Know of a certainty that the reward of this patience is great indeed, and the benefits derived from this trade are many. You must be the cause of consolation to his parents and to yours as well. Blessed are they who endure patiently. Praised be God, the Lord of all worlds.

Signed: Ṭarázu'lláh Samandarí

Letter from Hand of the Cause of God Mr John A. Robarts dated 22 February 1962:[4]

Mrs Manoutchehr Maani Entessari

My dear Bahá'í sister:

I have learned, with greatest sorrow, of the sudden passing to the Abhá Kingdom of your dear husband and at the same time of the birth of your darling little girl. She will be a joy to you always, a balm to your heart.

How incomprehensible are the mysteries of God to our finite minds! How could He have transplanted the glorious spirit of Manoutchehr, dedicated pioneer, Knight of Bahá'u'lláh, great servant of God, just when he seemed to be at the beginning of his devoted service to His Cause!

Your heart and mind must be tortured with such thoughts. But 'Abdu'l-Bahá assured us: 'If sorrow and adversity visit us, let us turn our faces to the Kingdom and heavenly consolation will be outpoured.'

'. . . He will send us heavenly calm.'

There is such comfort to be found in the teachings, the prayers, and I think especially in the Hidden Words. I recall, with much pleasure, the chats you and Manoutchehr and I had at the Nairobi conference. I shall continue to pray for him, and for you, and for your sweet little girl.

My wife joins me in deepest love and sympathies to you in your bereavement.

Affectionately yours,
John A. Robarts

# Bibliography


Abdi, Pouran Rouhani. Email of 26 February 2004.

'Abdu'l-Bahá. *Selections from the Writings of 'Abdu'l-Bahá.* Haifa: Bahá'í World Centre, 1978.

Amatu'l-Bahá Rúḥíyyih Khánum, Hand of the Cause of God. Letter written on behalf of Hand of the Cause of God Amatu'l-Bahá Rúḥíyyih Khánum by Hand of the Cause Mr Abu'l-Qásim Faizi. 6 February 1962.

*The Bahá'í World.* vols. 1–12, 1925–54. rpt. Wilmette, IL: Bahá'í Publishing Trust, 1980.

*The Bahá'í World.* vol. 13. Haifa: The Universal House of Justice, 1970.

*The Bahá'í World.* vol. 15. Haifa: Bahá'í World Centre, 1975.

*The Bahá'í World.* vol. 19. Haifa: Bahá'í World Centre, 1994.

Bahá'u'lláh. *Gleanings from the Writings of Bahá'u'lláh.* Wilmette, IL: Bahá'í Publishing Trust, 1983.

— *The Hidden Words.* Wilmette, IL: Bahá'í Publishing Trust, 1990.

— *Iqtidárát.* A compilation of the Tablets of Bahá'u'lláh. 1310 AH (1892–3 AD).

Faizi, Hand of the Cause of God Mr Abu'l-Qásim. Letter of 6 February 1962.

Gappy, David. Email of 12 April 2004.

'Glimpses of 'Abdu'l-Bahá', in *The Bahá'í World.* vol. 19. Haifa: Bahá'í World Centre, 1994.

*The Importance of Obligatory Prayer and Fasting.* Haifa: Bahá'í World Centre, 2000.

Ma'ání, Manúchihr. Diary, vols. 1, 2, 3, 6. Unpublished.

Nakhjavání, 'Alí. Letter of 5 February 1962.

Nicolas, A.-L.-M. *Madháhib-i-Milal-i-Mutimaddinih – Táríkh-i-Siyyid 'Alí-Muḥammad Ma'rúf bih Báb.* Paris, 1905.

Robarts, Hand of the Cause of God Mr John A. Letter of 22 February 1962.

Rouhani (Rúḥání), Mírzá Muḥammad Shafí'. *Kháṭirát-i Talkh va Shírín* (*Bittersweet Memories*) Hofheim-Langenhain: Bahá'í-Verlag, 1993. Bundoora, Victoria: Century Press, 2002.

Ruhe, David. S. *Door of Hope.* Oxford: George Ronald, 1983.

Samandarí, Hand of the Cause of God Ṭarázu'lláh. Letter of 18 February 1962.

Shoghi Effendi. *Messages to the Bahá'í World.* Wilmette, IL: Bahá'í Publishing Trust, 1971.

— *Tawqí'át-i Mubárakih 1927–1939.* Tehran: Bahá'í Publishing Trust, 119 BE.

# Notes and References

## Introduction

1. The fort of Kh͟ájih, situated about one kilometre to the southeast of Nayríz, was the scene of fierce fighting between early Bábís of the town under the leadership of Jináb-i Áqá Siyyid Yaḥyá Vaḥíd and the government forces.
2. The Battle of the Mountain took place in the southern mountains of Nayríz about two years after the first episode and was fought between the survivors of the first episode and the combined local and government forces.
3. Father's memoirs, entitled *Kh͟áṭirát-i Talkh͟ va Sh͟írín* (*Bittersweet Memories*), were published in Persian in 1993.

## Against Incredible Odds

1. A detailed account of the events that occurred in Nayríz consequent to Jináb-i Vaḥíd's teaching activities are covered in *Lama'átu'l-Anvár – History of the Soul Stirring Events in Nayríz* by Mírzá Muḥammad Sh͟afí' Rouhani (Rúḥání), whose life is discussed in this book. For more information in English about Jináb-i Vaḥíd and the events associated with the Bábí–Bahá'í Faith in Nayríz, see appendix 1.
2. Summarized from *Lama'átu'l-Anvár*, p. 17.
3. Summarized from ibid., pp. 17–18.
4. Civil registration is a relatively recent phenomenon. It was introduced in England and Wales as early as 1837 but in Iran it took effect almost a century later, in about 1930 during the reign of Riḍá Sh͟áh Pahlaví.
5. Jináb-i Vaḥíd, who was openly promoting the Bábí Faith in Nayríz, was opposed by the governor and attacked by his forces. He and his supporters took a defensive position in the nearby fort of Kh͟ájih after Mullá 'Abdu'l-Ḥusayn, Jináb-i Vaḥíd's old companion, became the first in Nayríz to receive bullet wounds because of his faith. During this episode Jináb-i Vaḥíd and many Bábís were martyred. Among those who offered up their lives for the Cause of the Báb

were father's great-grandfather Mullá 'Ali-Naqí, whose father was Mullá 'Abdu'l-Ḥusayn.

The governor of Nayríz continued to persecute the Bábís after the first event and threatened to kill them all. The Battle of the Mountain was triggered by the assassination of the governor by five Bábís in an unsuccessful attempt to prevent the massacre. Following this second episode, the son of Mullá 'Ali-Naqí and grandson of Mullá 'Abdu'l-Ḥusayn, named Mullá Muḥammad-S͟hafí' (father's grandfather), and his mother were among the captives sent to S͟híráz, together with the heads of the martyrs. They were later released and returned to Nayríz, where the family continued to live.

6. Provisional translation approved for publication by the Universal House of Justice.
7. Governor of Nayríz during the fort of K͟hájih episode.
8. One túmán is ten riyáls. The riyál was, and still is, the monetary unit in Iran.
9. *K͟háṭirát-i Talk͟h va S͟hírín*, p. 15.
10. The children of Mírzá 'Abdu'l-Ḥusayn, father's father, later adopted Rouhani as their family name; Mírzá Aḥmad, mother's father, adopted Vaḥídí as a family name; the third pilgrim, Mírzá Faḍlu'lláh, adopted 'Ináyatí as a family name.
11. *K͟háṭirát-i-Talk͟h va S͟hírín*, p. 18.
12. ibid. pp. 18–19. As family names were not yet current, an individual was identified by the name of his father.
13. ibid. p. 19.
14. ibid. p. 20.
15. ibid. pp. 24–5. Provisional translation approved for publication by the Universal House of Justice.
16. ibid. p. 27.
17. The Bahá'í principle of non-interference in political affairs was not yet enforced. Thus Bahá'ís occasionally held political posts during 'Abdu'l-Bahá's ministry.
18. Zaynu'l-'Abidín K͟hán was the governor of Nayríz in 1850 when the first battle between the Bábís of the town and armed forces took place. As he was held responsible for the massacre of the defenders of the fort of K͟hájih, as well as for the martyrdom of Jináb-i Vaḥíd and the atrocities committed against the survivors of that bloody episode, Zaynu'l-'Ábidín K͟hán was later murdered by some Bábís, thus fuelling the fire of animosity and vindictiveness of his family towards the Bábís of Nayríz. That animosity was later directed towards the Bahá'ís.

19. *Iqtidárát* is a book containing a collection of some of Bahá'u'lláh's writings.
20. Muḥarram is a month of mourning for S̲h̲í'í Muslims. Imám Ḥusayn, the grandson of the Prophet Muḥammad, was martyred in Karbalá, Iraq, during the month of Muḥarram.
21. Mullá S̲h̲afí' is Mullá Muḥammad-S̲h̲afí', who rose to prominence during the ministry of Bahá'u'lláh. He was the son of Mullá 'Alí-Naqí and grandson of Mullá 'Abdu'l-Ḥusayn, martyred in 1850 and 1852 respectively. Mullá Muḥammad-S̲h̲afí' was about twelve years old when Jang-i Jibal (War of the Mountain) ended and was among the captives who were sent to S̲h̲íráz together with the heads of the martyrs. Mullá Muḥammad-S̲h̲afí' attained the presence of Bahá'u'lláh in Bag̲h̲dád, rendered outstanding service to His Cause and wrote the original history of the Faith in Nayríz covering the first two episodes, to which Jináb-i Nabíl has referred in his Narrative.
22. In *K̲h̲áṭirát-i-Talk̲h̲ va S̲h̲írín*, p. 45. Provisional translation approved for publication by the Universal House of Justice.
23. This is a reference to the martyrdom in Iṣfahán of the King of Martyrs and Beloved of Martyrs, two devoted and renowned brothers, on 23 Rabí 'u'l-Avval 1296 AH (17 March 1879).
24. This is a reference to Núríján Bagum, the mother of K̲h̲ánum Laqá and grandmother of the late Adíb and Ḥabíb Taherzadeh.
25. This is a reference to father's father, Mírzá 'Abdu'l-Ḥusayn. As his mother was a Siyyidih, he was called Mírzá in childhood.
26. In *K̲h̲áṭirát-i-Talk̲h̲ va S̲h̲írín*, pp. 40–1. Provisional translation approved for publication by the Universal House of Justice.
27. Twelve carpets of the same size and design were made in Yazd and shipped to the Holy Land. Six were placed in the inner Shrine of the Báb and six in the outer Shrine of 'Abdu'l-Bahá. The original carpets bore a description woven into them, reading 'Donated by Mírzá Aḥmad of Nayríz for the Báb's Shrine'. When the design of the carpets was replicated and twelve new ones were made to replace the old, the name was removed. However, the Universal House of Justice graciously allowed two of Ṭúbá K̲h̲ánum's children (Mírzá Aḥmad's grandchildren) to contribute the cost of the new carpets.
28. Some early Bahá'ís practised bigamy, which they thought the provisions of the Kitáb-i-Aqdas permitted. The practice was initially tolerated until, through loving education, Bahá'ís came to understand 'Abdu'l-Bahá's interpretation of the text: that since it was not possible to uphold justice between two wives, only monogamy was allowed.

29. Provisional translations approved for publication by the Universal House of Justice.
30. They were first published under the title 'Glimpses of 'Abdu'l-Bahá' in *The Bahá'í World*, vol. 19, pp. 745–55.
31. Nayriz's fertile soil made it an ideal place for farming. Many of the inhabitants owned farms and earned a living by farming and trading in farm produce.
32. In his message of 6 March 1925 addressed to the Bahá'ís of Iran and sent through the members of the Central Assembly, Shoghi Effendi refers to the generous contributions made by the western friends, particularly those in the United States (*Tawqí'át-i-Mubárakih* 1922–6, p. 216).
33. *Kháṭirát-i Talkh va Shírín*, pp. 115–17. To give to the fund and not receive from it was a characteristic trait of the Bahá'ís of Iran. This trait was particularly strong among the friends of Nayríz. Unless they were absolutely desperate, they would not accept monetary or material assistance.
34. The Bahá'í relief fund set up for the victims of the flood, coupled with the sacrificial offerings and efforts of the Bahá'ís of Nayríz, made possible several significant achievements, such as compensation to needy victims, establishment of projects beneficial to Bahá'ís and non-Bahá'ís, construction of several houses for non-Bahá'ís, building a dyke to prevent future floods, establishing a promenade, acquisition of a site for the future Mashriqu'l-Adhkár, construction of a modern bath house, ownership of about one million square metres of land surrounding the fort of Khájih and construction of a room over the grave of 200 martyrs who had been buried in a mass grave. These in turn contributed to the establishment of good public relations between Bahá'ís and non-Bahá'ís and regular contact with local authorities.
35. In the period under discussion the husband was considered the head of the family and alone responsible for providing for the welfare and well-being of the family. He was also the decision-maker. Bahá'í men were more liberal minded than others but quite a distance from accepting women as their co-equals and full partners. Women were happy with the status quo, which provided them with protection and security. The situation gradually changed as Bahá'í men and women were educated in the nuances of equality and partnership. The change in the attitude of father and mother during the 60 years of their married life, when it came to their understanding of what the principle of equality meant, was phenomenal.

36. *Khāṭirát-i Talkh va Shírín*, p. 141.
37. *Arba'ín* means 40. It is a reference to the fortieth day after the martyrdom of Imám Ḥusayn, which is a day of mourning for Shí'í Muslims.
38. *Kháṭirát-i Talkh va Shírín*, p. 142.
39. ibid. p. 144.
40. ibid. p. 146.
41. ibid. p. 148.
42. ibid. p. 150.
43. ibid. pp. 152–3.
44. ibid. p. 155.
45. ibid. p. 156.
46. ibid. pp. 156–7.
47. ibid.
48. ibid. p. 157.
49. In ibid. pp. 176–7.
50. The Ḥaẓíratu'l-Quds of Shíráz in those days served both as a Bahá'í centre and a pilgrim hostel providing accommodation to Bahá'ís who came to the city for a few days to visit the House of the Báb or to attend to other matters.
51. Before reaching Shíráz and fulfilling her plan to visit Nayríz, Mrs Ransom-Kehler was taken ill in Iṣfahán and passed away there in 1933.
52. The Bahá'í laws of burial require that the dead be buried in coffins. For Shí'í Muslims who bury their dead without a coffin, this is a point of contention. There are also other differences between Bahá'í and Muslim laws of burial.
53. Ten children were born to my parents. After Mírzá 'Abdu'l-Ḥusayn, another son was born and named Mírzá Masíḥ. After him arrived a daughter named Shamsu'ḍ-Ḍuḥá, later known as Rawḥanieh, followed by Nayyirih, Pourándukht, Mahíndukht, Baharieh, Mawhibatu'lláh, Cyrus, who died in infancy, and Firishtih. They also suffered a miscarriage after their third child.
54. Mother was pregnant with my older sister, Mahíndukht.
55. 28 Sha'bán is the date of the Báb's martyrdom according to the lunar calendar.
56. *Kháṭirát-i Talkh va Shírín*, pp. 165–7.
57. Dentistry was in its elementary stage of development in Iran at that time. Father's teeth could not be saved. They were all extracted and replaced with dentures, which he wore to the end of his life.
58. All Bahá'í schools throughout Iran were ordered closed by the gov-

ernment in 1934. The official reason for it was the insistence of the Bahá'ís to keep them closed on Bahá'í holy days, nine in all.

59. *Kháṭirát-i Talkh va Shírín*, pp. 169–70.
60. Father had planted a beautiful garden near the fort of Khájih. It was called Bágh-i Ábpakhsh (water distribution garden) because water from canals dug for irrigation ran through it before being distributed to surrounding areas.
61. Shirkat-i Rústá'í was an important government-owned company in Fárs. It bought from local farmers the surplus of agricultural produce and exported abroad. As a farmer and trader, father had dealings with the company, hence was well-known to Mr Surúsh.
62. *Kháṭirát-i Talkh va Shírín*, p. 171.
63. ibid. p. 172.
64. ibid.
65. Dáráb is a small town in one of the four divisions by the same name that form the district of Fasá. It is situated to the southeast of Fasá and to the south of Nayríz.
66. *Kháṭirát-i Talkh va Shírín*, pp. 184–5.
67. ibid. p. 186.
68. A reference to Riḍá Sháh Pahlaví.
69. *Kháṭirát-i Talkh va Shírín*, p. 1.
70. ibid. p. 188.
71. ibid. p. 190.
72. One of the five major tribes living in Fárs.
73. *Kháṭirát-i Talkh va Shírín*, pp. 192–3.
74. Sixth grade was the final year of primary school. At the end of that grade pupils sat for qualifying exams. Those who passed could enter secondary school the following year. The curriculum for the girls' school included sewing.
75. He had been imprisoned in Ṭihrán for some time because of his belief in Bahá'u'lláh. After his release from prison, he lived in the Ḥaẓíratu'l-Quds of Ṭihrán and shared a room with father. In those days the Bahá'ís who visited Ṭihrán from other places in the country could have free accommodation in the Ḥaẓíratu'l-Quds, which was spacious, so a part of it served as a hostel for Bahá'í wayfarers, who paid for their subsistence.
76. *Kháṭirát-i Talkh va Shírín*, p. 195.
77. Bandar 'Abbás is a port on the Persian Gulf with a very hot and inhospitable climate, especially unpleasant in those days when electricity and other amenities did not exist.
78. *Kháṭirát-i Talkh va Shírín*, p. 196.

79. ibid. pp. 196–7.
80. A well-known Persian expression.
81. It was customary in Iran at bedtime to spread the bedding on floors covered with Persian carpets. During the day the bedding was folded, placed in a special wrapper and stacked up against a wall on one side of the room.
82. *Kháṭirát-i Talkh va Shírín*, pp. 199–200.
83. ibid. p. 200.
84. I believe the only means of public transportation in large cities was by horse-drawn carriages, called *durushkih*. Transportation outside the city was by means of trucks which moved back and forth infrequently.
85. Email of Pouran Rouhani Abdi, 26 February 2004.
86. *Kháṭirát-i Talkh va Shírín*, p. 215.
87. ibid.
88. About one-half of a cubic metre.
89. Email of Pouran Rouhani Abdi, 26 February 2004.
90. *Kháṭirát-i Talkh va Shírín*, p. 218.
91. Bahá'u'lláh, in *Importance of Obligatory Prayer and Fasting*, p. 26.
92. Bahá'u'lláh, *Hidden Words*, Arabic no. 51.
93. ibid. Persian no. 12.
94. As Shíráz was home to several Covenant-breakers of high stature, to protect the Bahá'í community, especially the youth, from their insidious schemes, at the instruction of the beloved Guardian, Mr Samandarí spent a considerable time in that city. While there, he lived a very simple life. His accommodation consisted of a room in the Bahá'í centre, which also served as a pilgrim hostel, where he received visitors.
95. *Kháṭirát-i Talkh va Shírín*, p. 221.
96. ibid. p. 222.
97. ibid.
98. Mr Nakhjavání, who was later elected to the Universal House of Justice in 1963 and served on the supreme administrative institution of the Bahá'í Faith for 40 years until his retirement in 2003, lived with his family in Shíráz for some time before pioneering to Uganda in 1951.
99. 'Abdu'l-Bahá, in *Bahá'í World*, vol. 19, p. 755.
100. Mr Abu'l-Qásim Faizi, who was designated by Shoghi Effendi a Hand of the Cause of God in 1957, had pioneered, together with his wife Gloria Khánum, to Bahrain in 1942.
101. Since Shíráz is a focal point of pilgrimage for the Bahá'ís throughout

the world, there used to be a Bahá'í pilgrim house or hostel in the city. I do not know its status after the Islamic revolution.

102. Paraphrased from Bahá'u'lláh, *Iqtidárát*, p.106; *Kháṭirát-i Talkh va Shírín*, p. 232.
103. *Kháṭirát-i Talkh va Shírín*, p. 241.
104. Pouran preferred medical studies for which she was well qualified. However, medical school required a substantial sum of money and took longer to complete. Considering the financial resources of a family with several school-aged children, that was not possible, nor did the government have a lending scheme to enable less well-off children to continue their studies.
105. A brief account of Pouran's life in Kenya is given in the last section of this book as part of my own pioneering experiences, for the change of her pioneering post was directly linked to the misfortune I suffered in that country.
106. A more elaborate account of the circumstances leading to my pioneering abroad, marriage and life as a married woman, a widow and a single parent in a foreign country as well as later developments can be read at the end of this book.
107. One of the wealthy believers in Ṭihrán had set up a commercial firm called Shirkat-i Firooz (Firooz Company), a trading company that sold imported goods. It had agents in several parts of Iran.
108. Colonel Yadu'lláh Vaḥdat was one of the devoted Bahá'ís of Shíráz who rendered invaluable services to the Bahá'í Faith in that city and in the province of Fárs. He was appointed an Auxiliary Board member in 1957. He was arrested by revolutionary guards in Shíráz in 1980. After about a year of imprisonment, he was executed in April 1981 for his belief in Bahá'u'lláh and for active Bahá'í service.
109. 'Abdu'l-Bahá, *Selections*, p. 228.
110. Shoghi Effendi, *Messages to the Bahá'í World*, p. 60.
111. ibid. p. 77.
112. The letter was sent through Mr A. Raḥmán, secretary of the Bahá'í group in Mahe.
113. Shoghi Effendi, *Messages to the Bahá'í World*, p. 105.
114. ibid. p. 85.
115. ibid. p. 97.
116. ibid. p. 106.
117. Diary of Manúchihr Ma'ání, vol. 6, p. 967.
118. ibid. p. 101.
119. For this remarkable achievement, see *Bahá'í World*, vol. 13, p. 631.
120. The Regional Spiritual Assembly of Central and East Africa, which

included Seychelles within its jurisdiction, was established at Riḍván 1956, with its seat in Kampala, Uganda.

121. Manú<u>ch</u> is the abbreviated form for Manú<u>ch</u>ihr. That is how he was addressed by members of his family when he was growing up in Iran.

122. This designation may have been in recognition of Manú<u>ch</u>ihr having introduced the Bahá'í Faith to the island of Praslin.

123. Princess Elizabeth Hospital, later renamed Kenyatta Hospital.

124. In those days disposable nappies did not exist. If they had, they would have been beyond my means.

125. There were three categories of people in East Africa during the colonial times: Africans, Asians and whites. Indians, Pakistanis and Arabs were called Asians; other Asians, such as Persians and Japanese, were called honorary whites!

126. The money sent from Iran by my family came through the company for which Manú<u>ch</u>ihr worked. That money was paid to me on a monthly basis, apparently as salary. On that basis, the Immigration Office had let me stay in the country.

127. Among those affected by the fire was the Fanánápazír family. Mr 'Ináyatu'lláh and Mrs '<u>I</u>shrat Fanánápazír and their three children were early pioneers in Shoghi Effendi's Ten Year Plan. They first pioneered to the Gambia, then Morocco. Finally, they settled as pioneers in Nairobi, in 1963. One of the highlights of our life in Nairobi was living next door to the Fanánápazírs for several years. Mr Fanánápazír was a prominent teacher who travelled extensively for the Faith. Mrs Fanánápazír, a loving Bahá'í knowledgeable in homeopathic medicine, was very kind and most helpful in many ways. At the time of the fire Mr and Mrs Fanánápazír were visiting Iran and their three children were studying abroad.

128. Although by then I had lived outside Iran for over ten years, <u>Sh</u>íráz was still shown in my passport as my place of residence. Therefore I could not claim or benefit from privileges extended to foreign residents.

129. After Shoghi Effendi passed away, Jam<u>sh</u>íd Ma'ání advanced claims incongruent with the principal beliefs of the Bahá'í Faith and was declared a Covenant-breaker.

130. The world administrative and spiritual centre of the Bahá'í Faith is in the twin cities of Haifa and 'Akká. Bahá'u'lláh, the Founder of the Bahá'í Faith, had been banished from Ṭihrán, His native land, in 1853. After successive banishments to different places within the domain of the Ottoman Empire, He was exiled in 1868 to the penal

colony of 'Akká, where He spent the last 24 years of His life. His burial at Bahjí in the vicinity of 'Akká fixed the permanent spiritual centre of His Faith in the Holy Land. During His lifetime Bahá'u'lláh visited Haifa several times and instructed His son, 'Abdu'l-Bahá, to bury the remains of His Herald, the Báb, who had been martyred in Iran in 1850, in a designated spot on the slopes of Mount Carmel in Haifa. Haifa serves as the Faith's administrative centre.

**Appendix 1**

1. Yaḥyá and Vaḥíd are equal in numerical value, which is 28.
2. When Vaḥíd accepted the Cause of the Báb, he wrote to his father-in-law, Shaykh 'Abdu'l-'Alí, a venerable judge, and some others of the ulamá of Nayríz an account of the Báb's mission and his acceptance of it. Some are believed to have shown interest in the nascent Faith and received Tablets from the Báb.
3. Guards watched over the body of Vaḥíd for a day. On the next, as a sign of respect for his ancestry, people buried it adjacent to the eastern wall of Buq'iy-i Siyyid Jalálu'd-Dín 'Abdu'lláh, known as the Siyyid. Vaḥíd's head was rescued by the black servant of the mother of Mírzá 'Abdu'lláh Khán, the Ḍawlatu'l-Ayálih, a prominent inhabitant of Maḥallih Bázár. She cleaned and anointed the head and hid it for a few days. She then had it buried, with the assistance of her servant, next to his body.
4. Nicolas, *Madháhib-i-Milal-i-Mutimaddinih – Táríkh-i-Siyyid 'Alí-Múḥammad Ma'rúf bih Báb.*

**Appendix 2**

1. Paradise Garden, an extensive agricultural area immediately adjacent to the Riḍván Garden; see Ruhe, *Door of Hope*, pp. 102–4.
2. The garden is no longer there; it has been dismantled and now forms a part of the gardens surrounding the Most Holy Spot.
3. A powerful chief of Persian origin, leader of the religious and political movement in Khurásán through which the Ummayads were overthrown and the Abbasids (Arabic family descended from 'Abbás, the uncle of Muḥammad) attained the throne. He died in 755.
4. Shaykh Faraju'lláh Kurdí is a well-known believer. He has been responsible for printing many Bahá'í books in Egypt and has rendered outstanding services. At the time he was in the process of publishing *Makátíb* ['Abdu'l-Bahá's writings], volume 3.
5. Bahá'u'lláh, *Gleanings*, p. 136.

6. Alma Knobloch became a Bahá'í in 1903 in the United States. With the consent of 'Abdu'l-Bahá, and assisted financially by her sister Fanny, Alma settled in Germany in 1907, the first pioneer to join Dr Edwin Fisher. She remained until 1921. See 'In Memoriam', *Bahá'í World*, vol. 9, pp. 641–3. Alma Knobloch died in 1943, Fanny in 1949.
7. Translator's note: The Bahá'í scholar 'Abdu'l-Ḥamíd Ishráq Kháварí in his *Muḥáḍirát* states that Ya'qúb-i Muttaḥidih was born in Káshán and raised in Hamadán. When he embraced the Faith the intensity of his love was such that he beseeched 'Abdu'l-Bahá on several occasions to bestow on him the honour of martyrdom. 'He is the only martyr from the Bahá'ís of Jewish background,' Ishráq Khávarí writes (there have been others since) and 'he was the last to give his life for the Faith during 'Abdu'l-Bahá's ministry'. To please his mother, Ḥájíyih Khánum, Mr Muttaḥidih had been about to marry but when he recognized that his request to be martyred was to be granted, he declined to marry and asked his mother, instead, to invite the Bahá'ís to a meeting after his death and offer them sweetmeats. She fulfilled her son's wish each year on the anniversary of his martyrdom, inviting the friends for prayers and then, with stooped posture and a brave smile, passing sweets among the guests.
8. A Bahá'í from India (originally from Khurásán) who, with Curtis Kelsey from the United States, installed the lighting plant for the illumination of the Shrines.
9. The future Edward VIII
10. Muṣṭafá Rúmí, posthumously appointed a Hand of the Cause by Shoghi Effendi. He died 13 March 1942.
11. The Houses of Worship in 'Ishqábád and Wilmette, Illinois
12. Mírzá Muḥammad Náṭiq
13. Translation authorized by the Universal House of Justice.
14. Mírzá 'Abdu'lláh Muṭlaq and Mírza Munír Nabílzádih, noted Bahá'í teachers.
15. Outer part of an eastern house, separate from the women's quarters and used for receiving guests.
16. After Bahá'u'lláh's ascension, 'Abdu'l-Bahá asked Jináb-i Nabíl to select excerpts from Bahá'u'lláh's writings for recitation at His tomb. Thus the Tablet of Visitation, which is read at His Shrine and at the Shrine of the Báb and which is also frequently used in commemorating their anniversaries, comprises excerpts from four Tablets revealed by Bahá'u'lláh and put together by Nabíl.
17. Translation authorized by the Universal House of Justice.

**Appendix 3**

1. This account of Manúchihr Ma'ání's teaching trip to the Praslin Island in October 1954 is based on volumes 1, 2 and 3 of his diary.
2. Mr David Gappy, a young Bahá'í from Seychelles, says in an email to the writer, dated 12 April 2004, that the length of time it took for the boat to go from Mahe to Praslin may have been different. He says, 'Today they travel at 60 km/h and it takes the same time.'
3. According to Mr Gappy, 'A lot of the places mentioned in the notes have changed their names over the years.'
4. On 17 February 1955 Mr Camille saw Manúchihr in Mahe and remembered him from his visit to Praslin several months earlier. He expressed an interest in learning more about the Bahá'í Faith. They had a lengthy discussion which ended with Mr Camille asking for Bahá'í literature. He received and read *Bahá'u'lláh and the New Era* and several other books before professing his belief in Bahá'u'lláh on 21 January 1956.

**Appendix 4**

1. Bahá'u'lláh, in *Bahá'í World*, vol. 15, p. 516.
2. Mr Cyrus Samandarí arrived in Mogadishu, Somalia, as a pioneer on 12 November 1955. He was taken ill in 1957 after Shoghi Effendi's passing, went to Nairobi for an operation in March 1958 and died there shortly thereafter. For more information, see his 'In Memoriam' in *Bahá'í World* , vol. 13, pp. 925–6.
3. Mr Luṭfu'lláh 'Alízádih pioneered to Nairobi where he died at the age of 66. See *Bahá'í World*, vol. 13, pp. 930–1.
4. Mr John Robarts was then living in Bulawayo, Southern Rhodesia (presently Zimbabwe).

# Index